Spooner

Sediments in Archaeological Context

Sediments in
Archaeological Context

Edited by

Julie K. Stein

and William R. Farrand

The University of Utah Press

Salt Lake City

06 05 04 03 02 01
5 4 3 2 1
Library of Congress Cataloging-in-Publication Data

Sediments in archaeological context / [edited by]
    Julie K. Stein and William R. Farrand.
        p.   cm.
Updated ed. of: Archaeological sediments in context. c1985.
Includes bibliographical references and index.
ISBN 0-87480-703-4 (cloth: alk. paper)—
    ISBN 0-87480-691-7 (pbk: alk. paper)
        1. Geology, Stratigraphic—Quaternary. 2. Geology,
Stratigraphic—Tertiary. 3. Excavations (Archaeology).
4. Antiquities, Prehistoric. I. Stein, Julie K.
II. Farrand, William R.
    QE696 .S44 2001
    551.3'04'02493—dc21   2001003860

Contents

Figures

Tables

Introduction

Julie K. Stein and William R. Farrand

Sediments in Archaeological Context is an updated version of the book *Archaeological Sediments in Context* published in 1985 and reprinted in 1988 by the Center for the Study of Early Man, Orono, Maine. The original 1985 book is now out of print and the editors believe an updated version is warranted. This title differs from the original title to reflect the emphasis of this book on the role of sediments in archaeology. The unifying principle here is our focus on *depositional environments* as inferred from the excavated sediments.

The audience for this book is every archaeologist who investigates sites in depositional contexts. In the past, archaeologists most likely noted the sedimentary context of their artifacts if the sites were in complicated depositional and weathering regimes. A new trend, however, has arrived where even those archaeologists excavating historic landscapes and architectural features are considering the sediments they encounter. The importance of sedimentary analysis has increased rather than decreased, and will likely continue to do so.

The growing importance of sedimentary analysis stems from the fact that, except for surface collections, every artifact and ecofact in archaeological analysis originates in the ground, i.e., in a sedimentary matrix. Archaeologists employ elaborate field methods for extracting these artifacts. They

- describe, at least rudimentarily, the matrix enclosing the artifacts while in the field,
- screen the matrix to separate the artifacts from the other matrix particles that are subsequently ignored,
- group artifacts into natural and arbitrary levels after non-artifacts are separated and thrown away, and
- draw plans and sections to record the groupings and the locations of the artifacts and to establish some stratigraphic phasing of the site.

These methods sometimes include a basic, often unsophisticated, description of the matrix. Systematic analysis of the matrix particles that encase the artifacts, however, would ensure that the context of the artifacts is recorded accurately and available for further interpretation.

This book concerns the analysis of the matrix particles referred to more appropriately and simply as sediments. The goal is to alert archaeologists, both professionals and students, to the potential of sediment analysis for answering archaeological questions, to convince them that describing sediments accurately, sampling them, and subjecting them to lab analysis will provide information worthy of the effort. It supplements the analysis of the artifacts themselves, thereby providing a description of the entire site complex and its physical environment.

The individual chapters give an overview of sedimentology without forcing the reader to master the geoscientific jargon and literature. More importantly, each author provides concrete examples of archaeological applications that illustrate the importance of studying sediments in archaeological contexts. Each chapter focuses on sediments within one type of depositional environment. We feel that the depositional environment is the best organizing principle for archaeological research because the depositional setting shapes sediments in archaeological contexts most profoundly. Interpreting sediments requires an understanding of all sedimentary processes operating within that depositional environment.

In each chapter the author cites primary literature relevant to sediments and archaeological research in a given depositional environment. We expect that individual readers may have to refer to more than one chapter to understand the environment in which their site sediments accumulated, as well as to investigate the literature cited.

The first chapter by Julie Stein focuses on sediments found in a cultural environment. She emphasizes the concepts of deposition and sediments found within archaeological sites and demonstrates their usefulness for archaeological research. The second chapter is by William Farrand who studies sediments within rockshelters and caves. The sedimentological analysis of rockshelter sediments has changed greatly in recent decades, from one focused heavily on particle-size analysis (granulometry) to one that incorporates chemical and mineralogical analyses, morphology of rock fragments, and post-depositional alteration, including soil formation.

The next two chapters are to be considered together. The third chapter is by Gary Huckleberry who introduces alluvial settings in dryland environments. He explains how rivers move sediments and how that transport in arid climates creates environments in which humans live. This chapter is an excellent introduction to rivers and allows individuals to familiarize themselves with the processes. The fourth chapter is by Bruce Gladfelter. He considers the sophisticated process of alluvial settings in more humid environments. Channelized flow is explained clearly and in detail. An individual interested in the complexities of this system will find all necessary information here. Although these chapters focus on alluviation in wetter and drier conditions, they also are arranged so that access to the complicated alluvial system can be gained incrementally, first through Huckelberry and secondly through Gladfelter.

The fifth chapter is by Craig Feibel who considers the unique interaction between people and lake margin environments. He discusses the contrast between open- and closed-basin lakes, and the nature of sedimentation at the lake margin that controls preservation or modification of occupation sites. In the sixth chapter Lisa Wells describes the sediments in marine coastal environments. Global climate, local tectonic activity, and tidal forces can influence sea-level fluctuations and dictate human settlements along marine coasts. The seventh chapter by Gail Ashley focuses on the special sedimentary environment of springs and wetlands, which have always been attractive to humans as water resources and biotic zones for exploitation.

As editors we are interested in providing an affordable book that could be assigned to students taking classes, or purchased by archaeologists needing access to sedimentological information. We hope that this volume will open doors for you in your archaeological pursuits.

1

Archaeological Sediments in Cultural Environments

Julie K. Stein

Today's archaeological methods were selected for their ability to extract isolated artifacts from the ground while maintaining their contextual associations, and not for their ability to record depositional histories of layers or sequences of strata. Artifacts as reflections of behavior have been the focus of archaeologists for the last one hundred years. The methods used for their collection are designed to separate them from non-artifacts and to record their position in space. Recently, archaeologists have broadened their interest from just the artifacts to include the depositional history of those artifacts. The methods, however, need to be broadened to reflect a shift from artifact-focus to layer-focus. Small additions to the basic methods for excavation will assist archaeologists in their ability to reconstruct not only the context of artifacts but also the depositional history of the entire layer and site in which the artifact was found. This chapter is an attempt to begin that broadening.

When archaeologists begin an excavation they lay out a grid, select certain squares, and dig the sediment and artifacts in arbitrary or natural levels. Everything from the ground is screened and saved together until a change is observed or a depth reached. The change signals to the excavator that all newly discovered artifacts should be separated from all previously excavated ones. The change is interpreted as an important difference in behavioral or natural processes, and called a change in context. The basis for this decision, therefore, is of great importance.

Archaeologists read subtle changes within the ground better than do most other geoscientists because they study the human past and are most comfortable addressing questions within the human scale (Stein 1993). The changes that most archaeologists note when they subdivide contexts relate to physical properties such as color, moisture, and presence/absence of large- or small-sized particles, observed at a certain "human" scale. The human scale encompasses

phenomena that are "accessible to humans directly through their unaided eye
. . . roughly 1/10 of a millimeter to a few kilometers in space, and from 1/10 of a
second to a few decades in time" (Morrison and Morrison 1982; Schumm
1991:47–48). Archaeologists identify subtleties smaller than most other geoscientists observe, and they dig more slowly with trowels and brushes, allowing
them to feel such changes as well as see them. Fieldwork in archaeology is designed to sample this human scale, and dictates the appropriate size for dividing
contexts. At the point of excavation, the cause of the change in context is not
important, only the fact that a change is observed.

The next task for an archaeologist is to interpret the meaning of the layers
and add that information to the analysis of the artifacts. This interpretation is
made with varying success depending on the site and the archaeological team.
Archaeologists often struggle with the interpretation of the layering because
most graduate training does not prepare them to make such interpretations.
Even with this disadvantage, there are many circumstances where archaeologists make this interpretation appropriately using uniformitarian principles.
Perhaps this is because archaeologists emphasize long stints of fieldwork, under apprenticeship/training conditions, that include observing processes operating in their area. They make a multitude of observations about the processes
they see and project those processes into the past. Archaeologists watch the
landscape, which allows them to interpret adequately many physical properties they observed in the site.

For example, an archaeologist might say, "This sand around the artifacts
came from that hill behind the site. I know this because all summer while we
excavated, sand washed down the hill during rainstorms and filled our excavation unit. It must have done that when the prehistoric people lived here too."
In such cases, the sand may be subdivided into layers based on darker or lighter
color, which is interpreted as more or less organic matter or charcoal derived
from the occupation. The interpretation of the layering is complete and most
likely correct.

Occasionally, however, the layering is too complex or sufficiently different
from present conditions to use modern analogs, and a specialist must be called
upon to make the interpretation. The archaeologist asks the geoscientist some
seemingly easy questions. "Tell me where this dirt came from, how it got here,
and how it has been altered, because I need to relate it to my interpretations of
the artifacts in each layer." The specialist is sometimes a geoarchaeologist who
is trained in the geoscientific techniques that relate to deposition and weathering at the scale of excavation used in archaeology. But at other times the specialist is a geoscientist who never before considered archaeological research or
worked at such scales. They all come, and they all try to help.

Using the vernacular of archaeologists, sites are composed of artifacts and features surrounded (or held) by matrix. These terms are not meaningful to most geoscientists, who do not have the artifact-centered perspective of archaeologists and who will not know the meaning of such words as features or matrix. They may not recognize which objects are artifacts and which are just gravel-sized rocks, or understand why separation of the gravel will translate into behavior.

Most geoarchaeologists suggest that the specialist should be able to appreciate archaeological as well as geoscientific principles and should be broadly familiar with a wide range of techniques (Barham and MacPhail 1995; Pollard 1999; Rapp and Hill 1998; Thorson 1990; Waters 1992). This, however, is not always possible or practical. Many times the archaeologist must struggle alone or with a nonarchaeological geoscientist and get whatever tidbit is offered. The answer to the archaeologist's plight (and the geoarchaeologist's plea) is to train all field archaeologists to recognize layering and to interpret some simplistic contexts, but also to train them to communicate with experts when unusual physical changes are observed.

This chapter is an attempt to start that process and to familiarize archaeologists with the basic principles associated with layering and to assist them in interpreting, or talking to experts about interpreting, layers they find in their sites. The following definitions are offered to enhance communication between the archaeologist and any geoscientist or geoarchaeologist that may be invited to participate in an excavation. In addition, these definitions point to considerations that expand archaeological practices and explain to all who examine archaeological sites what can be obtained if one examines sites in more than just a common sense or strictly uniformitarian approach.

Throughout this chapter the British Camp shell midden (45SJ24), in the San Juan Islands, Washington, will be used to illustrate concepts. This shell midden is on the shoreline of Garrison Bay and within the San Juan Island National Historic Park (Fig. 1.1). It was excavated by Stein from 1983 to 1991 and published in the books *Deciphering a Shell Midden* (Stein 1992a) and *Exploring Coast Salish Prehistory: Archaeology of San Juan Island* (Stein 2000b). Radiocarbon samples from the part of the site called Operation A indicate an occupation from about 1,000 years ago to the present (Stein et al. 2000). The site represents a place where people deposited abundant remains of shellfish, fish, terrestrial mammals, fire-cracked rock, stone and bone tools with their manufacture debris, and abundant matrix. The goal of the excavation was to explain a stratigraphic property found on many Northwest Coast sites, namely dark-colored sediment underlying lighter colored sediment. (The results are summarized in Stein 1996.)

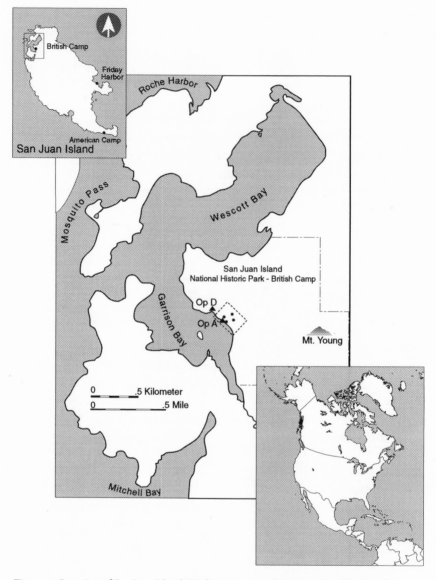

Figure 1.1. Location of San Juan Island, Washington, near the international border of
Canada and the United States.

The Deposit

Another term for layer is deposit. It is defined as a three-dimensional unit distinguished in the field on the basis of observable changes in some physical
properties (Stein 1987). Archaeologists are familiar with such units and have

called them elemental sediment units (ESU) (Fedele 1976:34), cuts (Fedele 1984:9), levels (Phillips et al. 1951:241), layers (Gasche and Tunca 1983:328; Stein 1990:514), and facies (Stein and Rapp 1985:154; Stein et al. 1992:97). These terms basically refer to the same thing: the unit identified in the field as representing similar context of artifacts and defined using any physical property at any scale that is convenient for the research question (Stein 1987, 1990, 1992b). An assemblage of artifacts removed from any given deposit constitutes the smallest unit of analysis possible. They are stored together because they have been defined as related using the definition of deposit, but can be combined with artifacts from other deposits for purposes of analysis. The deposit represents the smallest unit of context for any group of artifacts removed from the site.

The important aspect of this definition of a deposit is that any physical property can be selected as an important criterion for definition, and any degree of change in any of the physical properties can be selected as criterion for distinguishing one deposit from another. The guiding principle used to select the physical properties is based on any appropriate research question. For example, if weathering is suspected at a site, then properties such as color, silt and clay percentages, and carbonate content may be important. If shifting technology from hunting and gathering to agriculture is suspected at a site, then properties such as artifact content, soil chemistry, and house features may be important. If the site is the first to be examined in the region, then properties that are only the most extreme in their contrast may be important, or may even be arbitrarily chosen, such as depth below surface. The important aspect of this definition of a deposit is that the selection of physical properties (and therefore scale) is an arbitrary decision based on research questions, and not on a single correct physical entity (Stein 1993).

Because various physical properties can be selected to divide any particular site (depending on the research questions), there can be no one correct sequence. Two researchers could divide the same site into different numbers of deposits, both of which are justifiable (e.g., 40 deposits as opposed to 10 deposits). The number of deposits will depend on the question being addressed, the physical properties selected, and the scale convenient for recording (or mapping). The two archaeologists could be labeled "splitters" or "lumpers," but the point here is that the decision should be based on physical properties selected for their ability to answer the research question. One archaeologist could criticize another colleague for addressing an inappropriate research question, or addressing it with an inappropriate division of deposits, but not for simply identifying an inappropriate number of deposits.

Because deposits can be defined legitimately using a wide variety of physical properties and scales, the archaeologist should describe in detail the criteria and magnitude used to define deposits (e.g., Jacobsen and Farrand 1987; Farrand 2000). The deposits are being destroyed, and thus the properties observed, and the magnitude of difference in those properties, should be explicitly recorded.

Using the British Camp example, deposits were defined by eight properties (Fig. 1.2), three of which were the amount of shell, its fragmentation, and the color of the matrix (Stein et al. 1992:98–100). When the amount of shell changed from less than 50 percent abundance to greater than 50 percent, then a new deposit was identified. If the degree of fragmentation changed from less than 50 percent abundance to greater than 50 percent fragmented, a new deposit was identified. If the color of the matrix changed from brown to black, tan, or gray, a new deposit was identified. In some cases all three properties changed together, in others only one or two. In all cases, the change(s) signaled a new deposit, and the properties on which the decisions were based are described explicitly.

Stating explicitly the properties chosen allows another archaeologist to replicate the field procedure, or evaluate the grouping of artifacts and the appropriateness of the research question. Strangely enough, archaeological reports do not traditionally include the field criteria used to define the layers from which artifacts were derived. Such field criteria may be recorded in the excavation notes, but published literature is commonly silent on the most important criteria associated with excavation and artifact analysis. We should be more conscientious to report these data because the deposit is distinguished in the field and the physical properties that are selected on the basis of research questions disappear as the excavation proceeds. It is therefore important to publish those properties.

Sediments

A sediment has two definitions depending if you use a common definition from the English language, or if you refer to a sedimentological definition. It is also related closely to the definition of deposit. In common English language a sediment is matter that settles from a liquid (often associated with wine), or matter deposited by water. In sedimentological terminology it is "particulate matter that has been transported by some process from one location to another" (Reineck and Singh 1980; see discussion in Stein 1987:339). One appreciates immediately the problems occurring when two people communicate and one uses the English and the other the sedimentological definition. Transport by any agent is required in one, only water is implied in the other.

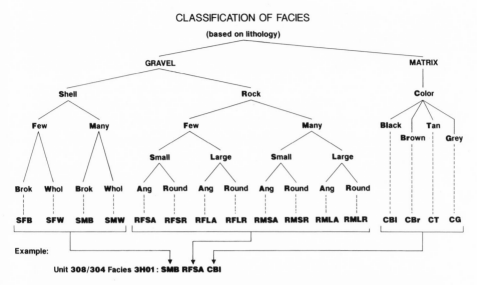

Figure 1.2. Classification of facies at British Camp, San Juan Island, based on lithology. Brok is the abbreviation for broken; Whol for whole; Ang for angular. Note that for each facies, the gravel is described on the basis of shell and rock, and the sand, silt, and clay (matrix) is described on the basis of color only. The example of Unit 308/304 facies 3H01 is described as containing many broken shells (SMB), few small angular rocks (RFSA), and black fine-grained sediment (CBI). Each facies is excavated using these lithological attributes. (Drafted by Timothy D. Hunt, reprinted from Stein et al. 1992, with permission from Academic Press.)

The sedimentological definition and its relationship to deposits requires some further explanation. It states that particulate matter was transported by an agent. First, the words particulate matter refer to any particle made of any mineral or organic material. Sedimentologists consider every object (no matter what its composition or shape) to be a sedimentary particle. So the phrase "particulate matter" is chosen to emphasize that all particles are sediments. Although not specifically stated, the definition is so inclusive that it accommodates artifacts as well as unmodified rock fragments. Artifacts are particulate matter that have been transported by some agent, initially at least by humans.

Second, the definition of sediment requires that the particle be transported. A question of scale immediately presents itself. How far does a grain have to move to be considered a sediment—a centimeter, meter, or kilometer? There is no exact answer. Sedimentologists typically concern themselves with research questions at the scale of basins, continents, and oceans (Stein and Linse 1993). Their answer would be that the particle has to move fairly far. But archaeologists concern themselves with research at the scale of people, houses, sites, and regions. Their answer would be different. The point of the definition is that the grains are called sediments only if they have been moved obviously from one location to another, and that the movement is detectable. The issue of scale is open, but subject to common sense.

Third, there is a technical, although subtle, difference between deposits and sediments. Deposits are groupings of particles that look different from what is above or below. They are defined by the field worker on the basis of physical traits. A sediment is the particulate matter within such a grouping that has been transported from one place to another. All sediments can be grouped into deposits, but not all deposits technically contain sediments. A deposit could contain decomposed bedrock weathered in place. This distinction is subtle and exemplified in the phrase "all sediment in each deposit," emphasizing that sediments are particles themselves and that the deposit is the grouping. In my opinion the term "deposit" is a more general reference to a layer. A sediment has a precise connotation related to the particles themselves. The literature, however, is full of examples when the two terms have been used interchangeably.

Fourth, this definition of sediment does not specify that the processes of transport have to be natural as opposed to cultural. People and animals can transport a sediment as effectively as water and wind. People carry bricks to walls, track sand with footwear, and throw bones in trash piles. Animals track sand on their paws and carry bones to trash piles as well as move bones out of trash piles. Water carries bones, and wind blows shells. The kind of transport agent is not important to the definition of sediment, only that a transport agent moves the object from a source to a deposition site.

Archaeologists have been trained to consider the entire archaeological record in terms of culture vs. nature. The very nature of defining a site as a place where artifacts are concentrated reinforces that dichotomy. Schiffer (1972, 1983, 1987) propelled the study of geoarchaeology to the forefront of the discipline by suggesting emphatically that archaeologists must interpret the deposits from which their artifacts come. He did, however, emphasize the difference between natural formation processes (n-transforms) and cultural formation processes (c-transforms), which has continued to influence archaeologists ever since (Stein 2001).

To emphasize the cultural-natural dichotomy influences inappropriately the interpretations of deposits toward one kind of particle—the artifact. Archaeologists have taken Schiffer's n-transforms and c-transforms concept, meant for artifact analysis, and applied the terms to entire deposits. This transfer from artifact to deposit is understandable given the historical emphasis on artifacts as opposed to deposits. But there are problems associated with this shift. Archaeologists have been asking the question, "Where did my artifacts come from and why do they look like that?" That is a question about artifacts not about deposition. Attributes of artifacts are related to technology, use, function, and style. To answer the question "where did my layer come from and why does it look like that?" requires looking at all the grains together and noting the variability or consistency of attributes between types of particles. The depositional history of the layers containing those artifacts is more likely recorded in the relationship of that artifact to the other particles in the deposit. Is the artifact the same size as all the particles? Is its orientation in the deposit vertical or horizontal, and different from the orientation of other artifacts? Are the edges of the artifact and all the grains rounded? Are all the grains oxidized or just the artifact? The new questions related to depositional history are best addressed by comparing attributes of all grains in a deposit—artifacts and non-artifacts, cultural and natural.

One would get better results by focusing on the entire depositional history of all kinds of particles. Each compositional type of particle could have a different history involving some natural and some cultural aspects. In deposits there may be particles transported by natural processes, and others transported by cultural ones that are grouped together for purposes of answering a certain research question. Classifying sediments as natural or cultural is not relevant to interpreting site formation processes from the perspective of a deposit. It may be relevant for interpreting particles, and certainly for individual artifacts, but not deposits.

Finally, the definition of sediment does not specify the rate of transport and deposition. Particulate matter could be transported by any agent and accumulate rapidly over minutes or slowly over hundreds of years (Ferring 1986). The definition says only that the grains were moved.

Principles of Sedimentation

The archaeologist, who realizes that the layers in the site are too complicated to interpret intuitively, calls the expert and asks, "Tell me about these layers. Why do they look like that?" What the archaeologist is really requesting is an interpretation of the depositional history for all sediment in each deposit according to the principles of sedimentation. I am sure archaeologists are not aware that what they ask involves a sophisticated principle. But it does.

Sedimentologists have figured out that a given deposit is either laid down (deposited) "under essentially constant physical conditions . . . (with) constant delivery of the same material during deposition" (a sediment) (Reineck and Singh 1980:96), or it was created by processes (weathering) whereby "rocks and minerals are altered to more stable forms under the variable conditions of moisture, temperature, and biological activity that prevail at the surface" (not a sediment) (Birkeland 1999:53).

To decipher a complicated site the specialist must jump in the trenches and look at the deposits closely, then walk around the site and region and consider all possible sources (even those that may be obscured or no longer exist), observe and reconstruct all possible transport agents, and reconstruct depositional environments for all particles in all deposits. Afterwards, the specialists must dig holes in areas beyond the area of artifact concentration (the site) to acquire control samples and determine the weathering history of the area, and search for all agents that may have mixed (turbated) deposits after they were laid down. The archaeologists may not understand why the specialist is running over the broad landscape and not sticking to the layers in each pit. The reason is simply that deposits are collections of sediments that come from one or many sources, are transported by any competent agent or group of agents, and are deposited whenever and wherever the competency of the transport agent is reduced and where a suitable "basin" is located (Stein 1987:340). Deposits also contain particles not transported but weathered in place or mixed. The specialists must reconstruct the depositional history by examining the whole region.

The tasks just described are necessary if one asked the simplistic question, "Tell me about these layers." This translates into sedimentological terminology of determining the "life history" of sediment (Hassan 1978). That life history (Fig. 1.3) is divided into four stages and defined by the principles of sedimentation: (1) source, (2) transport agent, (3) environment of deposition, and (4) post-depositional alteration (Krumbein and Sloss 1963; Blatt et al. 1972; Twenhofel 1950). The principles of sedimentation are used by sedimentologists and have been successfully applied to archaeological sediments (deposits) to answer the questions posed by most archaeologists (e.g., Goldberg et al. 1993; Nash and Petraglia 1987; Stein 1987).

Source

The first stage in the history of an archaeological sediment is represented by its source, either where bedrock was weathered to unconsolidated particles or where sediment was naturally deposited (Birkeland 1999). Particles in archaeological sites usually come from multiple sources. For example, bones come from animals acquired from hunting, fishing, animal husbandry, or wild animals that lived on the site at various times. Rocks used for tool manufacture may come from far away sources, and those used to heat water (hot-rock boiling technique) probably were from local sources. Sands, silts, and clay come

ARCHAEOLOGICAL RECORD
made of

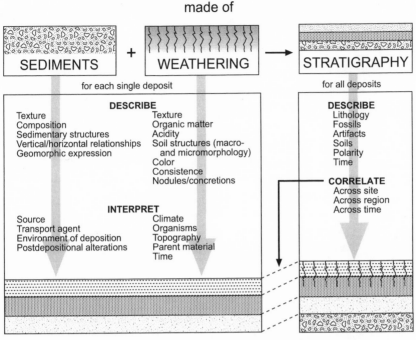

Figure 1.3. The archaeological record consists of sediments (particulate matter that was transported from one location to another). Sediments are characterized by describing five attributes, which in turn are used to interpret the depositional history of each single deposit (source, transport agent, environment of deposition, and post-depositional alterations). After deposition, sediments can be weathered. The effects of weathering are characterized by describing seven attributes, which are used to interpret the soil forming factors for each single deposit (climate, organisms, topography, parent material, and time). Stratigraphy is the comparison of many such deposits using the descriptions of lithology, fossils, artifacts, soils, polarity, and age. Stratigraphy uses these descriptions to correlate deposits across sites, regions, and/or time. (Drafted by Christopher Lockwood.)

from nearby, upslope, or upstream. Each material type must be examined separately and its source pinpointed.

The attribute that best addresses source is the composition of the grains in the deposit. Composition refers to the chemical substance of each particle in the deposit, and the grouping of those substances into meaningful categories (e.g., one each for minerals, rocks, plants, animals, and solutions). Most archaeologists separate artifactual particles in this way. For example, for each layer, they bag separately rocks and minerals, fauna, flora, and formed tools. The source of a deposit requires that all compositional types be examined (not just artifacts) and the sources of each compositional type of particle be determined. There will most likely be multiple sources from local and nonlocal areas represented in each deposit. These proportions are useful for contrasting deposits and their histories.

Sourcing artifacts is a familiar exercise for archaeologists. Bakewell (1996) determined the source of the fine-grained volcanic tool stone found at British Camp. Using petrographic and chemical techniques he identified the extrusive volcanic outcrop from which the stone was derived. Determining the source of other objects found in the British Camp midden is not as familiar an exercise for archaeologists. Latas (1992) located the source of the non-tool stone (e.g., fire-cracked rock) used in the hot-rock boiling technique at British Camp and found they all came from local sources (Fig. 1.4). Stein (1992c) determined that the sand, silt, and clay particles came from the underlying glacial-marine drift and the intertidal zone sediment. Ford (1992) identified the sources of the shellfish, and found that all but the sea urchins inhabit the bay in front of the site. These examples illustrate how sources for all kinds of objects can add to the understanding of the depositional history of each deposit.

Transport History

The second stage in the evolution of a sediment is its transport history. A transport agent is the process that brought the object from the source to the deposit. In archaeological sites, objects that are artifacts were usually transported by people. The definition of "site" is based on the presence and frequency of artifacts, so it is not surprising that people are an important transport agent in the depositional history of sediments at sites. The most common agents transporting non-artifact grains are wind for silt- and clay-sized grains; water for small gravel, sand, silt, and clay; gravity for all sizes of objects derived from steep slopes; and animals for a variety of other objects.

Transport processes are themselves not easy to classify. Sedimentologists have focused on many aspects such as the medium of transport, the vectors of force, even the environment where the transport occurred. The problem centers around the issue of focus. Is the agent of transport the water or the river? Visher (1969) believes it is the agent and not the environment, and relates particle-size parameters to three different ways (processes) of transport. He identifies rolling, saltation, and suspension. Rolling transport moves objects along the surface; saltation moves particles by bouncing them; and suspension moves them entirely within the medium of transport. Note that Visher does not refer to the kind of medium doing the transporting (e.g., water, wind, or ice). He focuses on the competence of the medium to overcome gravity and keep the particles from coming to rest on the surface.

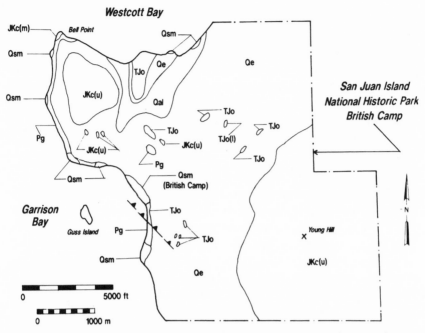

Figure 1.4. Geologic map of British Camp, San Juan Island, Washington. Shown on the map is the areal distribution of deposits within the park: shell middens (Qsm), alluvium (Qal), Everson Galciomarine Drift (Qe), Constitution Formation upper sandstone member (JKc[u]), Constitution Formation middle conglomerate member (JKc[m]), Orcas Chert ribbon chert (TJo), Orcas Chert limestone (TJo[l]), and Garrison Schist (Pg). Also shown is a low-angle thrust fault (line with saw-tooth edge). (Reprinted from Latas 1992, with permission from Academic Press.)

Archaeological artifacts are related most frequently to a transport agent not normally considered as relevant in sedimentology (i.e., people). People as transport agents are not considered explicitly in Visher's scheme, but people do transport objects and are important agents of transport at archaeological sites. When a person picks up an object and carries it, they become a transport agent, and their actions fit as suspension transport in Visher's scheme of classification. Visher's scheme defines the transport according to the number of times the particle comes in contact with the bed (the surface over which transport takes place). If the people are not rolling the objects, bouncing, or throwing them, then the objects are moved entirely within the medium doing the transport (a human being).

One of the most useful attributes to identify a transport agent is size. To transport an object is to pick it up off the ground, in other words to overcome gravity. Overcoming gravity is easy for small objects and difficult for large ones, and the size of an object tells you the competence needed to move it. The size of a single grain is a start, but even more interesting is the comparison of sizes of all the particles in a deposit. Are they all the same size? Are there only large and very small ones? Is there a continuum of sizes represented? Measuring grain sizes is called particle-size analysis, or granulometry, and is usually discussed in terms of frequency of grains in certain size categories. Particle-size data are most often displayed in histograms with the sizes arranged along the horizontal axis from the coarsest (large) fraction at the left to the finest (small) fraction on the right (Fig. 1.5).

The distribution of lithic grain sizes gave Madsen (1992) additional information about various deposits at the British Camp shell midden. He, like others, used size distributions of various material types (including microartifacts) to determine transport agents as well as depositional events associated with behavior (Buck 1990; Dunnell and Stein 1989; Fladmark 1982; Hull 1987; Metcalfe and Heath 1990; Rosen 1986, 1991, 1993; Sherwood and Ousley 1995; Sherwood et al. 1995; Stafford 1995; Stein and Teltser 1989; Vance 1986, 1989). Focus has recently shifted to the microscopic portion of the size continuum, and I suggest starting with Sherwood (2001) for a complete explanation of the advantages of using microartifact analysis.

The depositional history of a deposit requires reconstructing all transport agents for all particles.

Environment of Deposition

The third stage involves the environment of deposition (or the place where the sediment comes to rest). This is invariably the place where the archaeologist finds the deposit. This is the place where the transport agent lost its competence to transport and dropped the object. The environment of deposition is often referred to as the depositional event—a time when constant conditions prevailed.

A geoscientist would say that each deposit has integrity as a unit because as a group it was brought to its resting place by one specific depositional event. That event, however, could represent multiple sources and transport agents and a variety of particle types and sizes. A specific deposit is said to belong to a group because the specific event that produced it was constant over the period of time it accumulated. It looks internally more alike than the material deposited by earlier or later events.

A deposit therefore records an individual event, inferred from physical attributes, and represents a time when depositional conditions remained similar. No reference to duration or rate, however, is implied in the depositional event,

GRAIN-SIZE FREQUENCY CURVE

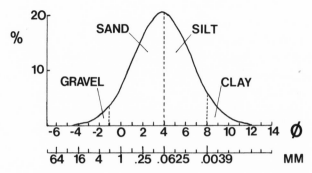

Figure 1.5. This generalized grain-size distribution curve graphically depicts the individual percentages of each grain-size class in a given sample. The size class of the particle, plotted on the horizontal axis, is expressed in two equally acceptable scales; millimeters and phi units (a logarithmic scale in which each class limit is twice as large as the next smaller class limit). Note that grain size is always drawn with the size range arranged from the coarsest (large) fraction at the left to the finest (small) fraction on the right. Nomenclature (gravel, sand, etc.) for size classes derived from sedimentology. (Figure redrawn from Stein and Rapp 1985.)

nor is any reference to homogeneity or singularity of source or transport agent. The deposition could have occurred over a long time, in short bursts, or in one millisecond. This environment of deposition, the deposit, is merely a group of objects from similar sources dropped by transport processes more similar to each other than to those above, below, or adjacent to it.

Observations important for explaining the change in competence are the shape of the deposits, their lateral and vertical extent, and the boundaries that separate them from other deposits (Gladfelter 1977).

Each particle in the deposit has a separate history, yet as a deposit all particles share only one depositional event: the last one that brought them all together. A Permian fossil, a rounded grain of quartz, a potsherd, and a fragment of charcoal all have separate individual histories, and these histories may be investigated by noting selected attributes of each individual object. Such attributes have been left on the particle during previous depositional events, and preserved through subsequent events. The attributes relevant to the target (or last) depositional event are only those related to the deposit as a whole (e.g., the grain-to-grain relationship, the textural distribution, the frequencies of mineral types). Each particle has a unique past, but the environment of deposition results from the final depositional event that collected many different particles and left them together. Viewing the deposit as an environment of deposition means focusing not just upon the particles called artifacts, or any individual particle for that matter, but also upon the depositional event that brought the artifacts and all the other particles together in the deposit.

The artifacts share with all other particles in the deposit a relationship called the depositional event or environment of deposition. Transport agents for all particles may have been the same, and the sources of the particles may be similar or different. The artifacts most assuredly have a history aligned with the people who made them, but that history is only partially relevant to the depositional event that created the deposit as a whole. The environment of deposition of artifacts alone has been the traditional concern of archaeologists, when in fact, the environment of deposition of all particles can provide equally valuable (albeit different) information.

I am not suggesting that the environment of deposition of artifacts be ignored, or that it is less important than the history of the whole deposit. Rather I am suggesting that the artifactual particle's attributes should not automatically be given precedence over other information relevant to depositional events. The environment of deposition, however, is most powerful when used as a unit of analysis separate from, and complementary to, the unit of analysis defined as the individual particle. Attributes used to investigate particles are not always appropriate for investigating deposits, and archaeologists are not always familiar with other means for investigating deposits besides examining the histories of individual particles. Yet, environment of deposition is really what archaeologists want to know.

Post-Depositional Alterations

The fourth stage, post-depositional alterations, is really separate from deposition. It occurs, by definition, after deposition takes place. Many kinds of post-depositional alterations occur. For example, diagenesis refers to physical and chemical changes in sediment after it was deposited and buried under another layer of sediment. Bioturbation is the mixing of sediment by biological organisms after deposition (Wood and Johnson 1978). Chemical alteration is the breakdown of rocks, minerals, and organic matter (Birkeland 1999). These are just some of the events that occur after deposition and affect the physical properties of a deposit. The principles of sedimentation require that the properties related to post-depositional events be distinguished from those related to deposition.

The most important post-deposition alteration for archaeological deposits is weathering. Weathering is the physical and chemical alteration of rock and minerals at or near the Earth's surface (Birkeland 1999:53). Although weathering is integral to many scientific disciplines, the study of soils (pedology) is one that focuses on weathering and greatly impacts archaeology. Pedology is "the area of soil science devoted to the study of soils in their natural setting; their morphology, genesis, and classification" (Holliday 1992:102). "Soils are the result of the complex interaction of a variety of physical, chemical, and biological processes acting on rock or sediment over time" (Holliday 1992:102) or, in other words, weathering (Brady and Weil 1999; Buol et al. 1997).

Soils should not be confused with sediments. Soils develop in sediments near the surface of the Earth through weathering under the influence of plants, other biological elements, and atmospheric conditions. Similar to the term "sediment" the word "soil" has two definitions; in common English language a soil is "the earth or ground, the portion of the Earth's surface in which plants grow, or a country or foreign place." In pedology it is "a natural body consisting of layers (horizons) of mineral and/or organic constituents of variable thickness, which differs from the parent materials in their morphological, physical, chemical, and mineralogical properties and their biological characteristics" (Birkeland 1999). There are other definitions, such as those of agricultural soil scientists who consider soil as a medium of plant growth, or engineers and some geologists who define soil as any unconsolidated sediment, including loose or weathered rock or regolith (as opposed to cemented rock).

The processes of weathering, as inferred by pedologists, have been grouped into those processes that (1) add materials to the soil, (2) transform materials within the soil (through chemical alterations), (3) transfer materials (either up, down, or sideways) through the soil, and those that (4) remove materials from the soil (Simonson 1959). These are the soil-forming processes, or processes of weathering a sediment or rock (see Fig. 1.3).

The attributes relevant to these processes include color, texture, consistency, structure, acidity, percentages of organic matter, calcium carbonate, sesquioxides, iron, and quantity and nature (interconnectivity) of voids (Buol et al. 1997). Note that some of these attributes overlap with those used by sedimentologists for studying deposition (Fig. 1.3). Many of them, however, are unique to pedology, and relate specifically to the interaction of physical, chemical, and biological processes associated with weathering.

Pedologists are not interested only in the additions, transformations, transfers, or removals of material from the soil. Their goal is to use these processes to infer the environment at the time the processes operated (i.e., the environment under which the soil formed). The processes (what is added, transformed, transferred, and removed) are controlled by environmental *factors,* which operate over time. These factors define the *state* of the soil system

(Tandarich and Sprecher 1994; Retallack 1994). Soil scientists are dedicated to understanding the soil-forming environment, so they classify contemporary, directly observable environments according to the factors relevant to their weathering, and use them to infer which factors were operating in the past (Holliday 1990; Johnson and Hole 1994).

One of the most valuable attributes noted in soils is vertical differentiation, called horizons. Horizons reflect changes in mineralogy, texture, and chemistry usually caused by weathering. In archaeological investigations, soil horizons must be differentiated from depositional sedimentary strata (Mandel and Bettis 2000).

The fourth stage of sediment history also includes processes that interrupt horizon development and mix (homogenize) the sediment near the surface. These post-depositional alterations are referred to as pedoturbations (Hole 1961) and include the effects of burrowing animals, trees, freezing and thawing, and other processes. Wood and Johnson (1978) were the first to alert archaeologists to the importance of these processes, and much research has since addressed these effects (Bocek 1986; Erlandson 1984; Johnson 1989, 1990; Johnston and Watson-Stegner 1990; Rick 1976; Stein 1983; Stone 1989).

Archaeologists now recognize that not only does post-depositional turbation mix artifacts deposited in layers near the surface but also it sometimes imparts patterns to artifact distributions that were not originally related to the depositional history. For example, in California, Bocek (1986) and Erlandson (1984) found that gophers create one set of burrows so as to travel below the surface and another deeper set in which to nest and breed. If gophers inhabit artifact-bearing deposits, then artifacts fall to the base of these two burrow systems and accumulate on the floors. If the gophers abandon the burrows, then the roofs collapse and the artifacts are left in two stratified concentrations, when originally they were distributed equally throughout the profile.

Archaeologists use artifact distributions to interpret prehistoric behaviors. Yet people are not the only producers of such spatial patterns. Study of post-depositional alterations includes the careful analysis of all turbation processes that impact the original deposit and spatial pattern of all particles in those deposits.

Depositional Events and Archaeology

Clearly, reconstructing the depositional history of each deposit identified in an archaeological site during excavation is a huge job that could be streamlined by grouping kinds of particles and deposits together. Rather than examining every grain in every deposit for all four stages of sedimentation, the geoarchaeologist could group deposits that share similar depositional histories, or similar sources. This grouping is an analytical device to help manage a huge number of observations. It is dictated by the research question and by the scale that is appropriate for the depositional history of the locale.

For example, one could imagine a situation where physical properties changed often and hundreds of deposits were identified during excavation. The specialist later discovered that most of the physical properties used to separate deposits were related to post-depositional alterations caused by weathering and the archaeologist's research question did not focus on weathering events. The research was targeting depositional events related to the transport of artifacts (in particular). The specialist should recommend to the archaeologist to group the deposits into larger depositional units relevant for interpreting the depositional history of the artifacts and particles surrounding those artifacts, and not to focus on the deposits altered by weathering that occurred after the artifacts were deposited. The specialist identified the best physical parameters for the given research question and shifted the definition of deposits. The shift results in fewer deposits subject to analysis. These fewer, larger depositional units are then examined for their depositional history, and each source, transport agent, and environment of deposition is identified.

At the British Camp site I discovered a variation of such a scenario (Stein 1992c, 1996, 2000b; Whittaker and Stein 1992). Northwest Coast shell middens located near the shore have a distinctive two-toned color scheme with dark-colored matrix on the bottom and light-colored matrix at and near the surface (Fig. 1.6). I proposed that the color was not related to depositional events but rather to postdepositional alterations. By excavating the site in many smaller layers, I proved that the only physical property that related to the dark/light dichotomy was water and chemical weathering. The layering was not behavioral. Yet for years archaeologists had been using the color scheme to separate artifacts and assess context. Using the smaller layers I can now group them on the basis of depositional event, artifact content, or any other criteria, rather than being forced to only compare the artifacts from the two color-determined layers.

Grouping deposits in various ways is the purview of the discipline called stratigraphy, and its application to archaeology has been described in many publications (Browman and Givens 1996; Cremeens and Hart 1995; Farrand 1984a, 1984b, 1993; Harris 1979, 1989; Harris et al. 1993; Stein 1987, 1990, 1992b, 2000a). Stratigraphy is "the science dealing with the description of all rock bodies forming the Earth's crust—sedimentary, igneous, and metamorphic—and their organization into distinctive, useful, mappable units based on

Figure 1.6. The sediment at the base of this profile is darker than the sediment in the upper portion because it has been wetted. Most people assume that rainwater wets sediment starting at the surface and that the upper sediment should be dark (wet) and the lower sediment should be light (dry). At many shell middens, located close to the modern shoreline, the opposite stratigraphy is observed. The lower layer is dark (wet) because the relationship of the land and sea level has changed over the last 2,000 years. The change resulted in a lowering of as much as 1 m of the land at the shoreline into the water. This zone of saturation includes the lower parts of hundreds of shell middens. The water brings with it increased rates of chemical decomposition. The lower layers of shell midden are losing their shell due to chemical degradation, and along with the shell goes the bone. In another 1,000 years we may have only stone artifacts left to recover (reprinted from Stein 2000b, with permission from University of Washington Press).

their inherent properties or attributes. Stratigraphic procedures include the description, classification, naming, and correlation of these units for the purpose of establishing their relationship in space and their succession in time" (Salvador 1994:137).

Stratigraphy differs from the study of depositional histories because it includes correlations across space and time. Correlations are made using any particle type or property of a deposit. Depositional histories can be one such property, but so can fossils, magnetic polarity, artifacts, or climatic reconstructions. Stratigraphy provides methods and rules for correlation and interpretation of many deposits and properties of deposits.

Control Samples

I emphasize control samples because they are the most frequently overlooked kinds of samples in all of archaeology. Deposits from archaeological sites are interpreted best if the depositional history is compared to nearby deposits where no artifacts are found. Samples collected as "controls" should be located at geomorphic positions (elevation, slope, and aspect) with faunal and floral assemblages similar to those found at the archaeological site. Commonly the archaeological site is so obviously different from surrounding areas because of cultural disturbances and additions of artifacts that a control area can only approximate site conditions. In some cases control samples can be obtained from strata within the site that appear to be devoid of cultural material. There always exists, however, a danger that these layers were in some way manipulated by people.

To determine the source of any sediment in any deposit from the site, the first question asked concerns the available sediment in the regions. If a river is nearby, a sample from the channel, natural levee, and floodplain should be considered. If the site is within a rockshelter, a sample of the overhang, the sediment above the overhang, and the substrate below should be collected. Samples should be taken of bedrock, beaches, intertidal substrates, or any source from which sediments could have come. These samples could be the most important key to interpreting the depositional history of your site's deposits. Do not leave the field without them.

Conclusion

To summarize, a deposit is a three-dimensional unit that is distinguished in the field on the basis of observable changes in some physical properties. By separating it from other deposits, each is considered to represent a separate depositional event, namely, the result of the derivation of sediments from one or many sources, the transport of that material by any competent agent or group of agents, and the deposition of the sediments whenever and wherever the competency of the transport agent is reduced and where a suitable "basin" is located (Stein 1987:340).

The request "tell me about these layers," requires the interpretation of all processes that brought the constant delivery of the same material under essentially constant physical conditions (Stein 1987:339). It requires the reconstruction of the depositional event that produced every deposit, using the principles of sedimentation. If archaeologists realize this, they will understand why specialists jump in and out of excavation trenches, examine the whole landscape, dig for control samples away from the site, and examine earthworms and gophers closely. All these behaviors are targeted toward identifying deposits and applying the principles of sedimentation.

Acknowledgments

The ideas expressed here were developed while teaching many University of Washington students of geoarchaeology. I would like to thank them all for their questions and contributions over the years. My understanding of deposit, deposition, sediment, and artifact have been formed by these bright and demanding scholars, in particular Paul Buck, Sarah Sherwood, Angela Linse, MaryAnn Emery, Debora Kligmann, Daniel Bush, Robert Kopperl, Barbara McKay, Roger Kiers, Debby Green, Jennie Deo, Kate Gallagher, Scotty Moore, and Christopher Lockwood. This manuscript has been greatly improved by the comments of Bill Farrand, Debora Kligmann, Rolfe Mandel, Vance Holliday, Kate Gallagher, and Christopher Lockwood. Finally, I wish to thank Academic Press and the University of Washington Press for permission to reprint figures.

References Cited

Bakewell, E. F.
1996   Petrographic and Geochemical Source-Modeling of Volcanic Lithics from Archaeo-
          logical Contexts: A Case Study from British Camp, San Juan Island, Washington.
          Geoarchaeology: An International Journal 11:119–140.
Barham, A. J., and R. I. MacPhail (editors)
1995   *Archaeological Sediments and Soils: Analysis, Interpretation and Management.* Institute
          of Archaeology, University College, London.
Birkeland, P. W.
1999   *Soils and Geomorphology.* 3rd ed. Oxford University Press, New York.
Blatt, H., G. V. Middleton, and R. C. Murray
1972   *Origin of Sedimentary Rocks.* Prentice-Hall, Englewood Cliffs, New Jersey.

Bocek, B.

1986   Rodent Ecology and Burrowing Behavior: Predicted Effects on Archaeological Site
        Formation. *American Antiquity* 51:589–603.

Brady, N. C., and R. R. Weil

1999   *The Nature and Properties of Soils.* 12th ed. Prentice Hall, New Jersey.

Browman, D. L., and D. R. Givens

1996   Stratigraphic Excavation: The first "New Archaeology." *American Anthropologist*
        98:80–95.

Buck, P. E.

1990   Structure and Content of Old Kingdom Archaeological Deposits in the Western
        Nile Delta, Egypt: A Geoarchaeological Example from Kom el-Hisn. Unpublished
        Ph.D. dissertation, Department of Anthropology, University of Washington, Seat-
        tle, Washington.

Buol, S. W., F. D. Hole, R. J. McCracken, and R. J. Southard

1997   *Soil Genesis and Classification.* 4th ed. Iowa State University Press, Ames, Iowa.

Cremeens, D. L., and J. P. Hart

1995   On Chronostratigraphy, Pedostratigraphy, and Archaeological Context. In *Pedologi-
        cal Perspectives in Archaeological Research,* edited by M. E. Collins, B. J. Carter, B. G.
        Gladfelter, and R. J. Southard, pp. 15–33. Soil Science Society of America, Special
        Publication 44. Madison, Wisconsin.

Dunnell, R. C., and J. K. Stein

1989   Theoretical Issues in the Interpretation of Microartifacts. *Geoarchaeology: An Inter-
        national Journal* 4:31–42.

Erlandson, J. M.

1984   A Case Study in Faunalturbation: Delineating the Effects of the Burrowing Pocket
        Gopher on the Distribution of Archaeological Materials. *American Antiquity*
        49:785–790.

Farrand, W. R.

1984a   Stratigraphic Classification: Living within the Law. *Quarterly Review of Archaeology*
        5:1.

1984b   More on Stratigraphic Practice. *Quarterly Review of Archaeology* 5:3.

1993   Discontinuity in the Stratigraphic Record: Snapshots from Franchthi Cave. In *For-
        mation Processes in Archaeological Context,* edited by P. Goldberg, D. T. Nash, and
        M. D. Petraglia, pp. 85–96. Monographs in World Archaeology No. 17. Prehistory
        Press, Madison, Wisconsin.

2000   *Depositional History of the Franchthi Cave: Stratigraphy, Sedimentology, and Chronol-
        ogy.* Indiana University Press, Bloomington.

Fedele, F. G.

1976   Sediments as Palaeo-Land Segments: The Excavation Side of Study. In *Geoarchaeol-
        ogy: Earth Science and the Past,* edited by D. A. Davidson and M. L. Shackley, pp.
        23–48. Westview Press, Boulder, Colorado.

1984   Towards an Analytical Stratigraphy: Stratigraphic Reasoning and Excavation. *Strati-
        graphica Archaeologica* 1:7–15.

Ferring, C. R.

1986   Rates of Fluvial Sedimentation: Implications for Archaeological Variability. *Geoar-
        chaeology: An International Journal* 1:259–274.

Fladmark, K. R.

1982   Microdebitage Analysis: Initial Considerations. *Journal of Archaeological Science*
        9:205–220.

Ford, P. J.
1992   Interpreting the Grain Size Distributions of Archaeological Shell. In *Deciphering a Shell Midden,* edited by J. K. Stein, pp. 283–326. Academic Press, San Diego.
Gasche, H., and O. Tunca
1983   Guide to Archaeostratigraphic Classification and Terminology: Definitions and Principles. *Journal of Field Archaeology* 10:325–335.
Gladfelter, B. G.
1977   Geoarchaeology: The Geomorphologist and Archaeology. *American Antiquity* 42:519–538.
Goldberg, P., D. T. Nash, and M. D. Petraglia
1993   *Formation Processes in Archaeological Context.* Monographs in World Archaeology No. 17. Prehistory Press, Madison, Wisconsin.
Harris, E. C.
1979   *Principles of Archaeological Stratigraphy.* Academic Press, London.
1989   *Principles of Archaeological Stratigraphy.* 2nd ed. Academic Press, New York.
Harris, E. C., M. R. Brown III, and G. Brown (editors)
1993   *Practices of Archaeological Stratigraphy.* Academic Press, London.
Hassan, F. A.
1978   Sediments in Archaeology: Methods and Implications for Paleoenvironmental and Cultural Analysis. *Journal of Field Archaeology* 5:197–213.
Hole, F. D.
1961   A Classification of Pedoturbations and Some Other Processes and Factors of Soil Formation in Relation to Isotropism and Anisotropism. *Soil Science* 91:375–377.
Holliday, V. T.
1990   Pedology in Archaeology. In *Archaeological Geology of North America,* edited by N. P. Lasca and J. Donahue, pp. 525–540. Geological Society of America, Centennial Special Vol. 4. Boulder, Colorado.
Holliday, V. T. (editor)
1992   *Soils in Archaeology: Landscape Evolution, and Human Occupation.* Smithsonian Institution Press, Washington, D.C.
Hull, K. L.
1987   Identification of Cultural Site Formation Processes through Microdebitage Analysis. *American Antiquity* 52:772–783.
Jacobsen, T. W., and W. R. Farrand
1987   *Franchthi Cave and Paralia: Maps, Plans, and Sections,* Fascicle 1, *Excavations in Franchthi Cave, Greece.* Indiana University Press, Bloomington, Indiana.
Johnson, D. L.
1989   Subsurface Stone Lines, Stone Zones, Artifact-Manuport Layers, and Biomantles Produced by Bioturbation via Pocket Gophers (*Thomomys bottae*). *American Antiquity* 54:370–389.
1990   Biomantle Evolution and the Redistribution of Artifacts. *Soil Science* 149:84–102.
Johnson, D. L., and F. D. Hole
1994   Soil Formation Theory: A Summary of its Principal Impacts on Geography, Geomorphology, Soil-Geomorphology, Quaternary Geology, and Paleopedology. In *Factors of Soil Formation: A Fiftieth Anniversary Retrospective Proceedings of a Symposium.* Sponsored by Division S-5 of the Soil Science Society of America, edited by R. Amundson, J. Harden, and M. Singer, pp. 111–126. Soil Science Society of America, Madison, Wisconsin.

Johnson, D. L., and D. Watson-Stegner
1990   The Soil-Evolution Model as a Framework for Evaluating Pedoturbation in Archae-
        ological Site Formation. In *Archaeological Geology of North America,* edited by N. P.
        Lasca and J. Donahue, pp. 541–560. Geological Society of America, Centennial Spe-
        cial Vol. 4. Boulder, Colorado.

Krumbein, W. C., and L. L. Sloss
1963   *Stratigraphy and Sedimentation.* W. H. Freeman, San Francisco.

Latas, T. W.
1992   An Analysis of Fire-Cracked Rocks: A Sedimentological Approach. In *Deciphering a
        Shell Midden,* edited by J. K. Stein, pp. 211–238. Academic Press, San Diego.

Madsen, M. E.
1992   Lithic Manufacturing at British Camp: Evidence from Size Distributions and Mi-
        croartifacts. In *Deciphering a Shell Midden,* edited by J. K. Stein, pp. 193–210. Acad-
        emic Press, San Diego.

Mandell, R. D., and E. A. Bettis III
2000   Use and Analysis of Soils by Archaeologists and Geoscientists: A North American
        Perspective. In *Earth Science in Archaeology,* edited by P. Goldberg, V. Holliday, and
        C. Reid Ferring, pp. 173–. Kluwer Academic/Plenum, Norwell, Massachusetts.

Metcalfe, D., and K. M. Heath
1990   Microrefuse and Site Structure: The Hearths and Floors of the Heartbreak Hotel.
        American Antiquity 55:781–796.

Morrison, P., and P. Morrison
1982   *Powers of Ten.* Scientific American Library, New York.

Nash, D. T., and M. D. Petraglia (editors)
1987   *Natural Formation Processes and the Archaeological Record.* BAR International Series
        352. London.

Phillips, P., J. A. Ford, and J. B. Griffin
1951   *Archaeological Survey in the Lower Mississippi Valley, 1940–1947.* Papers of the Peabody
        Museum of Archeology and Ethnology No. 25, Harvard University, Cambridge,
        Massachusetts.

Pollard, A. M.
1999   *Geoarchaeology: Exploration, Environments, Resources.* Geological Society, Special
        Publication No. 165. London.

Rapp, G. R. Jr., and C. L. Hill
1998   *Geoarchaeology: The Earth-Science Approach to Archaeological Interpretation.* Yale
        University Press, New Haven, Connecticut.

Reineck, H. E., and I. B. Singh
1980   *Depositional Sedimentary Environments.* Springer-Verlag, New York.

Retallack, G. J.
1994   The Environmental Factor Approach to the Interpretation of Paleosols. In *Factors of
        Soil Formation: A Fiftieth Anniversary Retrospective Proceedings of a Symposium.* Spon-
        sored by Division S-5 of the Soil Science Society of America, edited R. Amundson,
        J. Harden, and M. Singer, pp. 31–64. Soil Science Society of America, Madison,
        Wisconsin.

Rick, J. W.
1976   Downslope Movement and Archaeological Intrasite Spatial Analysis. *American An-
        tiquity* 41:133–144.

Rosen, A. M.

1986   *Cities of Clay: The Geoarchaeology of Tells.* University of Chicago Press, Chicago, Illinois.

1991   Microartifacts and the Study of Ancient Societies. *Biblical Archaeologist* 54:97–103.

1993   Microartifacts as a Reflection of Cultural Factors in Site Formation. In *Formation Processes in Archaeological Context,* edited by P. Goldberg, D. T. Nash, and M. D. Petraglia, pp. 141–148. Monographs in World Archaeology No. 17. Prehistory Press, Madison, Wisconsin.

Salvador, A.

1994   *International Stratigraphic Guide: A Guide to Stratigraphic Classification, Terminology, and Procedure.* 2nd ed. The Geological Society of America, Boulder, Colorado.

Schiffer, M. B.

1972   Archaeological Context and Systemic Context. *American Antiquity* 37:156–165.

1983   Toward the Identification of Formation Processes. *American Antiquity* 48:675–706.

1987   *Formation Processes of the Archaeological Record.* University of New Mexico Press, Albuquerque.

Schumm, S. A.

1991   *To Interpret the Earth: Ten Ways to Be Wrong.* Cambridge University Press, New York.

Sherwood, S. C.

2001   Microartifacts. In *Earth Science in Archaeology,* edited by P. Goldberg, V. T. Holliday, and C. Reid Ferring, pp. 327–351. Kluwer Academic/Plenum, New York.

Sherwood, S. C., and S. Ousley

1995   Quantifying Microartifacts Using a Personal Computer. *Geoarchaeology: An International Journal* 10:423–428.

Sherwood, S. C., J. F. Simek, and R. R. Polhemus

1995   Artifact Size and Spatial Process: Macro- and Microartifacts in a Mississippian House. *Geoarchaeology: An International Journal* 10:429–455.

Simonson, R. W.

1959   Outline of a Generalized Theory of Soil Genesis. *Soil Science Society Proceedings* 23:122–126.

Stafford, C. R.

1995   Geoarchaeological Perspectives on Paleolandscapes and Regional Subsurface Archaeology. *Journal of Archaeological Method and Theory* 2:69–104.

Stein, J. K.

1983   Earthworm Activity: A Source of Potential Disturbance of Archaeological Sediments. *American Antiquity* 48:277–289.

1985   Interpreting Sediments in Cultural Settings. In *Archaeological Sediments in Context,* edited by J. K. Stein and W. R. Farrand, pp. 5–19. Center for the Study of Early Man, Orono, Maine.

1987   Deposits for Archaeologists. In *Advances in Archaeological Method and Theory,* vol. 11, edited by M. B. Schiffer, pp. 337–393. Academic Press, Orlando, Florida.

1990   Archaeological Stratigraphy. In *Archaeological Geology of North America,* edited by N. P. Lasca and J. Donahue, pp. 513–523. Geological Society of America, Centennial Special Vol. 4. Boulder, Colorado.

1992a   (editor) *Deciphering a Shell Midden.* Academic Press, San Diego.

1992b   Interpreting Stratification of a Shell Midden. In *Deciphering a Shell Midden,* edited by J. K. Stein, pp. 71–93. Academic Press, San Diego.

1992c   Sediment Analysis of the British Camp Shell Midden. In *Deciphering a Shell Mid-
         den,* edited by J. K. Stein, pp. 135–162. Academic Press, San Diego.

1993   Scale in Archaeology, Geosciences, and Geoarchaeology. In *Effects of Scale on Archae-
         ological and Geoscientific Perspectives,* edited by J. K. Stein and A. R. Linse, pp. 1–10.
         Geological Society of America, Special Paper 283. Boulder, Colorado.

1996   Geoarchaeology and Archaeostratigraphy: View from a Northwest Coast Shell Mid-
         den. In *Case Studies in Environmental Archaeology,* edited by E. J. Reitz, L. A. New-
         son, and S. J. Scudder, pp. 35–54. Plenum Press, New York.

2000a   Stratigraphy and Archaeological Dating. In *Time after Time: A History of Archaeolog-
         ical Dating in North America,* edited by S. Nash, pp. 14–40. University of Utah Press,
         Salt Lake City.

2000b   *Exploring Coast Salish Prehistory: The Archaeology of San Juan Island.* University of
         Washington Press, Seattle.

2001   A Review of Site Formation Processes and Their Relevance to Geoarchaeology. In
         Earth Science in Archaeology, edited by P. Goldberg, V. T. Holliday, and C. Reid Fer-
         ring, pp. 37–51. Kluwer Academic/Plenum, New York.

Stein, J. K., J. N. Deo, and L. Phillips

2000   Radiometric Ages on the Northwest Coast: A New Settlement Pattern Revealed.
         Paper presented at the 65th Annual Meeting of the Society for American Archaeol-
         ogy, Philadelphia.

Stein, J. K., K. D. Kornbacher, and J. L. Tyler

1992   British Camp Shell Midden Stratigraphy. In *Deciphering a Shell Midden,* edited by
         J. K. Stein, pp. 95–134. Academic Press, San Diego.

Stein, J. K., and A. R. Linse (editors)

1993   *Effects of Scale on Archaeological and Geoscientific Perspectives.* Geological Society of
         America, Special Paper 283. Boulder, Colorado.

Stein, J. K., and G. Rapp Jr.

1985   Archaeological Sediments: A Largely Untapped Reservoir of Information. In *Contri-
         butions to Aegean Archaeology,* edited by N. C. Wilkie and W. D. E. Coulson, pp.
         143–159. Center for Ancient Studies, University of Minnesota, Publications in An-
         cient Studies 1. Minneapolis.

Stein, J. K., and P. A. Teltser

1989   Size Distributions of Artifact Classes: Combining Macro- and Micro-Fractions.
         Geoarchaeology: An International Journal 4:1–30.

Stone, T.

1989   Origins and Environmental Significance of Shell and Earth Mounds in Northern
         Australia. *Archaeology in Oceania* 24:59–64.

Tandarich, J. P., and S. W. Sprecher

1994   The Intellectual Background for the Factors of Soil Formation. In *Factors of Soil For-
         mation: A Fiftieth Anniversary Retrospective Proceedings of a Symposium.* Sponsored by
         Division S-5 of the Soil Science Society of America, edited by R. Amundson,
         J. Harden, and M. Singer, pp. 1–14. Soil Science Society of America, Madison, Wis-
         consin.

Thorson, R. M.

1990   Archaeological Geology. *Geotimes* 35(2):32–33.

Thorson, R. M., and V. T. Holliday

1990   Just What is Geoarchaeology? *Geotimes* 35(7):19–20.

Twenhofel, W. H.
1950   *Principles of Sedimentation.* McGraw-Hill, New York.
Vance, D. E.
1986   Microdebitage Analysis in Activity Analysis: An Application. *Northwest Anthropological Research Notes* 20:179–189.
1989   The Role of Microartifacts in Spatial Analysis. Unpublished Ph.D. dissertation, Department of Anthropology, University of Washington, Seattle.
Visher, G. S.
1969   Grain Size Distributions and Depositional Processes. *Journal of Sedimentary Petrology* 39:1074–1106.
Waters, M. R.
1992   *Principles of Geoarchaeology: A North American Perspective.* University of Arizona Press, Tucson.
Whittaker, F. H., and J. K. Stein
1992   Shell Midden Boundaries in Relation to Past and Present Shorelines. In *Deciphering a Shell Midden,* edited by J. K. Stein, pp. 25–42. Academic Press, San Diego.
Wood, W. R., and D. L. Johnson
1978   A Survey of Disturbance Processes in Archaeological Site Formation. In *Advances in Archaeological Method and Theory,* vol. 1, edited by M. B. Schiffer, pp. 315–381. Academic Press, Orlando, Florida.

2

Archaeological Sediments
in Rockshelters and Caves

William R. Farrand

In the minds of the general public and of earlier generations of archaeologists, caves have long been considered traditional, even stereotypical habitation sites for prehistoric humans. Now we clearly recognize that early humans lived not only in rockshelters and caves, but it is probable that open-air sites were much more numerous than cave sites. Rockshelters and caves may never have been more than seasonal habitations or transient refuges, but they still play a very important role in furnishing data on prehistoric human paleoecology. Rockshelters and caves have been called "highly efficient sediment traps" by Collcutt (1979), who has written an excellent critique of cave sediment analysis. Another useful overview of the importance of cave studies is furnished by Straus (1990). The reasons for this importance lie largely in the geologically specialized character of the rockshelter/cave niche, that is, relatively rapid sedimentation, protection of the deposits from erosion and weathering, the self-sealing nature of major roof falls, ease of recognition of such sites in the landscape, and their attractiveness for nonhuman fauna during times of nonoccupation by humans.

Detailed study and climatic interpretation of cave sediments is at most about 60 years old (Laïs 1941), and still in a disorganized and youthful state. A number of national "schools" have been active, especially in France (Bonifay 1956, 1962; Campy 1990; Laville et al. 1980; Miskovsky 1974), in Germany (Brunnacker 1983), in Switzerland (Schmid 1958, 1963), in South Africa (Brain 1981), and in China (ZeChun 1985). However, no organized body of theory ever emerged to provide a uniform framework for the interpretation of the sediments or for their regional correlation.

Rockshelter sediment study in the United States is not as widespread or as developed as in Western Europe. For example, Collins (1991) summarizes studies in Texas by surveying 55 different rockshelters, only one of which had been (as of that date) subjected to detailed sediment analysis, such as outlined in this chapter. However, there are some other rockshelters that provide excellent examples of detailed analysis, such as Meadowcroft in Pennsylvania (Donahue and Adovasio 1990), Rodgers in Missouri (Ahler 1976), and Gatecliff in Nevada (Davis 1983). The reason for fewer detailed studies in North America probably lies in the reality that human occupation of American rockshelters and caves is much more recent and the sediment fills are much thinner in general than in the Old World. Most American sites are very late glacial or postglacial in age (less than 12,000 years) and have undergone less extreme climatic changes.

Rockshelters and Caves

This chapter is concerned with rockshelters (areas under projecting rock ledges) and cave mouths that afford greater or lesser protection to man and beast from the weather, whether it be the cold, rain and snow, or unbearable solar radiation. Such sites normally have broad connections with the outside environment and are illuminated by daylight, but not necessarily direct sunlight. The outside climate or weather is nevertheless damped to some degree, and the degree of protection will be a function of the size, configuration, and orientation of the rockshelter or cave. Although my remarks in this chapter apply more or less equally to rockshelters and cave mouths, the latter may differ functionally from rockshelters. In caves, karstic processes may be still active, bringing imports of silts and clays or producing floods from the cave interior that erode the cave mouth sediments upon occasion, for example, Yarimburgaz (Farrand and McMahon 1997) and El Miron (Straus and Gonzalez Morales 2000; Straus et al. 2001). Cave sites commonly are preserved much longer in the landscape than rockshelters because of their greater structural stability. Relatively few rockshelter sites occupied prior to the penultimate glaciation (isotope stage 6) are preserved (see below). Dark cave interiors are not discussed in this paper because largely different sedimentary environments and controls are involved there. They are not in direct connection with the outside climate that we desire to reconstruct, and they usually were not sites of human habitation. (This environment is well discussed by Ford [1976], among others.)

Even within a relatively small geographic area with a rather uniform regional climate, each rockshelter tends to be a unique entity, complicating the correlation of sedimentary features from one to another. This point has been made repeatedly, beginning with the early workers of the present generation cited above. The sedimentary ensembles within nearby rockshelters may vary because of bedrock variability, exposure, local relief, size and shape, and of course, the intensity and continuity of human habitation.

Figure 2.1. Bedrock cliff face just west of Abri Pataud, Les Eyzies, France, illustrating the massive character of this horizontally bedded rock. In contrast to the situation in Figure 2.2, this configuration is not conducive to collapse of the bedrock. Note also the incipient rockshelter niche and the hydration spalling debris. (Photograph by W. R. Farrand.)

Bedrock type is an important control. Many rockshelters and caves are in limestone or dolomite bedrock. Even among superficially similar limestones, however, there may be a considerable difference in their susceptibility to weathering, as documented by experiments on freeze-thaw action (Guillien and Lautridou 1974, 1980) and in the insoluble component of the limestone (sandy vs. lithographic or micritic limestone). Moreover, the kind and dip of the stratification may differ, as well as the degree of joint (fissure) development. Consider the differences between massive (homogeneous), horizontally stratified bedrock (e.g., Abri Pataud, Fig. 2.1) and one that is thinly bedded, highly jointed, and dipping at a steep angle (e.g., Franchthi Cave, Fig. 2.2). The latter will obviously be much more susceptible to mechanical breakdown than the former, producing more abundant angular rubble *(éboulis),* all other things being equal.

In addition to limestone and dolomite bedrock, rockshelters and caves may form in other rock types. Lava tube caves are perhaps uncommon, but interesting (Wood 1974). Lava tubes form when viscous lava flows across the landscape. The lava on top, exposed to the air, as well as the lava at the base of the flow, may congeal while the lava inside them continues to move, eventually leaving an empty cavity or tube. Much later, erosion may expose the

Figure 2.2. The entrance to Franchthi Cave, Greece, showing nearly vertically dipping lime-stone bedrock, a highly unstable situation. The large pile of limestone blocks under the en-trance is an example of breakdown facilitated by such weak bedrock structure. (Photograph by W. R. Farrand.)

lava tube and, if large enough, humans may use the tube for shelter or habitation. Examples are found in Hawaii used for royal refuges and rituals (Kennedy and Brady 1997) and in the Snake River Plain in Idaho (Moody and Dort 1990).

A number of rockshelters, but not deep caves, commonly form in sandstone bedrock. A useful summary of sandstone shelters in the eastern United States published by Donahue and Adovasio (1990) surveys their distribution and general controls on sedimentation in these shelters, but concentrates on the detailed study of the Meadowcroft Rockshelter in western Pennsylvania. Sandstone rockshelters usually originate by river downcutting that creates steep to vertical valley walls, then undercutting of weaker bedrock strata by the river creates an initial rock overhang. That overhang is gradually enlarged by subaerial weathering that induces grain-by-grain disintegration of the sandstone, along with frost weathering under appropriate climates, gradually leading to collapse of roof blocks.

The height of a rockshelter above a local stream, or above sea level in the case of a coastal site, will be an important control on the entry of fluvial or marine sediments into the site. For example, two coastal caves in the Levant, Et-Tabun (Farrand 1979) and El-Bezez (Sweeting 1983), differ slightly in their relations with marine phenomena. The former has a bedrock sill that prevented the entry of marine waters into the cave. The latter was flooded by the sea so that marine beach deposits are directly intercalated with cave habitation sediments. Thus, in the latter case direct correlation with a given sea level can be demonstrated, not simply assumed. Other sea caves developed in karst in coastal Alaska demonstrate similar relations (Dixon et al. 1997).

The horizontal extent of the overhang (the "depth" of the shelter) and the height of the brow above the floor control the degree of damping of the outside climate, a deep shelter with a low brow providing the greatest protection. Furthermore, direction of exposure relative to sunlight and prevailing winds will influence the microclimate within the shelter and thus determine its desirability for habitation and the season of habitation. The intensity of habitation, either at any one time or repeated habitations, may also vary from site to site in a manner unrelated to the natural sedimentary processes going on there, being dictated in part by cultural considerations.

Finally, the relations outlined in the preceding paragraphs are not constant with time. Obviously a nearby stream or sea level may rise or fall with changing climate or because of other geomorphic controls, but the rockshelter itself usually evolves as well. The general pattern (Fig. 2.3) involves a deepening of the shelter as the back wall is attacked by weathering, either by freeze-thaw or by solution or both, because of the moister microclimate found there. Eventually the brow or part of the ceiling of the shelter collapses because of the increasing lack of support. Thus, large blocks of rock, up to several meters across, may fall onto the shelter floor. Since the brow is particularly susceptible to such collapse, a reduction of the depth of the shelter results. During this same time, sediments of varied provenience accumulated on the shelter floor, and now they protect the bedrock of the floor from further attack by weathering or erosion.

A useful example comes from the Abri Pataud where one can see that this cycle repeated itself a number of times (Fig. 2.4). The weathering of the back wall continued, but at a slightly higher level each time, creating a step on the bedrock floor. Ultimately collapse occurs again, and so forth, leaving a buried bedrock floor that rises in steps. In the later stages the overhang is progressively

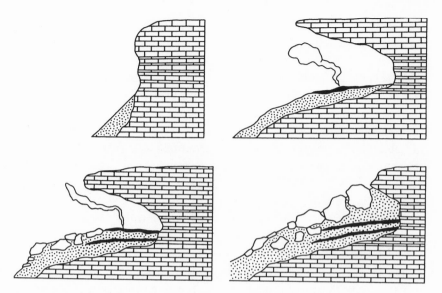

Figure 2.3. Evolution of a hypothetical rockshelter (after Laville et al. 1980, with permission of Academic Press, Inc.).

reduced, and the shelter is choked with its own sedimentary fill to the point where it merges with the normal talus or colluvial slope of the valley side (Fig. 2.3). Other examples are illustrated schematically for two other French rockshelters by Collins (1991).

Furthermore, rockshelters are relatively short lived. Collins's analysis of rockshelters in the French Perigord, based on data from Laville et al. (1980), indicates the average span for filling those shelters was less than 25,000 years and 34 percent were filled in less than 10,000 years.

The sedimentologist and the archaeologist must realize that such an evolution has occurred. For example, consider a stratigraphic sequence of three hearths at different depths but vertically superimposed at the same grid coordinates in an excavation. One must take into account that the lowest hearth may have been near the back wall under a low ceiling, the intermediate one just inside the brow under a high ceiling, and the uppermost one may have been open to the sky. Functional interpretation of human utilization of space within the site must take such changes into account.

In concluding these general remarks, it must be stressed that no two rockshelters are exactly alike. They may have different intrinsic (bedrock) characters and different relations to the outside environments, and they may be at different points in their natural evolution. Each one must be studied by itself without extrapolation of attributes or conclusions drawn from other sites,

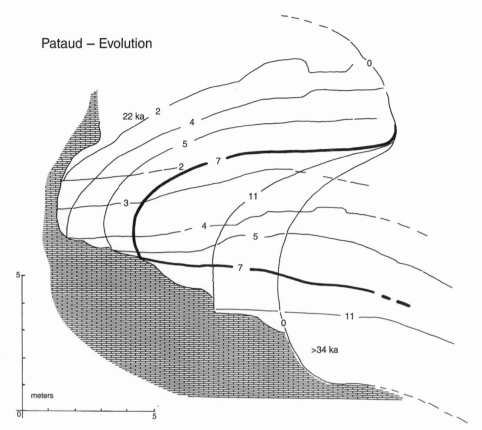

Figure 2.4. Reconstructed sagittal profiles through Abri Pataud, France. The numbered lines show the position of the floor, backwall, and ceiling of the shelter at times of different occupations from 34,000 to 22,000 years B.P. Line 0 is the presumed original configuration of the initial bedrock niche; numbers 2 through 11 are reconstructed profiles at the times of given occupations, with 11 being the oldest and 2 the youngest. The configuration at the time of occupation 7 is emphasized by a heavier line for convenience. As the floor was gradually filled with sediment, the shelter was progressively enlarged, with a greater overhang, up to the time of occupation 3. After that time, successive collapses of the brow reduced the sheltered area to its present configuration shown by the solid pattern.

even those close by. When the sedimentary sequence is understood for a given site and its paleoenvironmental inferences drawn, then and only then can comparisons and correlations among the sites be meaningful.

Sediment Sources

Sediments in caves are either endogenous or exogenous. Endogenous sediments within a cave are derived from the ceiling and walls by dissolution, frost action, and collapse. Exogenous sediments are carried in by running water, blown in by the wind, moved in by mass movements, introduced by karstic drainage from the cave interior, or brought in by humans.

This mixture of sediments must be sorted out by the sedimentologist, but it is a complex task because the deposits are quite immature in the sedimentologist's sense, that is, hardly moved at all from their source, poorly sorted granulometrically, relatively unweathered or otherwise unmodified, as well as being deposited simultaneously by several mechanisms, such as rock fall, wind, and human agency.

Other problems that need to be considered relate to interpretations and comparisons of those interpretations. Curves drawn from sediment data commonly have lots of "noise" and must be interpreted conservatively. In addition, appreciation of bedrock variability is essential because limestone, sandstone, and lava-tube caves do not form or evolve in a similar manner; thus, some aspects of their fillings are intrinsically different. Also basic climatic differences complicate comparisons, for example, between sites in a humid, frost-prone climate (Western Europe) and those in a semi-arid or Mediterranean climate where frost is rare.

One must employ as many different analytical techniques as possible in order to approach a synthetic interpretation of the origin and paleoenvironmental significance of cave and rockshelter sediments. On the other hand, in view of the large number of samples to be processed, economic considerations limit the application of techniques to those most rewarding in terms of time, money, and procedures commonly available in most laboratories. Publications in English that treat systematically the techniques commonly applied to cave and rockshelter sediments can be found in Laville et al. (1980), Farrand (1975a, 1975b, 1995), and Campy and Chaline (1993). These works apply to sites in the "periglacial" environment of Western Europe, but it has become clear to me that additional analyses and different interpretive approaches are required in other climatic regions, such as the semi-arid Near East (Farrand 1979, 2000; Farrand and McMahon 1997; Goldberg 1973; Mandel and Simmons 1997; Woodward and Bailey 2000) or South Africa (Brain 1981; Butzer 1976).

Principles of Sediment Analysis

To begin with, some remarks are in order about sediment study in archaeological sites in general, remarks that are not restricted to cave sites but pertain to any naturally stratified site. Sediments are the result of all kinds of deposition at a given site; they are deposited by natural geological processes, by the activity of animals, and by the activities of humans during their habitation of the site. The sediments thus constitute the prime evidence of the site stratigraphy; they contain all the other evidence of use or abandonment of the site, such as human artifacts and structures, remains of plants and animals used as food by humans, as well as all other fossils (e.g., microfauna, pollen).

Sedimentary strata are real units, each with a definable top and bottom (either sharp or gradational), that encompass all the physical space within the site. Moreover, sediments are always present in a stratified site, whereas artifacts or fossils may be lacking in any given stratum. Therefore, stratigraphy based on the sediments (i.e., lithostratigraphy of the geologist) is the most logical means of organizing all the other data gathered from the site. It follows, then, that the site sediments must be studied in detail so that this basic stratigraphy may be faithfully recorded and understood as clearly as possible.

In addition to serving as the basis for describing the site stratigraphy, sediment study can furnish information on past environments that existed at or near the site. Sediment study interprets the kinds of sedimentary processes at a site and variations in their rates, and the modification (weathering, erosion, and human activity) of sediments subsequent to their deposition. The integration of such information leads to reconstruction of the site environment in the past and, depending on the specific situation, may allow qualitative statements about the amplitudes and rates of environmental change. Obviously, interpretations based on sedimentology must be integrated with those based on other lines of evidence, such as fossils.

In summary, the goals of sedimentological analysis are:

1. a detailed description of all the strata in an archaeological site, that is, something more informative than "brown cave earth";
2. a lithostratigraphic framework for comparison of other stratigraphies;
3. a reconstruction of the local physical environment during and between occupations of the site;
4. (from 3) an interpretation of past climate of the area;
5. (from 3 and 4) a means of correlation from trench to trench within a site and among sites in the same climatic locale.

Finally, the geologist must see the sediments in situ. I personally refuse to work on sediments that I did not collect or at least did not see taken out of the ground. An unconsolidated sediment put into a sample bag becomes a "sack of dirt" unless tied to field observations. One cannot appreciate (in a sack of dirt) features such as:

1. sedimentary structures: stratification, especially thin laminations, cross-bedding, ripples, mud cracks, etc.;
2. contact relations: sharp, clear, or completely gradational, including possible unconformities (hiatuses);

3. color relations: uniform, mottled, banded;
4. lateral relations: facies changes, proximity to walls, hearths, roof collapse for example.

All of these relations should play a role in determining the choice of sampling locations, preferably a continuous column from top to bottom of the stratigraphic sequence at one or several locations, depending on perceived lateral variations, within the site.

Controls on Sedimentation

As outlined above, rockshelters and cave mouths are efficient sediment traps, and the end result of rockshelter evolution is the burial and protection of the earlier formed sediments to a much greater degree than in open-air sites. On the other hand, problems for the sedimentologist reside in the immature nature of the sediments and their mixed proveniences. Before interpreting the sediments in detail, it is necessary to keep in mind the possible sources of the sediments and the possible modifications that they might have undergone. Figure 2.5 represents schematically the interaction of processes that control sedimentation and modification. Working backwards from the integrated sediment that one excavates (the double box in Figure 2.5), we must realize that a number of possible changes (dashed lines) might have occurred since the primary sediment was deposited, changes that obscure the natural sedimentary processes to a greater or lesser degree. In an archaeological site, human activities are certainly not the least of these impacts, as can be seen by the addition of various kinds of debris and physical disruption (e.g., digging of pits or hearths) of the primary stratification. Climatically controlled weathering and pedogenesis can also effectively mask the character of the original sediment; and the geomorphology of the site or its immediate environs can promote changes, such as slumping, subsidence into swallow holes, gullying by surface runoff, and so forth.

If one is successful in revealing the character of the primary sediment, still there are problems in determining the major factors that influenced the deposition of that sediment. For example, a layer of windblown sediment in a site implies first and foremost the availability of dry sand and silt that can be picked up by the wind, the strength of the wind being a secondary consideration. However, the dry source material may be the result either of climatic dryness or of seasonally dry floodplain surfaces within a generally humid climatic setting (e.g., glacier-fed braided streams).

Although this chapter is not concerned directly with paleontology, fossils are integral components of sediments. Therefore, it should be kept in mind

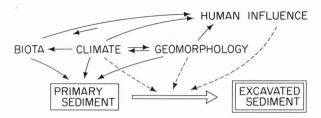

Figure 2.5. Interaction of controls on primary sedimentation and subsequent modification of sediments in sites (Farrand 1985, with permission of the Center for the Study of First Americans).

that the fossil content of rockshelter sediments may derive from several sources and may not be an indicator of the shelter's microclimate. This factor is most obvious in habitation layers where almost all the fauna and flora is introduced by humans. Moreover, in the absence of humans the vertebrate microfauna is largely introduced by raptorial birds, and carnivores also can drag bones of their prey into the shelter as well. Pollen is blown in from vegetation outside the shelter and may be selective as a function of the configuration and turbulence inside the shelter; however, the regional pollen rain may be overwhelmed by that from vegetation carried into the shelter by humans. In sum, very few fossils clearly indicate the microclimate within a rockshelter or cave, bats being an obvious exception. On the other hand, most fossils incorporated in the cave sediments can be important indicators of regional climate in the vicinity of the cave or rockshelter.

Depositional and Modification Processes

The agents responsible for depositing or altering sediments in a rockshelter are listed in Table 2.1, and the environmental factors influencing those agents are suggested in Figure 2.6. Note that a given general process may be responsible for both deposition and modification, but usually at different moments in time. Most of these processes need no detailed explanation here; see Laville et al. (1980) and Farrand (1975a, 1975b, 1995). Some clarification may be helpful, however, in the case of pedogenesis and especially for the interpretation of cryoclastic processes, collapse, and solution (hydration) weathering, all of which may produce coarse, angular rock rubble.

Pedogenesis

The role of pedogenesis, or soil formation, in rockshelters and cave mouths has not received much discussion, in part perhaps because one of the prime factors in pedogenesis is vegetation. Little vegetation grows on the floors of

Table 2.1. Rockshelter Processes

AGENT	DEPOSITION	ALTERATION
Cryoclastism	Frost slabs, spalls, grain-by-grain accumulation	Split/fissured stones, smaller spalls, debris
Collapse	Large blocks and shattered fragments	Crushed debris (of all kinds)
Solifluction	Hillslope sludge (from outside), colluvium	Displacement of earlier deposits (inside cave)
Cryoturbation	None	Churning of strata, rounding of stones
Flowing Water	Flood deposits, karstic imports, surface runoff	Erosion, gullying, travertine
Wind	Well-sorted sand and silt; loess	None
Solution (including hydration, weak acids)	Hydration spalls, grain-by-grain disaggregation; dripstone, travertine	Leaching of $CaCO_3$, rounding of stones, cementation
Pedogenesis	None	Chemical/mineralogical changes, leaching, cementation, root disturbance
Humans and Animals	Artifacts, bones, garbage, body wastes, imported rocks (manuports) and dirt, structures, hearths	Physical disturbance, digging, burrowing, house cleaning, chemical alteration; decreased pH

rockshelters and caves except in some cases just inside the drip line. Deeper rockshelters and caves receive only subdued daylight, which is not conducive to the growth of higher vegetation. However, moisture, oxygen, and acidity from decaying organic matter introduced by humans are available for weathering sediments on the cave floor at times when the sediment accumulation rate is strongly reduced or drops to zero.

Weathering short of full-blown pedogenesis is common in rockshelter and cave sediments. Most commonly this takes the form of solution by water moving through the air-sediment interface. That water may be somewhat acid from decaying organic matter, and the result is dissolution of fine-grained matrix carbonate and corrosion of the surfaces of limestone clasts leading to rounding of the clasts and chalky residues on clast surfaces ("white rocks"). Examples will be discussed in connection with Franchthi Cave below.

Truly pedogenic horizons do occur in some rockshelter sites, especially where the shelter is broadly open to the external environment. In the sedimen-

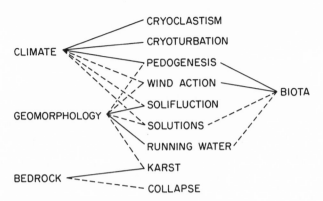

FACTORS INFLUENCING DEPOSITIONAL PROCESSES

Figure 2.6. Factors influencing depositional processes. Dashed lines indicate less direct influence (Farrand 1985, with permission of the Center for the Study of First Americans).

tary fill of the Abri Pataud (Dordogne, France) one major and several minor levels were conspicuously reddened by oxidation. Pataud "Level 3/4: Red" is not only "red" (Munsell 7.5YR 5/7, strong brown) but also shows leaching of carbonates and a progressive increase with depth of secondary clay, and the clay mineralogy reflects neoformation characteristic of pedogenesis (Farrand 1975a, 1975b). It is also interesting to note that the oxidative reddening in this level fades progressively as one approaches the back wall of the shelter where the effect of the external climate is reduced. This pedogenesis occurred during an interstadial warm interval. Examples of interglacial soil formation are found in other rockshelters, such as Combe Grenal (Dordogne, France) reported by Laville et al. (1980:55).

Pedogenic horizons, and weathered horizons in general, are very important in deciphering site-formation history. They imply a time of stability with little or no sediment accumulation, thus a time gap (hiatus) in the filling of the shelter. Such hiatuses are discussed below.

Freeze-and-Thaw Activity

The interpretation of the coarse, angular rock fraction of rockshelter sediments is still not resolved. The role of freeze-and-thaw appears to have received too much stress and too little critical evaluation, although its interpretation has become much more subtle since the excellent work of the Caën laboratory was published (Guillien and Lautridou 1974, 1980). Even the term *éboulis* seems to be too narrowly defined by some of the French workers themselves. The French dictionary defines *éboulis* as a mass of collapsed or fallen rock debris without any specification of upper or lower size limits or genesis. Laville et al. (1980) restrict the term, however, to the coarse stone fraction of rockshelter sediment, differentiating it from the matrix of the same stratum. Furthermore, Laville et al.(1980:5l) attach a genetic implication, stating explicitly that éboulis are "detached by frost weathering."

In fact, when a rock fall occurs (no matter what the cause) there will be the simultaneous production of large and small clasts—boulders to fine sand and silt, and maybe even clay-sized debris. The Caën laboratory reports clearly document the decreasing clast size and the increasing amount of fines produced by repeated freeze-and-thaw (see Guillien and Lautridou 1974). In terms of process, the matrix is an integral part of the éboulis; it should not be treated as a separate entity.

More important than terminology is the fact that not all the coarse fraction of rockshelter sediments is contributed by frost action. A collapse of rock from the brow or ceiling that has been weakened through the process of backwall retreat, whatever the cause—freeze-and-thaw, solution, river undercutting—will produce coarse, angular rock rubble (éboulis in the broad sense) of all sizes from blocks several meters across to a matrix of fine particles. This éboulis may resemble very closely that produced by freeze-and-thaw, so the question of distinguishing one from the other becomes important.

In the view of most previous works, the larger the size of the éboulis fragments, the more "severe" the freeze-and-thaw activity (Laville et al. 1980:53). If so, one can imagine the confusion that could result in the interpretation of levels where a slab of the ceiling crashed to the shelter floor, breaking into numerous, angular fragments in the same size range as freeze-and-thaw éboulis. Although the collapse debris may be the end result of the long period of frost action, its presence in the shelter deposits does not necessarily imply intense frost action at the time that it fell. In fact, the collapse could occur during a mild interval long after a period of frost climate. Thus, abundant coarse, angular debris does not necessarily imply a contemporaneous period of rigorous climate.

Part of the challenge in the interpretation of angular rock fragments revolves around the question of the maximum size of blocks that can be detached from the bedrock wall directly by freeze-and-thaw. The Caën laboratory used cubes of rock initially 10 cm on a side, and these were readily broken apart after several hundred freeze-and-thaw cycles or less. At the other extreme, roof blocks up to 10 or more meters in one or more dimensions would seem intuitively much too large to be the direct results of frost action. A reasonable guess is that the limit between these two processes may lie between a decimeter and a meter or so. Above this limit bedrock lithology and structure become the controlling factors on the size of angular debris. This is an important problem that remains to be resolved.

Moreover, my experience in the warm, semi-arid Near East and Greece suggests that some angular rock debris in the 2 to 20 cm range may not have been produced either directly or even indirectly by freeze-and-thaw, although it resembles cryoclastic *éboulis*. Deposits of such debris occur in climates now without frost. I have observed such rock debris in the Judean Desert and the Wadi Khareitoun not far from Bethlehem, in Holocene deposits in the Cave of Jebel Qafza near Nazareth, in Franchthi Cave at sea level in southern Greece, and in the United States in the same latitudes in Bonfire Shelter in southwest Texas (see also Collins 1991). Moreover, unless the temperature depression during the last glaciation was very much greater than other phenomena indicate, frost was very unlikely in these areas during late Pleistocene time. A drop of 15° or 20° C would be required to bring freezing temperatures to the Judean Desert localities (Farrand 1981).

Therefore, I believe that we should be looking for other mechanisms to explain the production of large clasts in rockshelters. In Franchthi Cave in southern Greece, the bedrock is strongly fissured as a result of tectonic movements. The fissures delineate rock fragments still in place on the bedrock wall that have the morphology and size essentially identical with *éboulis* clasts found in the Holocene strata in the cave fill (Farrand 2000, pl. 6b). Hydration weathering is another likely candidate (Hudec 1973; White 1976). Although, to my knowledge, hydration spalling of fine-grained limestone has not been demonstrated experimentally or observed unequivocally, it seems to me that expansion upon wetting after a prolonged warm, dry season is a reasonable mechanism to produce *éboulis*. In fact, I have observed present-day spalling in rock niches (incipient rockshelters) near the Abri Pataud (Fig. 2.1 and Farrand 1975b, pl. 5) that is more suggestive of hydration than of frost action. Hydration spalls are initially slabby, but they break into more and more equidimensional forms with time. Moreover, modern "frost weathering" shown by Laville et al. (1980, fig. 3-1), which they attribute to frost, is probably due to hydration, given that sustained freezing of the ground is rare in present-day Dordogne.

In a simplified attempt to distinguish freeze-and-thaw *éboulis* from nonfrost debris, I present cumulative grain-size curves (Fig. 2.7) from (a) the Caën data, (b) from frost-influenced sites (Pataud, Yabrud), and (c) from sites in areas free of frost (Qafzeh, Franchthi). I can detect no significant differences. More work, especially experimentation, is clearly needed.

In summary, coarse, angular rock debris in rockshelters may have been generated by freeze-and-thaw, by roof collapse, by hydration spalling, or by other

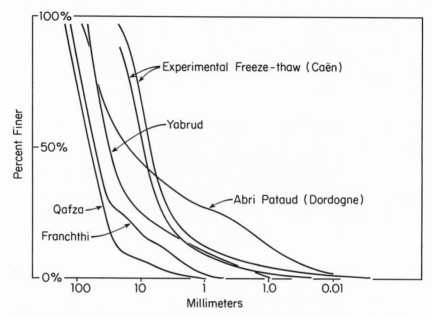

Figure 2.7. Cumulative curves of rockshelter granulometry. The samples from Qafza and Franchthi caves are of Holocene age; those from Yabrud and Abri Pataud are of glacial age (after Farrand 1985, with permission of the Center for the Study of First Americans).

mechanisms. Earthquakes may be the mechanism that ultimately brings the *éboulis* down in many caves. Thus, interpretation of *éboulis* uniquely in terms of varying intensity of freeze-and-thaw seems to be oversimplified, even in climatic regions with frost, and may lead to overlooking other important paleoclimatic controls of sedimentation.

Presentation of Data

As emphasized at the outset, interpretation of rockshelter sediments is complicated by (a) several different mechanisms in action and (b) sediments coming from several sources simultaneously. There is also the need to evaluate the impact of post-depositional modification by natural and human agencies. Therefore, a composite diagram is necessary in which one can see the synoptic status of as many parameters as possible at a given time and then follow their evolution through time. An example from Franchthi Cave is given in Figure 2.8.

There are, however, aspects of such so-called global diagrams that may be misleading, depending on the way in which the diagram is constructed. Most commonly zigzag diagrams are utilized in which the stratigraphic arrangement of the sediment samples is the vertical axis; and the horizontal axis depicts variations in granulometry, calcimetry, roundness, concretions, heavy minerals, and so forth. The horizontal axis for each column may be either the weight percentage of that particular variable, an index (e.g., sorting, roundness), or a direct measure, such as pH or median grain size (mm). Clearly, scaling factors are important in order to emphasize properly the change in a parameter with respect to stratigraphic depth ("time"), but care must be taken not to exaggerate change in a particular parameter by means of an inappropriate scale. This is a delicate choice in some cases, and one that requires a lot of intuitive common sense on the part of the user.

A special word of caution is pertinent concerning the choice of vertical scale as well. In the first place, the collection of samples is neither random nor (or rarely) uniform with respect to depth. The geologist, in consultation with the excavating archaeologists, would like to sample each lithostratigraphic layer or stratum in the section that appears to differ from over- and underlying layers; these units may be thicker or thinner than archaeological excavation levels or spits. In layers that are relatively thick, but visibly homogeneous, one should collect two, three, or more samples in order not to miss some subtle changes that are not evident to the naked eye. Time and money rarely allow one to sample continuously from top to bottom of the stratigraphic sequence. Therefore, one commonly ends up with an irregular vertical spacing of samples.

Commonly earlier workers plotted samples on an arbitrary vertical scale (e.g., one sample every centimeter on cross-section paper). Clearly, it would be more realistic and informative to plot the samples with their true vertical relations to each other, that is, to plot their depths below grid datum or above sea level (as in the Franchthi diagram, Fig. 2.8). Still better, especially if hiatuses, unconformities, or paleosols are recognized in the stratigraphy, the samples should be plotted against time on the vertical axis in order to appreciate the rate of change of the analyzed parameters. An example of the differences between arbitrary, true depth, and time scales is taken from Franchthi Cave (Fig. 2.9), where it can be seen that different parts of the stratigraphic sequence may be either telescoped or compressed. Absolute dates are not always available or abundant enough, however, so a true vertical time axis may not be possible for some sites. Some indication of possible time gaps, if suspected, should be built into the diagram, nevertheless.

Finally, on zigzag diagrams, if only one sample is taken from each layer recognized in the field regardless of its thickness, then a literal reading of a uniform rate of change from peak to adjacent trough can be quite misleading (Fig. 2.10, left). Unconnected histograms (Fig. 2.10, center) will be more realistic because they show values measured for a given depth without implying a rate of change. Even better would be plotting of histograms of variable width (Fig.

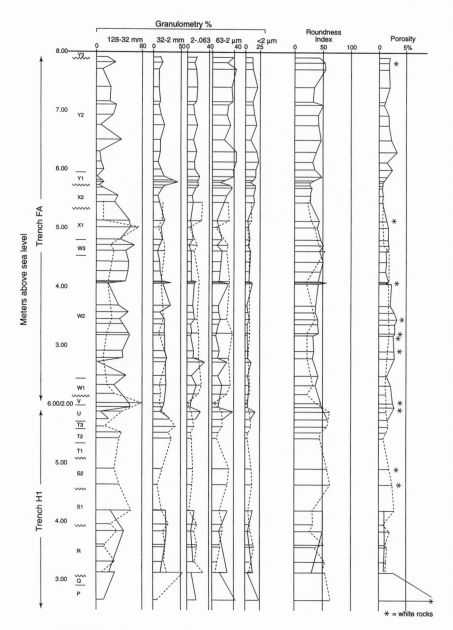

Figure 2.8. Global sediment diagram from Franchthi Cave, Greece (Farrand 2000, with permission of Indiana University Press).

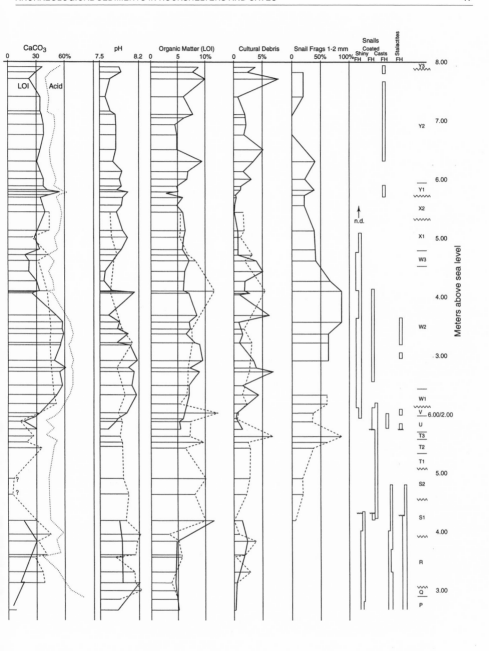

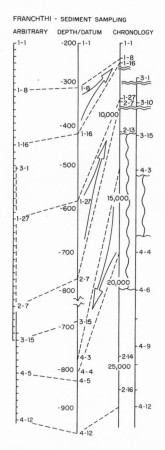

Figure 2.9. Visual effects of different vertical scales on stratigraphic plots of Franchthi Cave, Greece. The wavy lines, horizontal and vertical, indicate hiatuses in the "Chronology" column (after Farrand 1985, with permission of the Center for the Study of First Americans).

2.10, right), the width corresponding to the stratigraphic thickness of the sampled layer as determined in the field.

Interpretation of Data

Now that some words have been said about the origin of the sediments and their subsequent modification, and about diagrams by which a synoptic view of the sedimentary parameters through time is presented, I conclude this chapter with some comments on what the data mean. The remainder of the chapter will deal with examples of interpretation. Of all the many variables

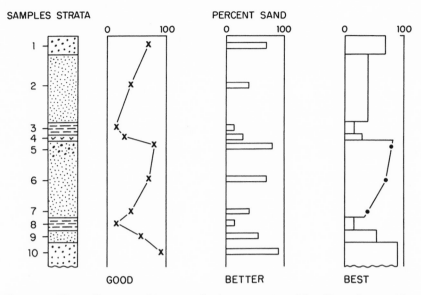

Figure 2.10. Zigzag diagrams vs. histograms for the presentation of data (Farrand 1985, with permission of the Center for the Study of First Americans).

measured and graphed, I shall choose only three categories for the purpose of illustrating some different aspects of interpretation:

1. Total granulometry (particle-size distribution), which is almost universally used as a basic descriptor of a given sediment, and it reflects strongly the nature of the primary sediment;

2. the ensemble of roundness and porosity of the rock clasts, considered together with the calcium carbonate ($CaCO_3$) of the fine fraction, that commonly provides a good means of evaluating modification by weathering; and

3. the heavy mineral assemblage, which may shed light on the provenience of the sediment or provide a measure of chemical weathering throughout the section.

Granulometry

Granulometry is the study of the frequency distribution of the size of particles, from large clasts to fine clay, in a sedimentary deposit. It is also known as particle-size analysis or grain-size analysis. We have already seen that zigzag diagrams can be used to show the variation of particle size with depth (Franchthi, Fig. 2.8, and Tabun, Fig. 2.15). However, these diagrams hide more

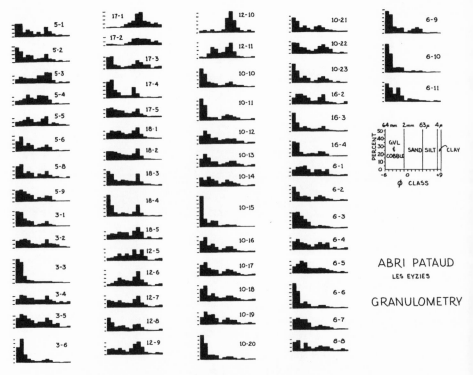

Figure 2.11. Granulometric histograms, Abri Pataud, France (after Farrand 1985, with permission of the Center for the Study of First Americans).

subtle variations that are extremely important in the final analysis of the origin(s) of the sediment. If the granulometry of a given rockshelter sediment sample is plotted in the form of a histogram of frequency vs. particle size, a polymodal distribution is the usual result (Figs. 2.10, 2.11, 2.12). I shall illustrate this with three examples of polymodal granulometry, but the modes in each case have different implications.

First, in the Abri Pataud (Fig. 2.11) we see four persistent modes—rock fragments (32–100 mm), granules (4–8 mm), medium sand, and fine silt plus clay, the latter being abundant in only a few samples. At Tabun Cave in Israel (Fig. 2.12), only three modes are persistent—sand, silt, and clay. There are no rock fragments in the Tabun sediments except in the uppermost levels (Layers B and C) where they occur mainly as head-sized boulders, much larger than the normal upper limit of sampling (arbitrarily set at either 100 or 128 mm). In Franchthi Cave in Greece (Fig. 2.13) five modes recur with regularity—large rock fragments, smaller rock fragments, coarse sand, silt, and clay—and in

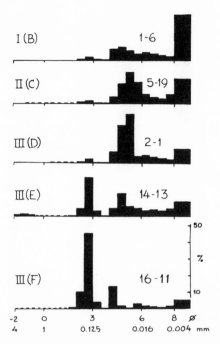

Figure 2.12. Granulometric histograms, Et-Tabun Cave, Israel (after Farrand 1985, with permission of the Center for the Study of First Americans).

Stratum W2 (sample 3-8, Fig. 2.13) a sixth mode in the medium sand range is
also distinct and characteristic of that lithostratigraphic unit.

A primary task of the sedimentologist is to identify these recurring modes
with a sedimentary source or process. Although modes in a given size interval
may be found at different sites, one cannot attribute their origin automatically
to a single process. For example, the rock fragments at the Abri Pataud appear
to be largely frost debris, whereas at Franchthi one can attribute them to a
highly tectonically fractured bedrock from which fragments have been detached by solution or by earthquakes.

The sand mode in Tabun Cave is undoubtedly eolian sand blown in from
the neighboring marine littoral zone. In the Abri Pataud, the sand mode in
any given stratum came most likely from grain-by-grain disintegration of the
sandy limestone bedrock or from sand blown in from the adjacent floodplain, or it may be a mixture of sand from those two sources. Particle size or
degree of sorting does not resolve this question at the Abri Pataud, but the
heavy minerals (see below) clearly identify the dominance of one or the
other provenience in different strata. Another interesting analysis of the sand

FRANCHTHI - TYPICAL HISTOGRAMS

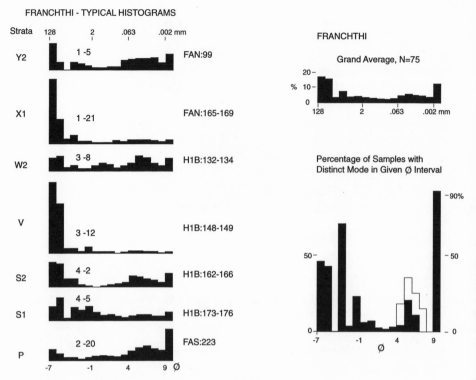

Figure 2.13. Granulometric histograms, Franchthi Cave, Greece (Farrand 2000, with permission of Indiana University Press).

component by Mandel and Simmons (1997) also utilizes grain size and mineralogy to distinguish bedrock, eolian, and colluvial sources on input to Aetokremnos rockshelter in Cyprus. The provenience of the sand mode in Franchthi Cave has not yet been positively identified. It cannot be derived from the bedrock, which contains no sand. It may be eolian in part; but it is conceivable that it was largely imported, intentionally or not, by the human inhabitants since it is abundant only in strata with the greatest intensity of human activity.

The clay mode in the Abri Pataud is important only in levels where other evidence of in situ weathering is abundant. In Tabun Cave, in contrast, the abundance of the clay-sized fraction (in the upper levels B and C) is clearly attributable to inwashing through the "chimney" that broke through the vault of the inner chamber only at the time when Tabun C sediments began to accumulate. Similarly, the prominent clay mode at Franchthi (Stratum S2, and especially Stratum P in Fig. 2.13) appears to be reworked *terra rossa* soil that has washed in through karstic fissures and passages, not a product of in situ weathering.

For the present purposes it is not my intention to demonstrate the correctness of the interpretation of each of these modes, but merely to illustrate that the polymodality is characteristic, and for a given site certain modes are persistent. Therefore, they must be important clues to differentiate sedimentary mechanisms that were operating simultaneously at a given moment in the past. If we can identify a given mode with a given process (e.g., rock fragments with freeze-and-thaw or fine sand with eolian activity as at the Abri Pataud), then we have a means of evaluating the evolution of the sedimentary fill, and by extension the environment existing during a prehistoric occupation.

Roundness, Porosity, and Carbonate Content

These parameters may be used singly or together as indicators of post-depositional weathering. Clearly when all three variables reinforce each other, the inference of weathering is all the more sound. Roundness (the wearing down and smoothing of sharp angles and edges of original rock fragments) may be produced either by chemical attack or by mechanical abrasion. If the porosity of the same rock fragments has increased measurably above that of the bedrock from which they derived, then the hypothesis of chemical rather than mechanical weathering is favored. Moreover, if the $CaCO_3$ content of the fine-grained matrix in the same bed has been reduced below the usual or average value found throughout the section, this fact also points in the same direction, namely enhanced chemical attack (leaching) in that level. For examples of the coherence of these three weathering indicators, see the upper one-third of Stratum W2, Strata V and U, and Stratum S2 in Franchthi Cave (Fig. 2.8). In addition, in these strata the included snail shells and limestone clasts ("white rocks") are conspicuously chalky as a result of leaching.

The pH Factor

In general, pH is a parameter where the interpretation is not straightforward, being controlled by parent material, weathering history, ambient moisture, organic material, and human activities. It is usually expected that the pH will show a decrease in the same levels where $CaCO_3$ is low, as might be expected if leaching had occurred. However, at the Abri Pataud the pH appears to fluctuate largely as an inverse function of intensity of human habitation, that is, more activity, lower pH, because of the organic wastes associated with

human activities (Farrand 1975b, tables 1, 2, 3). The pH is also complicated by
the presence of very fine-grained pedogenic carbonate accumulated during incipient soil formation that tends to increase pH where it might otherwise be
expected to be low.

Heavy Minerals

Turning to heavy minerals as an example of mineralogical analysis, we find
that they may be useful in at least two different ways, sediment provenience
and weathering history. Heavy minerals are usually dark-colored mineral
grains (ferromagnesian minerals, zircon, rutile, garnet, and others listed in Figure 2.14) with densities distinctly greater than those of the more common sand
grains (quartz, feldspar, calcite, mica). They commonly occur in low abundance, commonly less than 1 or 2 percent of the sand fraction. At the Abri
Pataud, which is situated at the foot of a limestone cliff adjacent to a wide,
sandy floodplain, there are a number of conspicuously sandy beds. At first
glance all the sands appear to have originated in the same way, differing only in
color which may be attributable to different degrees of weathering or to human contamination. However, the heavy-mineral suites are strikingly different
from bed to bed.

Figure 2.14 shows heavy minerals from two sources (10-11 from the sandy
limestone, 15-1 from the river floodplain) and from two sediment samples from
the Abri Pataud fill (10-2, 10-10). Some layers in the fill have heavy-mineral
suites very much like those in the sandy component of the limestone; others
are similar to heavy-mineral suites of the floodplain (Fig. 2.14, sample 10-2);
still others can be interpreted as mixtures from these two sources (Fig. 2.14,
sample 10-10).

The outcome of this analysis allows us to evaluate the relative contribution
of grain-by-grain disintegration of the bedrock wall, which was probably occurring more or less continuously, and of the input of quantities of sand blown
into the shelter from the floodplain, which varied with time and external conditions. See also a similar study by Mandel and Simmons (1997) in Cyprus.

A different example of the use of heavy minerals comes from Tabun Cave
where most of the lower two-thirds of the fill is eolian sand and silt, and the
sandy fraction of the uppermost beds (B and C) is undoubtedly of similar origin. Here the bedrock has no sandy component at all. Although the only conceivable source of the sand is the Mediterranean shoreline a few kilometers
away, one sees a systematic and abrupt change in the heavy-mineral suites in
the Tabun section ("Epi + Hb" column in Figure 2.15). The upper levels are
largely dominated by hornblende and epidote; but these two minerals that are

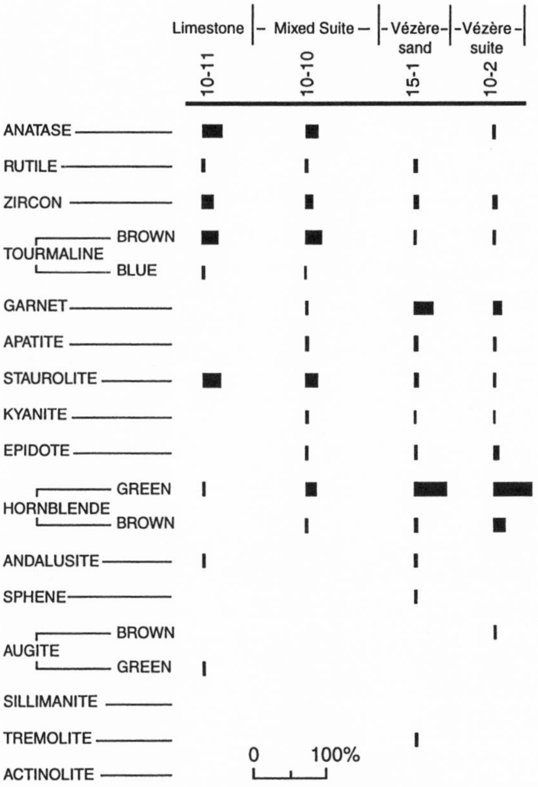

Figure 2.14. Heavy-mineral suites, Abri Pataud, France.

readily attacked by chemical weathering disappear almost completely below the base of Layer C, below which only weathering-resistant species (rutile, zircon, tourmaline, staurolite) dominate the heavy-mineral suites.

The obvious conclusion to be drawn is that the absence of hornblende and epidote in the lower beds is the result of weathering that was more or less contemporaneous with the deposition of those beds. In contrast, weathering did not play an important role during sedimentation of Layers B and C. Moreover, this interpretation is supported by other data, particularly the phosphates (Fig. 2.15). These phosphates are derived from the decay of animal bones present originally in the lower beds. No bones are found in the portions of Layers D through G that remain in the site, although bones were recovered from the outer (open-air) portions of the same beds during the 1929–1930 excavations.

Our conclusion is that both the nonresistant heavy minerals and the bones were destroyed by chemical weathering that occurred before the onset of Layer C deposition, which incidentally was contemporaneous with the opening of

ET-TABUN

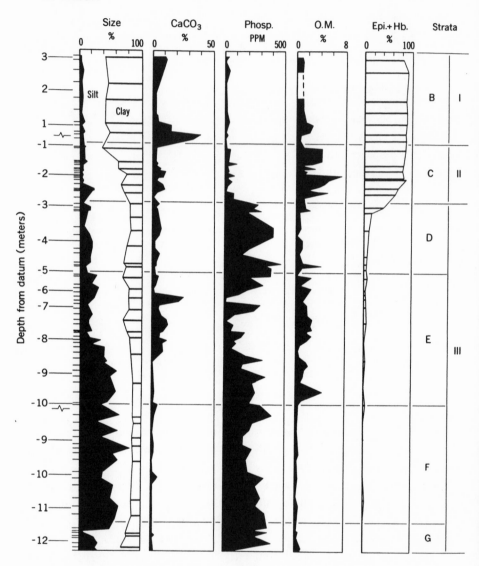

Figure 2.15. Summary sediment diagram, Et-Tabun Cave, Israel (after Farrand 2000, with permission of Indiana University Press).

the Tabun chimney (Jelinek et al. 1973). (See also the previous discussion of the clay mode at Tabun.)

Micromorphology

In recent years a new and complementary approach to the study of archaeological sediments has come into its own. Adapted from a longstanding method used in the study of rocks and soils, micromorphology is the technique of excising intact blocks of sediment from strata in a site, impregnating them with resins in a vacuum, and then, when they have solidified, slicing thin sections that can be studied under the microscope. A comprehensive treatment of micromorphology has been published by Courty et al. (1989). Moreover, it should go without saying that micromorphology can be applied to any stratified site, not just to rockshelters and caves (Macphail and Cruise 2001).

These thin sections reveal the internal relations (size, orientation, sorting, and mineral composition) of grains, cements, microfossils, and organic inclusions, as well as microlaminations and alterations of grains, among other features. These features will appear in their undisturbed state, that is, undisturbed by the process of routine sediment sampling necessary for bulk sedimentological analyses, such as those described in this chapter. The thin sections may reveal, however, disturbances of the sediments after they were originally deposited but before the site was excavated (e.g., past frost heaving or worm burrows).

As I said above, micromorphology is a complementary approach to classical sediment analysis. It sheds light on important relations that are not preserved in bulk samples, but the relatively small size of the two-dimensional thin sections—even "giant" thin sections up to 13.8 by 6.8 cm—may not reveal quantitative relationships of particle-size distributions, sorting, skewness, and other parameters, as readily as the latter may be measured in bulk samples. In my opinion, both classical analysis of bulk samples and micromorphological study of thin sections should go hand-in-hand because neither method alone is sufficient for the complete sedimentological interpretation of a site.

Some recent examples of micromorphological studies in rockshelters and caves include the recognition of past burning episodes (Schiegl et al. 1996), implications for radiocarbon dating (Goldberg and Arpin 2000), and the environmental reconstruction of Near Eastern (Goldberg and Bar-Yosef 1998) and South African (Goldberg 2000) caves.

Continuity and Rate of Sediment Accumulation

Hiatuses

Inspection of the global diagram, as described above, can identify simultaneous changes in several parameters indicating an episode of chemical or physical weathering at a certain stratigraphic level. For example, certain levels with a reduction of overall particle size, increased rounding of the rock fraction, decreased $CaCO_3$ and pH, and chalky surfaces on pebbles and cobbles point to a time when the sediment was subjected to weathering. A corollary of this conclusion is that during the weathering interval sediment input was strongly reduced or ceased entirely, and therefore there is a time gap (hiatus) prior to the resumption of sedimentation and subsequent occupation of the cave. Time gaps can also be identified by visibly eroded surfaces observed in the excavations, by offsets in a series of radiometrically dated levels, or by discontinuities in artifact or faunal sequences (Farrand 1993, fig. 5).

Such gaps can represent a considerable percentage of the total time span of a given site; a striking example comes from Franchthi Cave (Fig. 2.16) where at least 50 percent of the interval between 22,300 and 6,000 B.P. is not represented by any sediments in the excavated part of the cave (Farrand 2000: 85–86). Unfortunately for the cultural history of the site, two important time gaps at Franchthi occur at the critical Paleolithic/Mesolithic and Mesolithic/ Neolithic boundaries, which means that the question of transition or replacement of cultural traditions cannot be addressed directly. For the most part, however, such time gaps are neither obvious nor easy to recognize in the field during excavation. One may have the false impression that sedimentation at the site was continuous through time, which is probably never the case for a deeply stratified site (see also Campy and Chaline 1993).

Sediment Accumulation Rate

Given a sufficient number of radiocarbon dates and the recognition of hiatuses from sedimentary parameters, one can plot a sedimentation rate curve, such as the one from Franchthi Cave (Fig. 2.17). If the chronological control is sufficiently detailed, one can determine that the rate of sedimentation varied throughout the total duration of use of the cave. In some cases there was considerable variation—of at least two orders of magnitude within a thousand years. These variations may have resulted from changes in either geogenic or anthropogenic sedimentation, or both (see above). These variations are worthy of serious consideration when evaluating the intensity of use of the site as measured by the density of artifacts or fauna. For example, the density of arti-

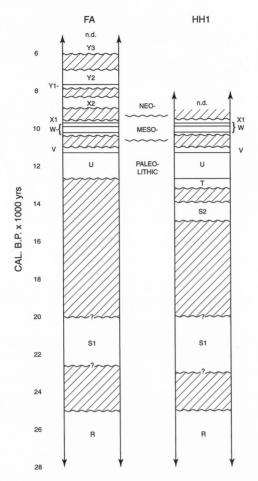

Figure 2.16. Stratigraphic columns from Franchthi Cave showing the durations of litho-stratigraphic units and intervening hiatuses. Note that the Neolithic/Mesolithic and Pale-olithic/Mesolithic boundaries each fall into a hiatus, about 300 years long (Farrand 2000, with permission of Indiana University Press).

facts in a certain 20-cm-thick stratum may be ten times as great as the density in another stratum of the same thickness, but the second stratum may have ac-cumulated ten times as fast as the first stratum. Thus, the number of artifacts accumulating per unit time would have been identical in the two cases.

Concluding Remarks

Obviously the foregoing is not an exhaustive treatment of all variables ob-served in the sedimentological study of rockshelter and cave deposits. The

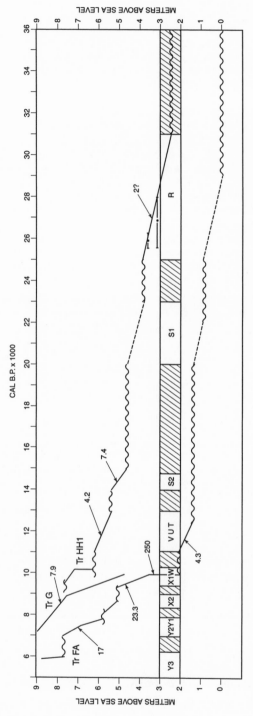

Figure 2.17. Sedimentation rate curves for Franchthi Cave, Greece, based on some 50 radiocarbon dates (modified from Farrand 2000, with permission of Indiana University Press). The dashed portions are speculative; there are no dates for Stratum S1. Rates are given in centimeters per 100 years.

ideas presented here are intended to show the complexity (polymodality, immaturity, multiple sources) of the sediments and the various approaches necessary in the interpretation of them. One particular variable (e.g., the abundance of rock fragments) may have quite a different meaning in one rockshelter from that in another. Above all, each rockshelter site must be examined thoroughly by itself before comparisons or correlations are made with other sites. The archaeologist is well advised to work together with the geologist—and vice-versa—in order to reach a reasonable conclusion on the sedimentary history and stratigraphy of a site.

This chapter has not been an attempt to explain how to do rockshelter sediment analysis or how to understand the geological basis of the many variables analyzed and displayed in the geological section of a site report. My goal has been to discuss some of the considerations essential to geological methodology in approaching the study of a rockshelter or cave-mouth site. On the other hand, perhaps I have not emphasized enough the necessity of interaction of the geologist with the archaeologists, paleontologists, ethnobotanists, and all other specialists engaged in the study of a given site. I believe firmly in the spirit of Butzer's contextual archaeology (Butzer 1978, 1982) that requires complete integration of all members of a team in all phases of a research project. Logistical difficulties, mainly the geographic distance between the home bases of various team members, too often render the realization of a truly contextual study utopian. Nevertheless, efforts can and should be made to work together as closely as possible and to understand each other's working hypotheses and logistical needs throughout the planning, execution, analysis, and synthesis phases of the project.

In the specific case of rockshelter sedimentology, the recognition of stratigraphic units, choices such as sample column locations and decisions on sampling frequency, should be mutual concerns of all members of the team. This approach is necessary to collect data pertinent to the testing of as many hypotheses as possible (not only those of the geologist) and not to destroy or overlook evidence required by other team members. Feedback between the archaeologist and the geologist concerning the relation of the latter's samples to archaeological "features" is equally essential.

Transcending these details, important as they may be, is the absolute necessity for the geologist to work side-by-side with the archaeologists on the site. As stated at the outset, the sedimentologist must see the sediments in situ in order to understand them fully. On the other hand, the site geologist (sedimentologist or whatever kind of specialist) should render more services to the project than just the collection and analysis of samples. He or she should be a team member with a certain expertise by virtue of his or her background and training, but this "expertise must transcend mere technology" (Schoenwetter 1981).

Ideally, the geologist should be on the site throughout the field operations in order to interact with any excavator in any trench at any time, whether to identify an exotic rock or to puzzle out a complicated stratigraphy. Any geologist can identify a rock; but one who is a member of the contextual team will be thinking in terms of why the rock is there, what properties made it desirable in the eyes of the prehistoric habitants, where did they have to go to obtain the rock, and so forth. This is geoarchaeology, and clearly it pertains to the study of any kind of archaeological site, not merely to rockshelters and caves.

Acknowledgments

The thoughts expressed in this paper stem from more than three decades of very fruitful collaboration with understanding and patient archaeological colleagues. Eugène Bonifay introduced me to the intricacies of rockshelter sediments, and I had the privilege of working side-by-side with the following excavation directors: H. L. Movius Jr. (Abri Pataud), A. J. Jelinek (Et-Tabun), T. W. Jacobsen (Franchthi Cave), R. S. Solecki (Yabrud, Jerf'Ajla), J. Tixier (Ksar'Aqil), B. Vandermeersch (Qafzeh), F. C. Howell (Yarimburgaz), and L. G. Straus (El Mirón), all of whom I consider to be enlightened interdisciplinary archaeologists. Financial support for the various projects came from the National Science Foundation, the National Endowment for the Humanities, the National Geographic Society, the Wenner-Gren Foundation for Anthropological Research, and the Centre National de la Recherche Scientifique (Paris). Thanks also to Rolfe Mandel and Vance Holliday for very helpful suggestions for improving the manuscript.

References Cited

Ahler, S. A.
1976   Sedimentary Processes at Rodgers Shelter. In *Prehistoric Man and His Environments: A Case Study in the Ozark Highland,* edited by W. R. Wood and R. B. McMillan, pp. 123–139. Academic Press, New York.

Bonifay, E.
1956   Les Sédiments Détritiques Grossiers dans le Remplissage des Grottes—Méthode d'Étude Morphologique et Statistique. *L'Anthropologie* 6:477–461.

1962   *Les Terrains Quaternaires dans le Sud-Est de la France.* Mémoire II. Publications de l'Institut de Préhistoire, Université de Bordeaux.

Brain, C. K.
1981   *The Hunters or the Hunted?* University of Chicago Press, Chicago and London.

Brunnacker, K.

1983   Die Sedimente in der Höhlenruine von Hunas. *Quartär-Bibliotek*, Band 4:53–89.

Butzer, K. W.

1976   A Re-Interpretation of the Swartkrans Site and Its Remains. *South African Journal of Science* 72:141–146.

1978   Toward an Integrated, Contextual Approach in Archaeology: A Personal View. *Journal of Archaeological Science* 5:191–193.

1982   *Archaeology as Human Ecology.* Cambridge University Press, Cambridge.

Campy, M.

1990   L'Enrégistrement du Temps et du Climat dans les Remplissages Karstiques: L'Apport de la Sédimentologie. *Karstologia Mémoires* 2:11–22.

Campy, M., and J. Chaline

1993   Missing Records and Depositional Breaks in French Late Pleistocene Cave Sediments. *Quaternary Research* 40:318–331.

Collcutt, S. N.

1979   The Analysis of Quaternary Cave Sediments. *World Archaeology* 10:290–301.

Collins, M.

1991   Rockshelters and the Early Archaeological Record in the Americas. In *The First Americans: Search and Research,* edited by T. D. Dillehay and D. J. Meltzer, pp. 157–182. CRC Press, Boca Raton, Florida.

Courty, M-A., P. Goldberg, and R. MacPhail

1989   *Soils and Micromorphology in Archaeology.* Cambridge University Press, Cambridge.

Davis, J. O.

1983   Geology of Gatecliff Shelter: Sedimentary Facies and Holocene Climate. In *The Archaeology of Monitor Valley,* 2. *Gatecliff Shelter,* edited by D. H. Thomas, pp. 64–87. Anthropological Papers of the American Museum of Natural History, vol. 59, part 1. New York.

Dixon, E. J., T. H. Heaton, T. E. Fifield, T. D. Hamilton, D. E. Putnam, and F. Grady

1997   Late Quaternary Regional Geoarchaeology of Southeast Alaska Karst: A Progress Report. *Geoarchaeology: An International Journal* 12:689–712.

Donahue, J., and J. M. Adovasio

1990   Evolution of Sandstone Rockshelters in Eastern North America: A Geoarchaeological Perspective. In *Archaeological Geology of North America,* edited by N. P. Lasca and J. Donahue, pp. 231–251. Geological Society of America, Centennial Special Vol. 4. Boulder, Colorado.

Farrand, W. R.

1975a   Sediment Analysis of a Prehistoric Rockshelter: The Abri Pataud. *Quaternary Research* 5:1–26.

1975b   Analysis of the Abri Pataud Sediments. In *Excavation of the Abri Pataud, Les Eyzies (Dordogne),* edited by H. L. Movius Jr., pp. 27–66. American School of Prehistoric Research, Bulletin 30. Peabody Museum, Harvard University, Cambridge.

1979   Chronology and Paleoenvironment of Levantine Prehistoric Sites as Seen from Sediment Studies. *Journal of Archaeological Sciences* 6:369–392.

1981   Pluvial Climates and Frost Action during the Last Glacial Cycle in the Eastern Mediterranean—Evidence from Archaeological Sites. In *Quaternary Paleoclimate,* edited by W. C. Mahaney, pp. 393–410. GeoAbstracts Ltd., Norwich, England.

1985   Rockshelter and Cave Sediments. In *Archaeological Sediments in Context,* edited by

J. K. Stein and W. R. Farrand, pp. 21–39. Center for the Study of Early Man, Orono, Maine.

1993   Discontinuity in the Stratigraphic Record: Snapshots from Franchthi Cave. In *Formation Processes in Archaeological Context,* edited by P. Goldberg, D. T. Nash, and M. D. Petraglia, pp. 85–96. Prehistory Press, Madison.

1995   L'Étude Sédimentologique du Remplissage de l'Abri Pataud. In *Le Paléolithique Supérieur de l'Abri Pataud (Dordogne): Les Fouilles de H. L. Movius, Jr.,* edited by H. M. Bricker, Chapter 2. Documents d'Archéologie Française, Paris.

2000   *Depositional History of Franchthi Cave-Sediments, Stratigraphy, and Chronology. Excavations in Franchthi Cave, Greece.* Fascicle 12. Indiana University Press, Bloomington.

Farrand, W. R., and J. P. McMahon

1997   History of the Infilling of Yarimburgaz Cave, Turkey. *Geoarchaeology: An International Journal* 12:537–565.

Ford, T. D.

1976   The Geology of Caves. In *The Science of Speleology,* edited by T. D. Ford, pp. 11–60. Academic Press, London.

Goldberg, P.

1973   Sedimentology, Stratigraphy and Paleoclimatology of Et-Tabun Cave, Mt. Carmel, Israel. Unpublished Ph.D. dissertation, University of Michigan, Ann Arbor.

2000   Micromorphology and Site Formation at Die Kelders Cave 1, South Africa. *Journal of Human Evolution* 38:43–90.

Goldberg, P., and T. Arpin

2000   Micromorphological Analysis of Sediments from Meadowcroft Rockshelter, Pennsylvania: Implications for Radiocarbon Dating. *Journal of Field Archaeology* 26:325–342.

Goldberg, P., and O. Bar-Yosef

1998   Site Formation Processes in Kebara and Hayonim Caves and Their Significance in Levantine Prehistoric Caves. In *Neanderthals and Modern Humans in Western Asia,* edited by T. Akazawa, K. Aoki, and O. Bar-Yosef, pp. 107–123. Plenum Press, New York.

Guillien, Y., and J-P. Lautridou

1974   Conclusions des Recherches de Gélifraction Expérimentale sur les Calcaires des Charentes. *Bulletin du Centre de Géomorphologie* 19:25–34. Centre National de la Recherches Scientifique, Caën.

1980   *Génèse des Abris sous Roche: Le Facteur Gel.* 105e Congrès National des Sociétés Savantesé Géographie, pp. 99–115. Caën, France.

Hudec, P. P.

1973   Weathering of Rocks in Arctic and Sub-Arctic Environment. In *Proceedings, Symposium on the Geology of the Canadian Arctic,* edited by J. D. Aitken and D. J. Glass, pp. 313–335. Geological Association of Canada, Toronto.

Jelinek, A. J., W. R. Farrand, G. Haas, A. Horowitz, and P. Goldberg

1973   New Excavations at the Tabun Cave, Mount Carmel, Israel, 1967–1972—A Preliminary Report. *Paleorient* 1:151–183.

Kennedy, J., and J. E. Brady

1997   Into the Netherworld of Island Earth: A Reevaluation of Refuge Caves in Ancient Hawaiian Society. *Geoarchaeology: An International Journal* 12:641–655.

Laïs, R.

1941   Höhlensedimente. *Quartär* 3:56–108.

Laville, H., J-P. Rigaud, and J. Sackett

1980   *Rockshelters of the Perigord.* Academic Press, New York.

Macphail, R. I., and J. Cruise

2001   The Soil Micromorphologist as Team Player. In *Earth Science in Archaeology,* edited by P. Goldberg, V. T. Holliday, and C. Reid Ferring, pp. 241–267. Kluwer Academic/Plenum, New York.

Mandel, R. D., and A. H. Simmons

1997   Geoarchaeology of Akrotiri Aetokremnos Rockshelter, Southern Cyprus. *Geoarchaeology: An International Journal* 12:567–605.

Miskovsky, J-C.

1974   *Le Quaternaire du Midi Méditerranéen.* Etudes Quaternaires-3. Université de Provence, Marseille.

Moody, U. L., and W. Dort Jr.

1990   Microstratigraphic Analysis of Sediments and Soils: Wasden Archaeological Site, Eastern Snake River Plain, Idaho. In *Archaeological Geology of North America,* edited by N. P. Lasca and J. Donahue, pp. 361–382. Geological Society of America, Centennial Special Vol. 4. Boulder, Colorado.

Schiegl, S., P. Goldberg, O. Bar-Yosef, and S. Weiner

1996   Ash Deposits in Hayonim and Kebara Caves, Israel: Macroscopic and Mineralogical Observations and Their Archaeological Implications. *Journal of Archaeological Science* 23:763–781.

Schmid, E.

1958   Höhlenforschungen und Sedimentanalyse. *Schriften des Institutes für Ur- und Frühgeschichte der Schweiz* 13. Basel.

1963   *Cave Sediments and Prehistory.* Basic Books, New York.

Schoenwetter, J.

1981   Prologue to a Contextual Archaeology. *Journal of Archaeological Science* 8:367–379.

Straus, L. G.

1990   Underground Archaeology. In *Archaeological Method and Theory,* edited by M. B. Schiffer, vol. 2, pp. 255–304. University of Arizona Press, Tucson.

Straus, L. G., and M. Gonzalez Morales

2000   The Fourth Excavation Campaign in "El Mirón" Cave (Cantabria, Spain), 1999. *Old World Archaeology Newsletter* 22(2):1–8.

Straus, L. G., M. Gonzalez Morales, W. R. Farrand, and W. J. Hubbard

2001   Sedimentological and Stratigraphic Observations in El Miron, a Late Quaternary Cave Site in the Cantabrian Cordillera, Northern Spain. *Geoarchaeology: An International Journal,* in press.

Sweeting, M.

1983   The Geological and Morphological Setting. In *Adlun in the Stone Age,* edited by D. A. Roe, Chapter 2. British Archaeological Reports International Series 159. Oxford.

White, S. E.

1976   Is Frost Action Really Only Hydration Shattering? A Review. *Arctic and Alpine Research* 81:1–6.

Wood, C.

1974   The Genesis and Classification of Lava Tube Caves. *Transactions of British Cave Research Association* 1:15–28.

Woodward, J. C., and G. N. Bailey
2000   Sediment Sources and Terminal Pleistocene Geomorphological Processes Recorded
        in Rockshelters Sequences in North-west Greece. In *Tracers in Geomorphology,*
        edited by I. D. L. Foster, pp. 521–551. John Wiley and Sons, London.
ZeChun, Liu
1985   Sequence of Sediments at Locality 1 in Zhoukoudian and Correlation with Loess
        Stratigraphy in Northern China and with the Chronology of Deep-Sea Cores. *Qua-*
        ternary Research 23:139–153.

3

Archaeological Sediments in Dryland Alluvial Environments

Gary Huckleberry

Drylands are places of great archaeological discovery. They are the setting for important developments in human history including hominid evolution in East Africa (Potts 1996) and the rise of complex societies in southern Mesopotamia (Adams 1965), Egypt (Hassan 1997), the Indus Valley (Kenoyer 1991), and the Andean coast of Peru (Kosok 1965). Although climate has changed through human history and many of these areas have alternated between conditions of relative moisture, they nonetheless reflect biological and cultural evolution that has been influenced in part by arid conditions. Drylands are sites of great archaeological discoveries also because aridity is conducive to the preservation and high visibility of the human biological and cultural record. It is no surprise then that archaeologists frequently find themselves in deserts studying the human past. Moreover, because water is the limiting resource, archaeologists commonly work in alluvial contexts in drylands. Streams and rivers are a magnet to biotic activity in deserts, including that of humans. For example, 95 percent of the population in modern Egypt lives within 20 km of the Nile, and this has likely not changed much during the last 5,000 years. Through history, desert peoples have focused their activities in riverine environments, and archaeologists seek to understand that history.

There are two aspects of streams and rivers, whether in humid or arid climates, that are of particular concern to archaeologists. One is how fluvial processes act to destroy, preserve, and modify the archaeological record. The other is how human subsistence is tied to the riverine environment. Both issues concern the behavior of the fluvial system, which can be reconstructed through the study of floodplain sediments and stratigraphy (Boggs 1987; Brakenridge 1988; Miall 1978; Reineck and Singh 1980). In terms of the basic mechanics of sedimentation and erosion, there is no difference between

humid and arid fluvial systems, and indeed many of the methodological and
theoretical approaches to studying the archaeological record in humid and
arid fluvial systems are the same (Brown 1997). However humid and arid fluvial systems differ in the magnitude and frequency of streamflow (Knighton
and Nanson 1997) and consequent changes in channel shape and size (Baker
1977; Bull 1991; Graf 1988; Wolman and Gerson 1978). Consequently, archaeologists who focus on physical site-formation processes in floodplains
(e.g., assessing the degree of post-depositional modification to artifacts and
features) and/or human adaptation to riverine environments (e.g., changes
in riparian biotic resources or irrigation systems) need to be aware of these
differences and have an understanding of dryland fluvial processes and resulting deposits.

In this chapter I focus on dryland fluvial processes and their geoarchaeological ramifications with examples taken from the American West. I will begin with an overview of how dryland streams differ from those in more humid
environments. I then divide the discussion into processes of floodplain formation, stability (including pedogenesis), and destruction, and how sedimentological and stratigraphic analyses can be used to reconstruct these processes in
order to better interpret the cultural record. I conclude with a consideration of
strategies for data collection and analysis. Given the complexity of arid landscapes, it is not possible to present all salient aspects of dryland fluvial
processes. I will emphasize valley floodplains rather than hillslopes or alluvial
fans, which represent important landscape components with their own characteristic fluvial dynamics and associated deposits (see Bull 1972; Gile et al.
1981; Hassan 1985; Nilsen 1985).

Definition of Drylands

There are many definitions for dryland environments. I will simply define it
here as any region characterized by a general lack of available moisture during
much of the year (see Graf 1988:4–10 and Cooke et al. 1993:2 for expanded
definitions). It is unknown what percentage of the earth's terrestrial environments is composed of drylands because definitions of drylands vary, and because dryland boundaries fluctuate through time due to natural climate
change and human activities (i.e., desertification). Drylands are generally
found in areas distant or isolated from maritime airflow and in areas dominated by persistent high pressure, particularly at and near 30° S and N latitude.
By one estimate, drylands make up over one-third of the earth's terrestrial surface (Cooke et al. 1993:5).

Characteristics of Dryland Streams

Although the focus here is on sediments in archaeological contexts, it is worth-
while to present a quick overview of the physical and behavioral traits of dryland rivers and their archaeological implications. Dryland rivers and streams
can be classified in different ways depending on what hydrological or geomorphic aspects are emphasized. Based on the frequency of streamflow, dryland
rivers and streams may be classified as ephemeral, perennial, or intermittent.
Given that drylands are regions of low annual precipitation, it is not surprising
that streamflow within drylands tends to be ephemeral. Ephemeral streams are
influent, that is, they lie over deep water tables and flow for short periods of
time when rainfall temporarily exceeds infiltration rates (Strahler and Strahler
1983:176). Perennial rivers also occur in drylands but have large, extralocal
catchment areas in more humid, commonly high-elevation environments
(Cooke et al. 1993:102). Some dryland streams are intermittent whereby channel segments intersect water tables resulting in alternating dry and flowing
reaches. Terms like ephemeral, perennial, and intermittent are useful for emphasizing the spatial and temporal variation in water as a limiting resource in
drylands.

Another way of classifying dryland rivers (and indeed all rivers) is by their
plan view geometry: braided, meandering, or anastomosing (Leopold and
Wolman 1957). This system of classification is useful for assessing river behavior because plan view geometry reflects the availability of water and sediment
load—two key factors in erosion and deposition (see Gladfelter, this volume).
Although all three channel shapes are found in drylands, braided stream patterns prevail because there is usually more sediment available for transport
than water available to carry it (though see Bull 1991:114–118 for exceptions).
The usual abundance of sediment load is linked to a paucity of vegetation
which otherwise retards runoff and helps to hold sediment in place (Langbein
and Schumm 1958). Braided streams are prone to rapid shifts in channel location due to sedimentation and consequent diversion of flow. Consequently,
such channels are not well suited for burial and long-term preservation of archaeological materials (Waters 1991:138).

Stream channels can also be characterized by their longitudinal profiles.
Most streams have a concave longitudinal profile, but dryland streams can
have segments with convex profiles due to an accumulation of sediment (Bull
1991:19–20; Schumm and Hadley 1957). Furthermore, ephemeral-stream
channels formed in unconsolidated materials can have alternating entrenched
and nonentrenched reaches resulting in a stepped longitudinal profile (Bull

1997). Such streams are usually quite dynamic in that streamflow changes from deep (entrenched reach) to shallow (nonentrenched reach) over short distances, and the locations of these alternating reaches can shift several hundreds of meters within decades (Graf 1988:218; Waters 1992:145–149). These entrenched channels usually contain steep-sided walls and are commonly referred to as "arroyos," particularly in the American Southwest where they are common. Arroyos are archaeologically significant in that they provide exposures of alluvial stratigraphy often containing deeply buried cultural material. Well-known Paleoindian sites in the western United States that were discovered in the walls of arroyos include Hell Gap in Wyoming, Lindenmeier in Colorado, Folsom in New Mexico, and Lehner, Naco, and Murray Springs in Arizona. Stratigraphy exposed by arroyos also provide insight into past hydrological conditions that can have important implications regarding paleoclimate and the development of prehistoric irrigation agriculture (see Floodplain Destruction below).

Another aspect of dryland rivers of geomorphic and archaeological significance concerns variability in streamflow. The annual peak discharge in dryland rivers is often several orders of magnitude greater than the mean annual discharge, resulting in a highly variable flow regime. In contrast, the difference between mean and maximum annual discharge is less in humid region rivers, and their floodplains are shaped by a more consistent discharge (i.e., a more persistent flow regime). The result is a more dynamic behavior for dryland floodplains where channel size and shape are determined by infrequent, large magnitude floods rather than any average discharge. Because flood frequency and magnitude change through time in response to climate change (e.g., Knox 1993; Webb and Betancourt 1992), so do channel and floodplain characteristics. Large floods result in channel downcutting or widening and modify the configuration of the floodplain. The recovery time for the dryland floodplain to return to its previous form is much longer than for streams in humid environments (Wolman and Gerson 1978). As a result, dryland streams display "disequilibrium" behavior whereby channel geometry is much more randomly determined by recent flood history, rather than by any "dominant discharge," which is more common with humid fluvial systems (Richards 1982:122–124).

Given that environments with predictable resources are most desirable in terms of human subsistence, periods of increased floodplain dynamics can create challenges for people who depend on the floodplain for survival. For example, along the Middle Gila River in central Arizona, increased frequency of large floods result in a more unstable braided stream channel whereas periods of relative low, large flood frequency result in a more stable, single channel meandering pattern. An increase in overbank flooding as inferred from ^{14}C-dated stratigraphy suggests that the Hohokam were challenged by eroded canal head-works and a shallow, braided channel poorly suited for water control beginning A.D. 1000 (Huckleberry 1995a). This may explain important settlement and canal alignment changes during the Sedentary to Classic period transition.

Climate and Dryland Alluvial Systems

River behavior is driven by the balance between streamflow and sediment load, and consequently changes in climate greatly affect depositional and erosional processes in all fluvial systems. Therefore, alluvial stratigraphy is a tool for helping to reconstruct climate. Unfortunately, the relationships between stream behavior and climate change are multifaceted and not universal (see Huckleberry and Billman 1998), and thus climatic interpretations from alluvial stratigraphy can be ambiguous. Nonetheless, some stratigraphic features in dryland floodplains are unambiguous indications of previously moist climates. Relict features indicative of more effective moisture may include soils (Holliday 1990; Monger 1995; Quade et al. 1998; Reider 1990), lacustral deposits (Waters 1989), spring deposits (Haynes 1995; Quade et al. 1995; Waters 1992:215–219), and fluvial deposits indicative of greater annual discharge (Baker and Penteado-Orellana 1977).

As an example, changes in sediment size record hydroclimatological changes associated with the latest Pleistocene-Holocene transition at the Sunshine Paleoindian site in east-central Nevada (Huckleberry et al. 1997; Fig. 3.1). Following recession of pluvial Lake Hubbs, the stream channel downcut into lacustrine sediment and backfilled with gravelly channel deposits (ca. 10,000–11,000 ^{14}C yrs B.P.). Stream competence diminished during the drier Holocene, and overbank alluviation became limited to very fine sand and silt intercalated with eolian sands. Although coarse-grained deposits were still present in the fluvial system, streamflow was too small and infrequent to mobilize them. Similar stratigraphic sequences elsewhere in Nevada point to glacial-interglacial climate change as a dominant force driving deposition and erosion in the basins.

Floodplain Construction

Floodplain deposition, erosion, and stability are of primary interest to archaeology because they affect the preservation, density, and spatial patterning of cultural materials in fluvial contexts (Rapp and Hill 1998:59–66; Waters 1992:92–103), and they influence the capacity for various human adaptive strategies. At geological time scales, sediment is merely in temporary storage in

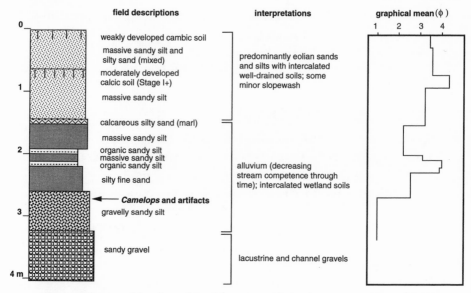

Figure 3.1. Stratigraphic column from the Sunshine Paleoindian Locality, Nevada (Huckleberry et al. 1997). Laboratory data courtesy of Amy Holmes.

floodplains during its episodic journey from uplands to the sea. Whether a floodplain is considered to be aggrading (i.e., floodplain growing through sedimentation), stable, or degrading (i.e., floodplain erosion) depends on the spatial and temporal scale considered (Schumm and Lichty 1965). Although such processes need not be spatially uniform within or between hydrologic basins at any one time, one can recognize periods of prevailing erosion or deposition (e.g., Haynes 1968), the latter occurring when sediment load is greater than the capacity of water to transport it.

There are many different conceptual models for describing floodplain formation—a product of the complex behavior of streams in diverse environments. Although admittedly simplistic (see Brown 1997:19), a useful system for characterizing floodplain formation is to divide floodplain deposits into two categories: lateral and vertical accretion (see Gladfelter, this volume, for a more complete definition of floodplain elements).

Lateral accretion deposits represent the relatively high energy channel environment whereby alluvium is dominated by coarse sediment (coarse sand to cobbles) and laid down by the lateral movement of the channel as it cuts into pre-existing bank deposits (Brakenridge 1988; Reineck and Singh 1980:265–287). Most of the sediment is transported as bedload (i.e., close to the channel bottom, rather than suspended load). Such deposition is prevalent in braided streams whereby an overabundance of sediment results in the deposition of bar deposits and consequent lateral deflection of the main paths of flow but can also be associated with meandering and anastomosing streams. When viewed in cross section, lateral accretion deposits are discontinuous and lenticular with a multitude of bedding patterns (Picard and High 1973). Gravelly deposits are commonly massive (i.e., lack internal bedding) and weakly graded (i.e., minimal vertical changes in particle size), and large clasts tend to have their long axes aligned downstream (i.e., imbricated) giving the deposit a fabric and indication of previous direction of flow.

Given a relatively high energy environment of deposition, it is not too surprising that lateral accretion deposits are not commonly associated with good archaeological preservation. Archaeological materials are commonly found in lateral accretion deposits but mostly in secondary contexts as "articlasts" (Gladfelter 1985) or as disturbed lags (Butzer 1982, fig. 7-1). An exception is the Granite Point site on the lower Snake River in Washington where early Holocene archaeological materials were found relatively in place in fluvial cobble deposits (Leonhardy 1970). More common, however, artifacts and ecofacts are reworked in high energy channel environments. At Whitewater Draw in Arizona, late Pleistocene mammoth, horse, camel, and bison remains were fluvially redeposited with early Holocene Archaic materials leading to confusion over the age of the ground stone assemblage. Geoarchaeological excavations many years later revealed the true stratigraphic relationships (Waters 1985, 2000). At the Sunshine site in Nevada, Great Basin Paleoindian materials have been found in association with extinct fauna (*Camelops* sp.) in a buried context (Jones et al. 1996; Fig. 3.1). The artifact and faunal assemblages are potentially contemporaneous, but the bones and artifacts occur in secondary contexts in channel sands and gravels. Although limited abrasion of the cultural and faunal material suggest a local origin, the ability to locate materials in primary context is hindered by the random nature of braided channel shifts.

In contrast to lateral accretion deposits, vertical accretion deposits are composed mostly of sediments that settle out of suspension in lower energy floodplain environments located away from the main channel. Such deposits are characterized by relatively fine (fine sand and finer) textures with tabular or blanket geometry and include bank (sometimes referred to as "overbank") and flood basin deposits (Reineck and Singh 1980:265–266). Horizontal, cross-stratification, and graded bedding as well as buried soils are common. Although more commonly associated with meandering and anastomosing streams, vertical accretion deposits can be found in association with braided stream systems, but usually represent a smaller portion of the floodplain stratigraphy.

There is a greater opportunity for archaeological preservation in vertical accretion deposits (Butzer 1982:101; Waters 1992:138–143). Not only are the sedimentological conditions favorable for the burial and preservation of cultural materials, but such deposits represent parts of the floodplain (e.g., levee and flood basin) that commonly serve as loci for cultural activities in drylands such as agriculture and habitation. Indeed, many prehistoric agricultural villages in the American Southwest are found in vertical accretion deposits in alluvial stream terraces (e.g., Eddy and Cooley 1983; Greenwald 1994; Mabry 1998). Moreover, vertical accretion deposits have the advantage of horizontal continuity making them favorable for tracing and correlating geological materials of known age (e.g., soils, volcanic tephra layers, and radiocarbon samples) to cultural materials or features of unknown age.

When working with vertical accretion deposits, it is important to try to distinguish separate episodes of deposition. Obviously, surfaces of human occupation or in situ cultural materials are not going to occur within the middle of a single flood deposit—they are going to occur at the contact between two temporally discrete deposits. The best evidence for separating depositional events are clear signs of surface stability such as archaeological features, mud cracks, and soil development. Less certain evidence for distinguishing depositional events include sudden changes in sedimentary texture, stone lines, and graded bedding (Baker 1989). Most alluvial deposits formed from a single flood grade upward from coarse to fine representing the transition from the peak discharge of a flood to the subsequent waning stages as water velocities diminish. Beds may coarsen upward without an increase in discharge if the amount of fine sediment in the hydrologic basin is reduced (e.g., Rubin et al. 1998), but such sequences are rare. Unfortunately, surges in streamflow during a single flood can result in multiple graded sequences within a single flood deposit. In such cases, it is easy to overestimate the number of floods (see discussion in Atwater et al. 2000 and Baker et al. 1991:249–250) and, accordingly, underestimate the rate of deposition, that is, interpret a greater amount of time in a given depth of stratigraphy than what is really represented.

Horizontal changes in particle size are also useful for interpreting flood history and determining the direction of streamflow. Typically, sediments grade horizontally from coarse to fine away from the main source of water flow. Hence, a transect from channel through levee to flood basin environments should result in decreasing mean grain size. This can help in reconstructing the direction of possible artifact displacement by overbank flooding. However, horizontal changes in particle size may be subtle and require laboratory analysis (see Data Collection and Analysis, below). Such an approach was used to identify depositional processes outside of prehistoric canal channels in the Phoenix Basin of Arizona (Huckleberry 1988; Fig. 3.2). Repeated application

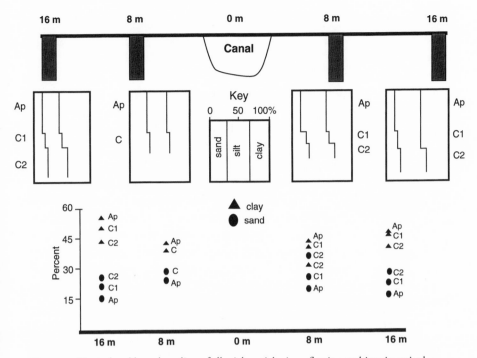

Figure 3.2. Vertical and lateral grading of alluvial particle size reflecting prehistoric agricultural processes associated with canal irrigation (Huckleberry 1988, fig. 5.22). Here, cultural deposition mimics natural alluviation.

of sediment-laden water in agricultural fields combined with slopewash from canal berms result in both vertical and horizontal textural grading. In this case, particle-size analysis was used to define a textural gradient indicating that humans repeatedly dredged the canal in order to maintain it for irrigation agriculture.

Other depositional processes besides lateral and vertical accretion can be associated with floodplain construction. The most common in dryland fluvial systems is alluvium redeposited by wind. Periodic flooding results in the deposition of sand and silt across a broad part of the floodplain, especially in braided streams. Following flood recession, the sediment soon dries and becomes available for wind transport and accumulates as either active dunes, coppice dunes (i.e., sands mounded at the base of vegetation), or sand sheets. Because flooding may recur, it is common for eolian deposits to interfinger with overbank alluvial deposits. Most eolian deposits appear massive or retain some cross-bedding, and show less textural variation than alluvium at the scale of a floodplain. Texturally, eolian sands usually contain fine to medium sand (Picard and High 1973:72), but texture will be heavily influenced by the nature of the parent material (Boggs 1987:364) (e.g., silty alluvium generates silty dunes). Given similar textures, distinguishing eolian and alluvial deposits can be problematic in the absence of preserved bedforms. Comparisons of the particle sizes of light and heavy mineral fractions may be useful for distinguishing water and wind-laid deposits (Leigh 1998).

In addition to eolian sediments, floodplains can contain deposits of colluvial sediment derived from adjacent hillslopes. Sedimentologically, such colluvium is best recognized by limited lithological variability (given its local origin), poor sorting, and greater clast angularity. Since hillslopes often grade into the edges of the floodplain, colluvium also tends to be coarser textured than adjacent alluvium. An exception to these general rules is where hillslopes are composed of older terrace alluvium in which case the colluvium shed from the hillslope will be similar to floodplain alluvial sediments. In such situations, one may need to rely on the geometry of the deposits to distinguish colluvium and alluvium. Colluvial deposits should thin away from the slope and across the floodplain (thinning in a direction opposite that of alluvial deposits derived from the channel).

Floodplain Stability

Floodplains are dynamic landforms prone to deposition and erosion, but parts of floodplains can become stabilized through stream downcutting resulting in the formation of terraces. Stream terraces may persist for hundreds of thousands of years and represent an important stable component of the landscape where surface archaeological materials are likely to be found. Alternatively, terraces may be short lived if rivers begin to backfill their floodplains due to tectonism, climate change, or internal hydrological adjustments. When this happens, terraces become buried providing a good opportunity for subsurface preservation of archaeological materials. Soils are the key markers for episodes of previous terrace surface stability (see Gladfelter, this volume). On one hand, soils provide challenges for archaeologists by removing primary alluvial bedding (Wood and Johnson 1978). On the other hand, soils provide insight into floodplain evolution and where former surfaces of human activity likely occurred. In either case, the ability to identify soils and buried terraces is a practical skill in alluvial geoarchaeology.

Rates of pedogenesis are generally slower in drylands than humid environments, but many local factors can accelerate the rate of soil formation, especially in floodplains. These include favorable parent material, high dust flux, and mesic microclimate. On low terraces still prone to periodic flooding or seasonally shallow water tables, the most common indicator of pedogenesis is

Figure 3.3. Alluvial paleosol on Black Mesa, Arizona. Humic zone at top of shovel represents a period of relative floodplain stability. (Gary Huckleberry photograph no. 319.)

humification, the build-up of organic materials (Buol et al. 1997) and the formation of an A horizon (Fig. 3.3). A horizons may be exaggerated in thickness if periodic deposition occurs at a slow enough rate such that each deposit of sediment becomes modified by pedogenesis before being buried by the next depositional event. Such soils are considered to be "cumulic" in that they thicken upward as the floodplain aggrades (Ferring 1992; Reider and Karlstrom 1987). If rates of deposition were to increase, then the soil might contain internal microstratigraphic bedding (e.g., Huckell 1998) or eventually merely become buried and removed from subsequent pedogenesis. Once buried, organic matter gradually breaks down through oxidation, although buried A horizons in dryland floodplains have been dated well back into the Pleistocene (e.g., Quade et al. 1998; Reider 1990).

Buried A horizons are excellent stratigraphic markers for identifying prehistoric human occupation surfaces. For example, the Marmes site in southeastern Washington contains stratified rockshelter and floodplain deposits with archaeological materials dating back to the terminal Pleistocene (Fryxell et al. 1968; Huckleberry et al. 1998; Sheppard et al. 1987). The floodplain portion of the site is composed of a Palouse River terrace with relatively uniform silty, overbank deposits overlain by cobbly, angular colluvium from the hillslope containing the rockshelter (Fig. 3.4). Within the overbank deposits are weakly

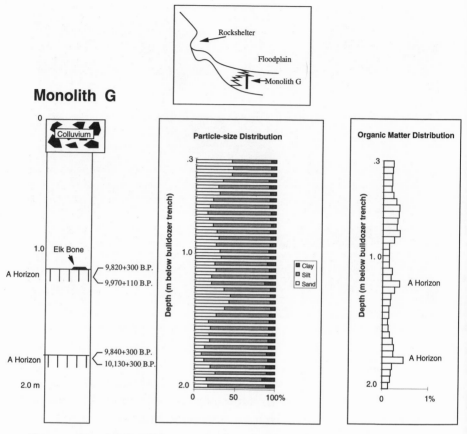

Figure 3.4. Monolith G and laboratory data from the Marmes Site, Washington (Huckleberry et al. 1998).

developed A horizons dated to approximately 10,000 ^{14}C yrs. B.P. These horizons represent surfaces of stability in the floodplain and probable locations for buried cultural materials. They were recognizable in the field only by slightly darker color due to higher organic matter content (later confirmed with laboratory analysis) and served to help direct excavations. Artifacts and charred human and faunal remains were found at the contact of the upper buried A horizon.

If given enough time and stability, more well-developed soils containing calcic, cambic, or argillic B horizons (Birkeland 1999; Buol et al. 1997; Holliday 1990) will form on alluvial terraces. The rate of formation for these pedogenic features can vary tremendously even within areas of similar climate and vegetation. For example, in the Sonoran Desert of the southwestern United

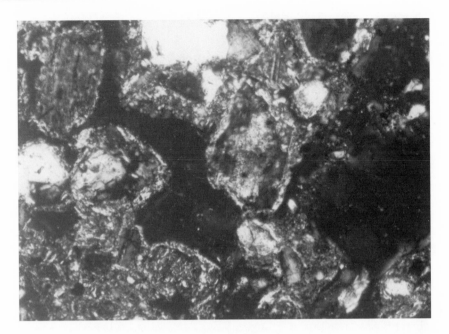

Figure 3.5. Photomicrograph of ABt horizon from archaeological site AZ U:6:244 (ASM), Mesquite Wash, Arizona. Clay coatings on sand grains indicate alluvial stability and soil formation. Cross-polarized light; field length = 870 μ.

States, soil formation is greatly affected by the rate of dust flux. An enhanced dust flux from the Phoenix Basin resulted in accelerated pedogenesis in alluvial soils located on the west slope of the Mazatzal Mountains (Huckleberry 1997). Soils only 1,000 years old have clay skin development (Fig. 3.5) similar to soils several thousand years older located at similar elevations in the region. Such local variability in the rate of alluvial pedogenesis should be kept in mind when constructing soil chronosequences and estimating the potential for buried cultural materials of a given age. If local pedologic factors can be characterized, however, then alluvial soils can be used as important chronological and climatological tools in archaeological research.

Floodplain Destruction

Sediments and soils are records of floodplain formation and stability. Erosion is marked by an absence of sediments. Therefore, one has to turn to stratigraphy for a record of past floodplain destruction. Gaps in the depositional record caused by erosion are marked by unconformities (Boggs 1987:526), and in unconsolidated alluvial deposits, these can be marked by an inset channel, abrupt

Figure 3.6. Buried paleochannel on Cowboy Wash, Ute Mountain, Ute Indian Reservation, southwestern Colorado. Channel cuts through latest Pleistocene alluvial paleosol. Base of channel contains a noncalibrated radiocarbon age of 3,670 yrs B.P. (Gary Huckleberry photograph no. 4948.)

change in particle-size, or stone lines (Ruhe 1959). In other cases, erosional contacts may be invisible. Floodplains erode when streamflow has a sediment carrying capacity that exceeds the amount of sediment entering the system. As previously mentioned, this may be because of a variety of natural and human disturbances, or may be part of the stream's natural ability to adjust its own geometry in order to best move sediment through the system (Cooke and Reeves 1976).

How erosion occurs within a floodplain varies. A lowering of base level or an increase in the discharge:sediment load ratio can drive a stream to downcut. Many floodplains in the American Southwest record episodes of past entrenchment in the form of buried Holocene paleochannels that have been revealed by historic and modern arroyos (Fig. 3.6). Entrenchment and expansion through nick-point retreat can occur rapidly (e.g., several hundreds of meters along the length of a channel during a single runoff event). As a result, the time-transgressive nature of past arroyo activity is often difficult to identify given the limited temporal precision provided by most dating methods. For example, with radiocarbon, most arroyo-cutting events appear instantaneous

Figure 3.7. Bank-cutting along Moenkopi Wash, Black Mesa, Arizona, during a flash flood. (Gary Huckleberry photograph no. 344.)

within a given watershed. However, Force and Howell (1996) were able to trace the upslope migration of arroyo cutting in McElmo Canyon as well as its impacts to prehistoric Puebloan communities in southwestern Colorado using ceramics. In the Four Corners region, ceramic seriation is calibrated with tree-ring dates, which can provide decadal temporal resolution.

Once a local base level of erosion is attained by stream downcutting, the channel will commonly swing laterally removing adjacent streambank deposits (Fig. 3.7). Whereas overbank flooding and surface stripping of a terrace can occur, especially in fine-textured floodplains with cohesive banks (Nanson 1986), most erosion in dryland floodplains is accomplished via lateral erosion of pre-existing alluvium. Eventually, the channel widens to a point where the hydraulic radius of seasonal peak discharge is reduced, thus reducing stream power, defined here as the ability of streamflow to pick up and remove sediment. When this occurs, the arroyo begins to backfill.

The amount of floodplain destruction that occurs with arroyo activity increases with the number of previous cycles of entrenchment and subsequent backfilling. This obviously can have a tremendous impact on the preservation and visibility of archaeological sites (Waters 1991, 2000). Stream power is maximum in small to intermediate-sized drainage basins of approximately 100 km² (Graf 1983). Streams associated with intermediate-sized drainage basins are more likely to have numerous cutting and backfilling episodes, thus complicating or obscuring the archaeological record. Such stream systems are more likely to have a variety of possible buried and exposed alluvial terraces with different aged fill (see Leopold and Miller 1954, fig. 2). Because sedimentation and erosion can vary spatially along a given stream due to localized hydraulic and geological variables (Schumm 1991), the height and sequence of alluvial terraces can likewise change in a downstream direction, making correlation based on topographic position difficult. Temporal correlations between terraces both within and between separate hydrologic basins are best made with numerical age criteria (e.g., radiometric or tree-ring dates) or calibrated age criteria (e.g., tephra or soil development).

Floodplain erosion and deposition are not restricted to systems of small- and intermediate-scale dryland streams. Higher order streams associated with larger catchment areas are also prone to erosion, and it may be expected that the archaeological record in such locations is also intrinsically biased with respect to differential preservation and visibility. Larger trunk streams carry tremendous volumes of water and sediment and have substantially larger floodplains. Their impact on the landscape with respect to erosion and deposition is potentially great. This may explain why Archaic and Paleoindian sites are so rare in floodplains of larger streams in southern Arizona: middle to early Holocene and latest Pleistocene surfaces are either buried or destroyed (Waters and Kuehn 1997). Human settlement patterns on the landscape have to be viewed with a realization that fluvial processes have modified the record, and that absence of evidence may be more geological than cultural in origin.

The timing and nature of floodplain destruction are directly relevant to aspects of human adaptation in drylands. The magnitude of impact that floodplain erosion has on human subsistence varies with adaptive strategy. Foragers may be impacted by destruction of riparian communities that contain important floral and faunal food sources (Kwiatkowski 1994). Floodwater farmers rely on relatively low energy overbank inundation to supply water and nutrients to field areas, and are vulnerable to downcutting, which can prevent overbank deposition. In the Four Corners region of the American Southwest, arroyos associated with drought have been invoked as contributing factors to large-scale changes in prehistoric Pueblo settlement patterns (Bryan 1941; Dean 1988). On larger perennial streams in the lower deserts of the American Southwest, floods and associated channel changes have likewise been invoked for prehistoric settlement changes by the Hohokam (Huckleberry 1995a; Nials et al. 1989). Canal irrigation farmers are vulnerable to both flood damage to their canal headworks and subsequent channel changes that can render their entire canal alignments obsolete. In north coastal Peru, a combination of El Niño floods and earthquakes may have radically altered river channel morphology causing the collapse of Moche irrigations systems (Moseley et al. 1983). Consequently, identifying previous episodes of floodplain degradation can be archaeologically significant not only in site preservation and visibility but also in terms of identifying episodes of environmental change that impact human subsistence and settlement patterns.

Data Collection and Analysis

A thorough geoarchaeological assessment of fluvial processes requires rigorous, systematic field recording of stratigraphy and sedimentology as well as an understanding of geomorphic context. It also requires a decision of whether or not sediment sampling and laboratory analyses are required, and if so, what type of analyses should be performed. Such a decision depends on an assessment of costs and benefits and the types of research questions being addressed (Holliday and Stein 1989). In many cases, laboratory analysis can be used to help support field interpretations and test hypotheses regarding environments of deposition, origins of sediment, and possible post-depositional processes.

For characterizing depositional units, particle-size analysis represents a foundation for interpretation. Sediment texture is a proxy for the energy of the depositional environment, and particle-size data can be a useful device for reconstructing depositional regimes. As an example, if an episode of increased floods as reconstructed in the tree-ring record played a role in Hohokam settlement pattern change in south-central Arizona by damaging canal systems and limiting food growing capacity (Nials et al. 1989), then there should be some geological evidence of such events. Particle-size analysis of canal sediments (Fig. 3.8) provides a means of identifying episodes of flooding (Huckleberry 1999). Grain size is an indirect measure of water velocity, and water velocities reconstructed from canal alluvial particle sizes that exceed levels an earthen canal can support are good evidence for uncontrolled flooding that likely damaged the canal. Such an approach provides local empirical evidence for prehistoric flooding and provides an independent means of testing the Hohokam flood hypothesis.

Particle-size data can also be used to infer origin of sediments (e.g., Fig. 3.2) or to help interpret whether stratigraphic features are cultural or natural. As an example of the latter, particle-size analysis was used to re-interpret stratigraphic features in overbank alluvial deposits in the Lake Ilo Basin of western North Dakota (Lenz 1997). Irregular-shaped bodies of sand intruded into horizontally bedded alluvium were originally interpreted as anthropogenic stone

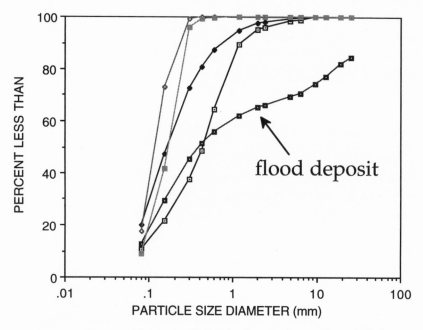

Figure 3.8. Cumulative particle-size distribution for alluvial sediments from a Hohokam canal (Huckleberry 1995b).

quarry pits. However, particle-size and chemical data were used to correlate the "quarry pit" matrix to a nearby liquefaction feature, which was a post-depositional intrusive body of sediment formed by hydraulic pressure (see Wood and Johnson 1978). The sediment analysis thus suggests that these are not cultural features but rather the product of natural, post-depositional disturbances.

Other types of laboratory analyses (see Stein 1985, 1987 for examples) may also be useful in geoarchaeological studies of dryland fluvial systems for purposes of determining the origin of fluvial sediments, characterizing depositional environments, or determining the degree of post-depositional alteration (e.g., pedogenesis). In such cases, laboratory analyses can be cost-effective if they can give greater support to interpretations of sediment history and be used to test specific research questions. If, however, laboratory analysis is performed without a research question in mind in an effort to simply generate numbers and give the impression of doing "science," then precious resources would be better spent elsewhere.

When laboratory analyses are performed in support of geoarchaeological research, it is important to remember that the best and most sophisticated laboratory methods are only as good as an understanding of the physical context of the sediments in relation to both the archaeological site and the landscape. Obviously, sediment without provenience is just dirt, but whereas it is common in archaeology to know the spatial relationship of the sediments at an archaeological feature or site scale, it may be less common that sediment context is analyzed at the landscape scale (see Stein and Linse 1993). Sediment sampling confined to one location, or limited to site boundaries may be inadequate to recognize mesoscale geological processes that affect both human behavior (e.g., floods and agriculture) or the preservation and visibility of the archaeological record (Freeman 2000). Sampling and analysis of control sediments outside of feature and site boundaries may be essential for distinguishing natural and cultural depositional and post-depositional processes (e.g., Lenz 1997; Stein 1985) or for identifying environmental events of human consequence such as vegetation changes (e.g., Monger 1995; Reider et al. 1988). Although financial and logistical constraints may limit such an extensive sampling strategy, it is nonetheless important to try to relate archaeological site sediments to the surrounding landscape. Only then can sediment charts and graphs, usually representing spatial scales of square meters, have meaning to processes that occur at larger spatial scales which may be more relevant to environmental history and human adaptation.

Conclusions

Rivers and streams are dynamic components of the landscape and provide a great challenge for study by historical scientists. There is no one simple model for dryland stream behavior much like there is no one simple model for human behavior. Nonetheless, the goal for archaeologists is to filter out the natural processes that affect the archaeological record in fluvial contexts so more reliable interpretations about human behavior can be made. By applying principles and methods of stratigraphy, sedimentology, geomorphology, and pedology, it is possible to place the sedimentary matrix in its appropriate spatial-temporal context, which is essential for interpreting the archaeological record (Butzer 1982; Rapp and Hill 1998; Waters 1992).

Dryland streams are different from those in humid environments, but the basic mechanics of sediment transport, deposition, and post-depositional modification are the same. What are different are the frequency and magnitude of geomorphic processes in drylands with respect to floodplain formation, stability, and destruction. Because these affect preservation of the archaeological record and limit the types of human adaptive strategies practiced in floodplains, archaeologists need to be cognizant of these traits.

Modern observations of fluvial processes in drylands can provide valuable evidence for historical reconstruction, but the primary data for understanding past floodplain formation, stability, and destruction are sediments. Thus, the geoarchaeological mantra holds true for dryland fluvial settings: the sedimentary matrix surrounding the cultural record may be as valuable as the cultural materials themselves. Systematic collection of field data combined with laboratory analyses is the most fruitful approach to, at a minimum, characterize the geologic context, but more importantly to provide a robust data set to test hypotheses regarding site history and human behavior. Given that dryland floodplains can change at human timescales and are natural magnets for cultural activity, considerable information regarding human prehistory still lies buried within alluvium. Many great archaeological discoveries remain to be made, and it is probable that many of these will take place in dryland fluvial contexts.

Acknowledgments

Many of the data presented here are the product of geoarchaeological investigations supported by CRM companies and agencies including the Arizona Department of Transportation, Maricopa County Department of Transportation, Archaeological Consulting Services, Ltd., Soil Systems, Inc., and Statistical Research, Inc. I would like to thank Andrea Freeman, Julie Stein, and two anonymous reviewers who helped with comments on an earlier draft of this manuscript.

References Cited

Adams, R. M.
1965   *Land behind Baghdad.* University of Chicago Press, Chicago.
Atwater, B. F., G. A. Smith, and R. B. Waitt
2000   The Channeled Scabland: Back to Bretz? Comment and Reply. *Geology* 28:574–576.
Baker, V. R.
1977   Stream-Channel Response to Floods, with Examples from Central Texas. *Geological Society of America Bulletin* 88:1057–1071.

1989   Magnitude and Frequency of Palaeofloods. In *Floods: Hydrological, Sedimentological, and Geomorphological Implications,* edited by K. Beven and P. Carling, pp. 171–183. John Wiley and Sons, London.
Baker, V. R., and M. M. Penteado-Orellana
1977   Adjustment to Quaternary Climatic Change by the Colorado River in Central Texas. *Journal of Geology* 85:395–422.
Baker, V. R., B. N. Bjornstad, A. J. Busacca, K. R. Fecht, E. P. Kiver, U. L. Moody, J. G. Rigby, D. F. Stradling, and A. M. Tallman
1991   Quaternary Geology of the Columbia Plateau. In *Quaternary Nonglacial Geology; Conterminous U.S.,* edited by R. B. Morrison, pp. 215–246. Geological Society of America, Boulder, Colorado.

Betancourt, J. L.
1990   Tucson's Santa Cruz River and the Arroyo Legacy. Unpublished Ph.D. dissertation, University of Arizona, Tucson.
Birkeland, P. W.
1999   *Soils and Geomorphology.* 3rd ed. Oxford University Press, New York.
Boggs, S., Jr.
1987   *Principles of Sedimentology and Stratigraphy.* Merrill Publishing Company, Columbus, Ohio.
Brakenridge, R.
1988   River Flood Regime and Floodplain Stratigraphy. In *Flood Geomorphology,* edited by V. R. Baker, C. Kochel, and P. Patton, pp. 139–156. John Wiley and Sons, New York.
Brown, A. G.
1997   *Alluvial Geoarchaeology: Floodplain Archaeology and Environmental Change.* Cambridge University Press, Cambridge, England.
Bryan, K.
1941   Pre-Columbian Agriculture in the Southwest, as Conditioned by Periods of Alluviation. *Association of American Geographers Annals* 31:219–242.
Bull, W. B.
1972   Recognition of Alluvial-Fan Deposits in the Stratigraphic Record. In *Recognition of Ancient Sedimentary Environments,* edited by J. K. Rigby and W. K. Hamblin, pp. 63–83. Special Publication 16. Society of Economic Paleotologists and Mineralogists.
1991   *Geomorphic Responses to Climatic Change.* Oxford University Press, New York.
1997   Discontinuous Ephemeral Streams. *Geomorphology* 19:227–276.
Buol, S. W., F. D. Hole, R. J. McCracken, and R. J. Southard
1997   *Soil Genesis and Classification.* 4th ed. Iowa State University Press, Ames.
Butzer, K. W.
1982   *Archaeology as Human Ecology.* Cambridge University Press, Cambridge.
Cooke, R., and R. Reeves
1976   *Arroyos and Environmental Change.* Oxford Research Studies in Geography. Clarendon Press, Oxford, England.
Cooke, R., A. Warren, and A. Goudie
1993   *Desert Geomorphology.* UCL Press, Bristol, Pennsylvania.
Dean, J.
1988   A Model of Anasazi Behavioral Adaptation. In *The Anasazi in a Changing Environment,* edited by G. J. Gumerman, pp. 25–44. Cambridge University Press, Cambridge.
Eddy, F. W., and M. E. Cooley
1983   *Cultural and Environmental History of Cienega Valley, Southeastern Arizona.* University of Arizona Anthropological Paper No. 43. The University of Arizona Press, Tucson.
Ferring, C. R.
1992   Alluvial Pedology and Geoarchaeological Research. In *Soils in Archaeology: Landscape Evolution and Human Occupation,* edited by V. T. Holliday, pp. 1–40. Smithsonian Institution Press, Washington, D.C.
Force, E., and W. Howell
1996   *Holocene Depositional History and Anasazi Occupation in McElmo Canyon, Southwestern Colorado.* Archaeological Series No. 188. Arizona State Museum, Tucson.

Freeman, A. K.

2000   Application of High-Resolution Alluvial Stratigraphy in Assessing the Hunter-Gatherer/Agricultural Transition in the Santa Cruz River Valley, Southeastern Arizona. *Geoarchaeology: An International Journal* 15:559–590.

Fryxell, R., T. Bielicki, R. Daugherty, C. Gustafson, H. Irwin, B. Keel, and G. Krantz

1968   Human Skeletal Material and Artifacts from Sediments of Pinedale (Wisconsin) Glacial Age in Southeastern Washington, United States. *Proceedings VIII International Congress of Anthropological and Ethnological Sciences,* vol. 3, *Ethnology and Archaeology,* pp. 176–181. Tokyo and Kyoto, Japan.

Gile, L. H., J. W. Hawley, and R. B. Grossman

1981   *Soils and Geomorphology in the Basin and Range Area of Southern New Mexico— Guidebook to the Desert Project..* New Mexico Bureau of Mines and Mineral Resources Memoir 39. Socorro, New Mexico.

Gladfelter, B. G.

1985   On the Interpretation of Archaeological Sites in Alluvial Settings. In *Archaeological Sediments in Context,* edited by J. K. Stein and W. R. Farrand, pp. 41–52. Center for the Study of Early Man, Orono, Maine.

Graf, W. L.

1983   Downstream Changes in Stream Power in the Henry Mountains, Utah. *Annals of the Association of American Geographers* 73:373–387.

1988   *Fluvial Processes in Dryland Rivers.* Springer-Verlag, New York.

Greenwald, D. (editor)

1994   *Early Desert Farming and Irrigation Settlements: Archaeological Investigations in the Phoenix Sky Harbor Center,* vol. 1, *Testing Results and Data Recovery Plan.* SWCA Anthropological Research Paper No. 4. SWCA, Inc., Flagstaff, Arizona.

Hassan, F.

1985   Fluvial Systems and Geoarchaeology in Arid Lands, with Examples from North Africa, the Near East, and the American Southwest. In *Archaeological Sediments in Context,* edited by J. K. Stein and W. R. Farrand, pp. 53–68. Center for the Study of Early Man, Orono, Maine.

1997   The Dynamics of a Riverine Civilization: A Geoarchaeological Perspective on the Nile Valley, Egypt. *World Archaeology* 29:51–74.

Haynes, C. V., Jr.

1968   Geochronology of Late-Quaternary Alluvium. In *Means of Correlation of Quaternary Successions,* edited by R. B. Morrison and H. E. Wright, pp. 591–631. Proceedings 7th INQUA Congress. The University of Utah Press, Salt Lake City.

1995   Geochronology of Paleoenvironmental Change, Clovis Type Site, Blackwater Draw, New Mexico. *Geoarchaeology: An International Journal* 10:317–388.

Holliday, V. T.

1990   Pedology in Archaeology. In *Archaeological Geology of North America,* edited by N. P. Lasca and J. Donahue, pp. 525–540. Geological Society of America, Centennial Special Vol. 4. Boulder, Colorado.

Holliday, V. T., and J. K. Stein

1989   Variability of Laboratory Procedures and Results in Geoarchaeology. *Geoarchaeology: An International Journal* 4:347–358.

Huckell, B. B.

1998   Alluvial Geomorphology and Geochronology. In *Archaeological Investigations of Early Village Sites in the Middle Santa Cruz Valley: Analyses and Synthesis,* edited by

J. B. Mabry, pp. 31–56. Anthropological Paper No. 19. Center for Desert Archaeology, Tucson, Arizona.

Huckleberry, G.

1988   Relict Irrigation Canals in the East Papago Freeway Corridor. In *Arizona Department of Transportation Archaeological Testing Program*, Part 2, *East Papago Freeway*, edited by D. G. Landis, pp. 109–168. Soil Systems Publications in Archaeology No. 13. Phoenix, Arizona.

1995a   Archaeological Implications of Late-Holocene Channel Changes on the Middle Gila River, Arizona. *Geoarchaeology: An International Journal* 10:159–182.

1995b   Hydraulics, Sedimentology, and Structure of the Pueblo Blanco Canals. In *Archaeological Excavations at Pueblo Blanco: The MCDOT Alma School Road Project*, edited by D. Doyel, A. Black, and B. MacNider, pp. 339–361. Report No. 90. ACS Cultural Resources, Tempe, Arizona.

1997   *Rates of Holocene Soil Formation in South-Central Arizona.* Open-File Report 97-7. Arizona Geological Survey, Tucson.

1999   Assessing Hohokam Canal Stability through Stratigraphy. *Journal of Field Archaeology* 26:1–18.

Huckleberry, G., C. Beck, G. T. Jones, and A. Holmes

1997   Further Excavations and Paleoenvironmental Data at the Sunshine Locality, Eastern Nevada. *Current Research in the Pleistocene* 14:162–163.

Huckleberry G., and B. Billman

1998   Floodwater Farming, Discontinuous Ephemeral Streams, and Puebloan Abandonment in Southwestern Colorado. *American Antiquity* 63:595–616.

Huckleberry, G., C. E. Gustafson, and S. Gibson

1998   Stratigraphy and Site Formation Processes. In *Marmes Rockshelter (45FR50) Preliminary Report*, edited by B. A. Hicks, pp. 44–98. Confederated Tribes of the Colville Reservation. Nespelem, Washington.

Jones, G., C. Beck, F. Nials, J. Neudorfer, B. Brownholtz, and H. Gilbert

1996   Recent Archaeological and Geological Investigations at the Sunshine Locality, Long Valley, Nevada. *Journal of California and Great Basin Anthropology* 18:48–63.

Kenoyer, J.

1991   The Indus Valley Tradition of Pakistan and Western India. *Journal of World Prehistory* 5:331–385.

Knighton, D., and G. Nanson

1997   Distinctiveness, Diversity and Uniqueness in Arid Zone River Systems. In *Arid Zone Geomorphology: Process, Form, and Change in Drylands*, edited by D. S. G. Thomas, pp. 185–203. John Wiley and Sons, London.

Knox, J.

1993   Large Increases in Flood Magnitude in Response to Modest Changes in Climate. *Nature* 361:430–432.

Kosok, P.

1965   *Life, Land, and Water in Ancient Peru.* Long Island University Press, New York.

Kwiatkowski, S.

1994   Prehistoric Biotic Communities and Ecosystem Dynamics near Pueblo Grande. In *The Pueblo Grande Project*, vol. 5, *Environment and Subsistence*, edited by S. Kwiatkowski, pp. 5–34. Soil Systems Publications in Archaeology No. 20. Phoenix, Arizona.

Langbein, W. B., and S. A. Schumm
1958   Yield of Sediment in Relation to Mean Annual Precipitation. *Transactions of the American Geophysical Union* 39:1076–1084.

Leigh, D.
1998   Evaluating Artifact Burial by Eolian Versus Bioturbation Processes, South Carolina Sandhills, USA. *Geoarchaeology: An International Journal* 13:309–330.

Lenz, B.
1997   Late Quaternary Sediment Liquefaction in the Lake Ilo Basin, Dunn County, North Dakota. Unpublished M.A. thesis. Northern Arizona University, Flagstaff.

Leonhardy, F.
1970   Artifact Assemblages and Archaeological Units at Granite Point Locality 1 (45WT41), Southeastern Washington. Unpublished Ph.D. dissertation, Washington State University, Pullman.

Leopold, L., and J. P. Miller
1954   *A Postglacial Chronology for Some Alluvial Valleys in Wyoming.* U.S. Geological Survey Water Supply Paper 1261. U.S. Government Printing Office, Washington, D.C.

Leopold, L. B., and W. G. Wolman
1957   *River Channel Patterns—Braided, Meandering, and Straight.* U.S. Geological Survey Professional Paper 252. U.S. Government Printing Office, Washington, D.C.

Mabry, J. (editor)
1998   *Archaeological Investigations of Early Village Sites in the Middle Santa Cruz Valley: Analyses and Synthesis.* Anthropological Paper No. 19. Center for Desert Archaeology, Tucson, Arizona.

Miall, A. D.
1978   Lithofacies Types and Vertical Profile Models in Braided River Deposits: A Summary. In *Fluvial Sedimentology,* edited by A. D. Miall, pp. 597–604. Canadian Society of Petroleum Geologists, Calgary.

Monger, H. C.
1995   Pedology in Arid Lands Archaeological Research: An Example from Southern New Mexico-Western Texas. In *Pedological Perspectives in Archaeological Research,* edited by M. Collins, B. J. Carter, B. G. Gladfelter, and R. J. Southard, pp. 35–50. Special Publication 44. Soil Science Society of America, Madison, Wisconsin.

Moseley, M., R. Feldman, C. Ortloff, and A. Narvaez
1983   Principles of Agrarian Collapse in the Cordillera Negra, Peru. *Annals of the Carnegie Museum* 52:299–327.

Nanson, G.
1986   Episodes of Vertical Accretion and Catastrophic Stripping: A Model of Disequilibrium Flood-Plain Development. *Geological Society of America Bulletin* 97:1467–1475.

Nials, F., D. Gregory, and D. Graybill
1989   Salt River Streamflow and Hohokam Irrigation Systems. In *The 1982–1984 Excavations at Las Colinas: Studies of Prehistoric Environment and Subsistence,* pp. 59–78. Archaeological Series 162. Arizona State Museum, Tucson.

Nilsen, T. H. (editor)
1985   *Modern and Ancient Alluvial Fan Deposits.* Van Nostrand Reinhold, New York.

Picard M., and L. High Jr.
1973   *Sedimentary Structures of Ephemeral Streams.* Elsevier Scientific Publishing Company, New York.

Potts, R.

1996   *Humanity's Descent: The Consequences of Ecological Instability.* William Morrow and Company, New York.

Quade, J., R. M. Forester, W. L. Pratt, and C. Carter

1998   Black Mats, Spring-Fed Streams, and Late-Glacial-Age Recharge in the Southern Great Basin. *Quaternary Research* 49:129–148.

Quade, J., M. D. Mifflin, W. L. Pratt, W. McCoy, and L. Burckle

1995   Fossil Spring Deposits in the Southern Great Basin and Their Implications for Changes in Water-Table Levels near Yucca Mountain, Nevada, during Quaternary Time. *Geological Society of America Bulletin* 107:213–230.

Rapp, G. R., Jr., and C. L. Hill

1998   *Geoarchaeology: The Earth-Science Approach to Archaeological Interpretation.* Yale University Press, New Haven, Connecticut.

Reider, R. G.

1990   Late Pleistocene and Holocene Pedogenic and Environmental Trends at Archaeological Sites in Plains and Mountain Areas of Colorado and Wyoming. In *Archaeological Geology of North America,* edited by N. P. Lasca and J. Donahue, pp. 335–360. Geological Society of America, Centennial Special Vol. 4. Boulder, Colorado.

Reider, R. G., G. Huckleberry, and G. Frison

1988   Soil Evidence for Postglacial Forest-Grassland Fluctuations in the Absaroka Mountains of Northwestern Wyoming, U.S.A. *Arctic and Alpine Research* 20:188–198.

Reider, R. G., and E. T. Karlstrom

1987   Soils and Stratigraphy of the Laddie Creek Site (48BH345), and Altithermal Occupation in the Big Horn Mountains, Wyoming. *Geoarchaeology: An International Journal* 2:29–47.

Reineck, H., and I. Singh

1980   *Depositional Sedimentary Environments.* Springer-Verlag, New York.

Richards, K.

1982   *Rivers: Form and Process in Alluvial Channels.* Methuen and Company, Ltd., London.

Rubin, D. M., J. M. Nelson, and D. J. Topping

1998   Relation of Inversely Graded Deposits to Suspended-Sediment Grain-Size Evolution during the 1996 Flood Experiment in Grand Canyon. *Geology* 26:99–102.

Ruhe, R.

1959   Stone Lines in Soils. *Soil Science* 87:223–231.

Schumm, S. A.

1991   *To Interpret the Earth: Ten Ways to Be Wrong.* Cambridge University Press, Cambridge.

Schumm, S. A., and R. Hadley

1957   Arroyos and the Semiarid Cycle of Erosion. *American Journal of Science* 255:161–174.

Schumm, S. A., and R. Lichty

1965   Time, Space and Causality in Geomorphology. *American Journal of Science* 263:110–119.

Sheppard, J. C., P. E. Wigand, C. E. Gustafson, and M. Rubin

1987   A Reevaluation of the Marmes Rockshelter Radiocarbon Chronology. *American Antiquity* 52:118–125.

Stein, J. K.

1985   Interpreting Sediments in Cultural Settings. In *Archaeological Sediments in Context,* edited by J. K. Stein and W. R. Farrand, pp. 5–20. Center for the Study of Early Man, University of Maine, Orono, Maine.

1987   Deposits for Archaeologists. In *Advances in Archaeological Method and Theory,* vol. 11, edited by M. B. Schiffer, pp. 337–395. Academic Press, New York.

Stein, J. K., and A. R. Linse (editors)

1993   *Effects of Scale on Archaeological and Geoscientific Perspectives.* Geological Society of America, Special Paper 283. Boulder, Colorado.

Strahler, A. N., and A. H. Strahler

1983   *Modern Physical Geography.* 2nd ed. John Wiley and Sons, New York.

Waters, M. R.

1985   *The Geoarchaeology of Whitewater Draw, Arizona.* Anthropological Papers of the University of Arizona No. 45. The University of Arizona Press, Tucson.

1989   Late Quaternary Lacustrine History and Paleoclimatic Significance of Pluvial Lake Cochise, Southeastern Arizona. *Quaternary Research* 32:1–11.

1991   The Geoarchaeology of Gullies and Arroyos in Southern Arizona. *Journal of Field Archaeology* 18:141–159.

1992   *Principles of Geoarchaeology: A North American Perspective.* The University of Arizona Press, Tucson.

2000   Alluvial Stratigraphy and Geoarchaeology in the American Southwest. *Geoarchaeology: An International Journal* 15:537–557.

Waters, M. R., and D. D. Kuehn

1997   The Geoarchaeology of Place: The Effect of Geological Processes on the Preservation and Interpretation of the Archaeological Record. *American Antiquity* 61:483–497.

Webb, R. H., and J. L. Betancourt

1992   *Climatic Variability and Flood Frequency of the Santa Cruz River, Pima County, Arizona.* U.S. Geological Survey Water-Supply Paper 2379. U.S. Government Printing Office, Washington, D.C.

Wolman, M., and R. Gerson

1978   Relative Scales of Time and Effectiveness of Climate in Watershed Geomorphology. *Earth Surface Processes* 3:189–208.

Wood, R. W., and D. L. Johnson

1978   A Survey of Disturbance Processes in Archaeological Site Formation. In *Advances in Archaeological Method and Theory,* vol. 1, edited by M. B. Schiffer, pp. 315–370. Academic Press, New York.

4

Archaeological Sediments
in Humid Alluvial Environments

Bruce G. Gladfelter

> An object seen in isolation from the whole is not the real thing.
> —Masanobu Fukuoka (1978)

Alluvium is sediment deposited by water, in or bordering a channel or as a fan at the edge of a valley bottom. It is of interest in archaeology for two reasons: (1) alluvium is a common matrix for artifacts, and floodplains and fans are common settings for archaeological sites, and (2) alluvium and its hydrogeomorphic context may indicate characteristics of past hydrological conditions and, consequently, of a paleoenvironment.

Alluvium is deposited when its concentration in water exceeds the capability of the fluid to carry it. Sustained deposition results in aggradation of an alluvial unit (formally labeled an allostratigraphic unit [NACOSN 1983], but this term is no longer widely used); prolonged erosion results in the degradation of an alluvial unit. Consequently, alluvium contains a gradational record that is discontinuous, broken by erosional interruptions that may be a singular event or a protracted interval of many events. The breaks in deposition are indicated by diastems that denote brief, hydraulic or hydrologic changes, or by unconformities that represent prolonged disruption of the "stability" of the entire fluvial system. The former case involves adjustments within the channel (autochthonous activity); the latter may implicate external factors (allochthonous activity). Not infrequently, climatic conditions are thought to be the allochthonous explanation, but there are additional or alternative reasons as well that can involve geologic, geomorphologic, or hydraulic factors.

An earlier paper addressed the physical properties of alluvium and artifacts in it from the perspective of both being in the storage mode of a sediment budget (Gladfelter 1985). The relevance of this perspective for archaeological interpretations and for past hydrologic environments was examined. The discussion in this chapter extends those themes to consideration of units of alluvium and their depositional setting by enlisting recent geoarchaeological examples, drawn mostly upon developments over the past 15 years or so that pertain to fluvial geomorphology and archaeology in the Midwest of the United States. Because of this, the temporal spectrum is the Holocene.

A pervading theme, sometimes implicit, is that alluvium and stream discharge comprise a dynamic system, called a cascading system, which is linked with a morphologic system consisting of the channel and the floodplain (and alluvial fans). The linked responses between these two systems vary in space and in time. The commentary examines this linkage by considering the relationship of climate and alluvium, and the notion of stability as it pertains to floodplains. Throughout the discussion the issues of time and scale reoccur. We must remain aware of the briefness and limited scale of the human perspective, both of which filter our observations of cultural and natural variability and, consequently, our interpretations of them. The magnitude and frequency of hydrologic events are scalar and temporal dimensions, respectively, that are in addition to the more commonly recognized factors of spatial and temporal variation (e.g., Stein and Linse 1993).

Alluvium in Humid Environments

An environment is humid if over the course of a year there is a surplus of moisture; arid environments have a deficit of moisture. The moisture surplus means that the water budget is positive. Thornthwaite (1948) defined the water budget as: $P = AE + \Delta ST + S$, where the demand for precipitation (P) is prioritized and allotted first to plants as actual evapotranspiration (AE), followed by any change in the storage of water in the ground (ST), and lastly surplus (S) as runoff if any water remains available. Assessed from the Thornthwaite perspective, while a moisture deficit may occur in part of a given year in a humid environment, characteristically there is a moisture surplus for the entire year. Intra-annual changes in surplus reflect the seasonal property of climate, but as long as water is available throughout a budget year, from either or both precipitation and storage, there is a positive water balance and channel flow is likely to be perennial.

The distinguishing characteristic of a humid environment that is adopted here is the occurrence of perennial discharge (Q). In such an effluent system, discharge is composed of runoff and base flow from storage. The temporal and spatial patterns of intra- and interannual moisture availability that are important to people, as well as other aspects of climate (daily cloud cover, length of growing season, degree of coincidence of insolation and precipitation, timing of events), are elusive in the record of the past.

The variation of these factors in the short term defines our weather. The distinction between weather and climate is important for many archaeological interpretations. For example, subsistence practices are adjustments to weather conditions—people's movements and use of space in a given environment exploit resources that are patterned after the weather. Weather is more influential in the day-to-day, seasonal, and even decadal subsistence behaviors of hunter-gatherers, pastoralists, and early agriculturalists than is their climatic environment. The larger system people construct for subsistence (e.g., tropical, desertic, high latitude, grassland, woodland, shrubland, ecotone) is an adaptation in tune with their overall environment and the climate. It may not be possible to recognize in the archaeological record what is a cultural adjustment and what is an adaptation.

The climatic scale or level of observation is more time transgressive than that of the weather (Fig. 4.1). Change at the weather scale in times past should be more difficult to recognize given its nature—sites of occupation that represent brief rather than continuous activity can be difficult to assess, and the representativeness of our sample perhaps cannot be known. At large time scales (e.g., Holocene), climate change and human adaptations must be generalized, while the known record on which generalization is based is a partial one in which we may be able only to discern trends. But what is obtained from the preserved record are accounts only of brief occurrences extracted from the continuity, and we cannot be certain as to what extent they are representative of that continuity. Our resolution is very much constrained by dimensional controls—in space and time—all of which operate to interfere with the interpretation of the record.

Effects on subsistence systems and complex societies can occur at all levels of climatic variation (e.g., Clark 1985). This accentuates the importance of distinguishing local from regional variance in the hydrologic system. Our interpretation of the hydroclimatic change also is affected by the temporal dimension that we assume. For example, when short periods (days to decades) or long periods (Quaternary) are considered, hydroclimatic variance is the greatest; elements of weather may be indicated by the former, but global circulation is implicated by the latter. At intermediate scales, variance is probably least (see McDowell et al. 1990).

The response time of the fluvial system and the memory of a gradational unit within it are related directly to the temporal and spatial scales, which can be insensitive to short-term variance thereby obscuring recognition of weather systems. Consequently, behavioral adjustments that might have occurred to accommodate such short-term variance are smothered, and there results a predisposition to identify in the archaeological record cultural adaptations that are responses to variance within a longer term, hydroclimatic period. Time is

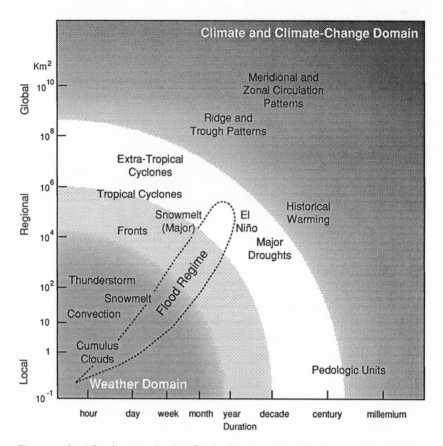

Figure 4.1. Spatial and temporal scales of hydroclimatic activity. The location of each label approximates its respective spatio-temporal dimension; a distinction is made between weather and climate. The location of labels is somewhat subjective, but not arbitrary (adapted from Clark 1985; Hirschboeck 1988; and McDowell et al. 1990).

the elusive dimension for both geomorphic and archaeological reconstructions (e.g., McDowell et al. 1990).

The Fluvial System

There are several reasons why an appreciation of the relationships among the dynamics of a river and alluvial forms are of archaeological interest. The rates, patterns, and magnitudes of fluvial activity establish the physical properties of the alluvial matrix of the archaeological material, the matrix that is used to reconstruct the prehistoric dynamics of the channel and system. It is important to understand these past dynamics on a floodplain because hydrologic circumstances influence decisions about occupation and exploitation of locations. Post-occupational, fluvial dynamics are of interest too because they can preserve or fragment the record of occupation and exploitation. Finally, the reconstruction of the hydrogeomorphic history of an alluvial system is a prerequisite for inferences about the paleohydrological environment, and for the prediction of locations of undiscovered sites.

Deposition of suspended alluvium in open channel flow is determined by its concentration; that is, the proportion of sediment (load) to the volume of water (discharge) such that changes in either or both effect a morphologic response within the fluvial channel. The alluvial stratigraphic record may retain such a response and provide insight about human occupation in an environment of the past.

Schumm (1968) constructed a set of quasi-equations linking the cascading (dynamic) system of the load and the discharge (Q) to the three-dimensional patterns of the morphologic properties of the channel—cross-sectional shape (width, depth, and their ratio, F), longitudinal gradient or slope (S), and plan form (L) of the channel. Either mean annual flood or mean annual discharge can be represented by Qw in the equations, and Qt is the proportion of alluvium that is bedload. Schumm's quasi-equations illustrate that "water discharge determines the dimensions of the channel (W, D, meander dimensions), but the relative proportions of bedload (sand and gravel) and suspended load (silts and clays) determine not only the shape of the channel but (also) width-depth ratio and channel pattern" (Schumm 1988:231).

The relationship of mean annual discharge and the load of the channel determine its morphological properties; note that if the proportion of bedload changes, the proportion of suspended load in the total load will vary accordingly. Meander wave length (L) and channel sinuosity (P) are related inversely (e.g., a less sinuous channel has a longer wave length), and the width-depth ratio (F) varies inversely with channel sinuosity:

$$Equation(1): Q_w^+ Q_t^+ \approx \frac{w^+ L^+ F^+}{P^-}(S^\pm d^\pm)$$

$$Equation(2): Q_w^- Q_t^- \approx \frac{w^- L^- F^-}{P^+}(S^\pm d^\pm)$$

$$Equation(3): Q_w^+ Q_t^- \approx \frac{d^+ P^+}{S^- F^-}(w^\pm L^\pm)$$

$$Equation(4): Q_w^- Q_t^+ \approx \frac{d^- P^-}{S^+ F^+}(w^\pm L^\pm)$$

Equations 1 and 2 say that when the volume of both discharge and load in the stream channel vary in the same direction, the channel adjusts its width,

wave length, and width-depth ratio (and perhaps gradient and depth, depending upon the actual proportions of bed and suspended loads) also in that direction, while sinuosity necessarily varies inversely. Equations 3 and 4 say that
when the concentration of alluvium changes (i.e., the proportions of discharge
and load vary), the depth and sinuosity of the channel vary directly according
to the direction of change in Q, while the width-depth ratio and slope vary inversely with sediment concentration according to the type of load (increasing
with increased bedload but decreasing with increased suspended load). The
width of the channel and its wave length adjust according to the magnitude of
changes in depth and sinuosity.

The Channel

Within a given reach of a stream channel, riffles and pools alternate along
its bottom, each spaced about five to seven times the width of the channel.
Riffles of coarser sediment, and bars in and along a channel, may be utilized at
low-water stages but any artifacts will be moved as part of the bedload at
higher discharges. Lithics recovered from these settings are assuredly not in
their primary matrix. Riffles are not exposed in a perennial channel but smaller
artifacts that may become concentrated there at low-water stages will be sorted
and scoured at subsequent higher discharges. In general, consequently, artifacts recovered from intra-channel deposits were moved from their point of
discard; the distance of travel commonly is assessed by the surface finish, degree of abrasion, and extent of "rounding" or morphologic modification of the
"articlast." These attributes may signal relative distances of transport, but there
is no method by which actual distance of travel can be determined.

Hydraulic variation within a channel, at a cross-sectional location and in
the downstream direction, and beyond it at overbank stages may be preserved
by sedimentary structures that vary with the caliber, density, shape, and spacing of clasts and the turbulence of the water. The surviving depositional structures and sediment can be used to infer the dynamics of the past fluvial system
that entrained, transported, and deposited the sediment. Facies models developed by sedimentologists become one basis for a reconstruction and differentiation of sedimentary environments on the floodplain (e.g., Miall 1996, with
references). Not infrequently, archaeologists invoke the proportional statistical
distribution of particle sizes within a sample of alluvium, and perhaps additional properties as well, to infer an environment of sedimentation. However,
even though moment statistics and other constructs are used in this way, statistical distributions of grain sizes do not by themselves define alluvial depositional environments (see references in Gladfelter 1985).

It may be useful to reconstruct the discharge of a channel that retains alluvium containing artifacts. An estimate of paleodischarge can disclose aspects of past environmental hydrologic conditions and of the behavior of the fluvial system with which artifacts and prehistoric activity are associated. Such estimates contribute to an assessment of the primacy of lithic artifacts found in alluvial contexts. Many equations have been derived to estimate paleodischarges based upon channel morphology (e.g., Wharton 1995) or properties of clasts in the alluvium (e.g., Brown 1997, appendix 1.3; Church 1978; Ethridge and Schumm 1977; Maizels and Aitken 1991; Williams 1984). No single equation has universal relevance.

The Floodplain

The drainage basin is the fundamental hydrogeomorphic unit. It is both the watershed and the source of sediment for the fluvial system that transmits both from the landscape. The drainage basin is, in both real and practical terms, the geomorphic context of archaeological material. It is an open system with alluvium in only temporary storage (e.g., Gladfelter 1985). The drainage basin also is the spatial integrator of hydroclimatic change with alluvial stratigraphic successions. Within it morphologic and dynamic components are linked by the interactions of geologic, hydrologic, hydraulic, and geomorphic factors, each of which may influence the system across a range of spatial and temporal scales.

A flood is an event that occurs when water overflows the confines of a channel; that is, the volume of discharge exceeds the cross-sectional area of the channel. A floodplain, as its name indicates, is a plain (i.e., area of gentle slope and modest relief) that is inundated by the flood. The plain is constructed of sediment from farther up valley that the stream has been unable to transport. The amount of stored alluvium in a floodplain is affected by the width of the valley bottom (Faulkner 1998). A valley floor without a floodplain will not store archaeological material, and valley margins without alluvial fans are without a direct linkage between erosion on an upland and aggradation on a floodplain, in which case attention must be directed to the smallest drainage basins because they are most sensitive to gradational activity that occurs on an upland.

The floodplain may be narrow, as in small basins or when width is constricted by bedrock, or broad as in large valleys with multiple meander belts (e.g., Guccione et al. 1998). In general, the larger the width of the floodplain, the greater the likelihood that archaeological material could be stored in or on the alluvium, and the more types of facies there are. Clearly the validity of this postulate depends upon the age of the sediments in a particular circumstance, and the proportions of bedload and suspended load in the system. Water in channels that have a high proportion of bedload has high levels of turbulence and this turbulent velocity is not conducive to the preservation of many archaeological materials, or to the recovery of artifacts in a primary context. Braided channel patterns of some wide floodplains are associated with coarse loads, which assures that archaeological evidence for the use or occupation of those surfaces ultimately will be reworked (see Best and Bristow 1993).

The floodplain of an alluvial system with mostly suspended load is of much greater archaeological interest than one that is dominated by bedload (Jackson 1981; Willis 1989). The lower turbulent velocity of suspended load systems means that the potential for artifacts to be entrained or disturbed is appreciably less. In addition, suspended load is deposited under lower energy circumstances that are conducive to the burial of artifacts and features.

Climate, Alluvium, and Archaeology

Spatial and temporal patterns of water and sediment yields are important to understand among other things: the completeness of the archaeological record on/in a floodplain or alluvial terrace; the prospect of recovering sites of a particular age on or within a floodplain or the geomorphic components of it; the interval of time represented by an alluvial matrix with artifacts and features; gradational patterns within the drainage basin that is the context of archaeological sites; and human and nonhuman impacts on the prehistoric landscape. However, the imprecision of the temporal resolution and spatial variability can limit any linkage to inferences about behavioral adjustments.

Fluvial Geomorphology and Climate

The storage of artifacts is a legacy of how sediment is routed through a drainage basin. In humid environments, most alluvium is moved by stream discharges associated with storms that occur every five or ten years. Although such events are of hydrogeomorphic significance, most morphologic adjustments by stream channels and floodplains are in response to ordinary flows of high frequency and low magnitude, those that have a low statistical recurrence interval (RI) of less than one year (i.e., RI = 0.92 years, or $Q_{0.92}$). This realization must be weighed, however, against the importance of extreme flood events (see Lewin 1989) that obliterate the record of lesser events. But, the spatial and temporal differentiations of extreme and routine events proves not to be straightforward. A regional storm (e.g., front) may produce a basinwide, cataclysmic response and features that survive over a long term, but a local storm (e.g., convection) may affect only low-order basins where hydrogeomorphic adjustments are short lived. This has been noted by Carling and Beven (1989). All of these factors contribute to the explanation of the gradational record that survives, and to the expectation of where deposits of an appropriate archaeological age and depositional environment might be found.

In any given circumstance, sediment yield varies directly with water yield, and inversely with the density of vegetation. Intraregional differences among gradational sequences may reflect, consequently, spatial variations in the magnitude, frequency, duration, and intensity of meteorological events. For example, storms of high intensity but short duration have more impact on water and sediment yields in smaller, low-order basins, whereas in large basins storms of long duration are more significant. Since the large-scale atmospheric circulation to which such events relate shows variation over intervals of decades, centuries, and millennia, hydrogeomorphic responses can be expected to vary at similar scales.

Spatial variation in flooding is tied to geomorphological as well as climatological factors. Properties of the regime of rainfall and orographic conditions are climatological (see Hayden 1988; Hirschboeck 1988); geomorphic factors are the properties of the drainage basin and the river channels in it (Kochel 1988). It is precisely these latter factors that account for most intra- and interbasin variability in alluvial sequences. In brief, the nonclimatic factors are: basin area and shape (hydrographs attenuate with increased basin area, greater equidimensionality of basin shape, and less relief), vegetation cover, thickness of soil or regolith, sediment delivery, and the situation of a basin within an ordinal hierarchy (e.g., de Boer 1992). Channel properties influence the fluvial response to climatic input: bedload, gradient, W/D, and pattern (i.e., equations 1–4 above).

These complexities of the fluvial system confound retrodiction of paleohydrologic and climatic conditions so that, even though linkages between hydrogeomorphic variables are known and for the most part understood, a prediction of where prehistoric occupations on a floodplain may be preserved is imperfect. Equally important is the realization that prehistoric sites surviving on and in a floodplain are only a partial representation of an original settlement pattern and, quite possibly, not a reliable legacy of a prehistoric settlement system.

Facies Models

Alluvium aggrades in the floodplain as the river channel shifts its location laterally, creating lateral accretion (or bottom stratum) deposits; when

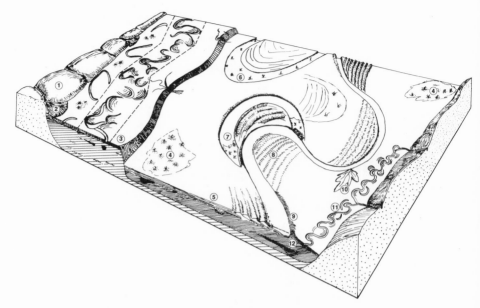

Figure 4.2. Schematic composite diagram of hydrogeomorphic features on the floodplain of a meandering river. See Table 4.1 for the explanation.

discharge overflows the channel and inundates the plain, vertical accretion (or top stratum) deposits aggrade (see Fig. 4.2 and Table 4.1). The deposition of lateral accretion sediments is within and proximal to the channel, while vertical accretion sediments aggrade beyond the channel in the floodbasin. Even though lateral accretion sediments frequently comprise the bulk of the sediment in the floodplain (but see Putnam 1994), their morphologic expression is subdued by overbank deposits, and archaeological sites that were close to a channel become eroded or buried. The different locations of sedimentation sometimes are referred to as high energy (lateral accretion) or low energy (vertical accretion) environments of deposition.

Alluvium aggrades in many different locations on a floodplain and the deposits at each setting comprise alluvial facies (e.g., Nanson and Croke 1992). The properties of the sediments depict the facies, which are then lateral subdivisions of an alluvial unit. Facies in a sedimentary unit signify different depositional environments across a floodplain surface for a particular period of time; facies exposed in a vertical geostratigraphic section in a floodplain indicate changes in the depositional environment at that place over a particular interval of time. The former allows for the reconstruction of a synchronic pattern of depositional environments, the latter of a diachronic pattern. Both reconstructions are important for interpretation of settlement patterns on a floodplain.

Table 4.1. Alluvial Contexts of Archaeological Material

GEOMORPHIC FEATURE OR SETTING[1]	ARCHAEOLOGICAL POTENTIAL
(1) Dissected upland of loess or bedrock forming a bluff above the valley.	Sites of any age may be found on the upland; older sites may be within a soil profile (e.g., Kuehn 1993; Stafford 1995; Van Nest 1993).
(2) Alluvial fan interdigitated with alluvium of the floodplain.	Sites may be preserved (and stratified) within fans constructed of fine alluvium, and on the surface. Age of sites may be contemporary with alluviation on the floodplain (interdigitated facies), or post-date the alluviation (e.g., Hajic 1990; Running 1995; Styles 1985; Van Nest 1993).
(3) Alluvial terrace with inactive meanders of older rivers. Features within the meander belt (dashed lines) are younger than the meander scars of an older river outside of the meander belt. A paleosol (Entisol) is developed on the vertical accretion deposits of the terrace. Alluvium of the floodplain on which these rivers flowed is buried beneath the younger alluvium of the contemporary floodplain.	Sites within the meander belt cannot be older than the meandering activity; sites inside of a particular meander loop cannot be older than the meander loop. Buried sites that survived paleomeandering activity will be old. Near-surface sites outside of the meander belt may be contemporaneous with its gradational activity or younger; older sites can be shallowly or more deeply buried in vertical accretion sediment (e.g., Gladfelter 1981; Hassen 1993).
(4) Backswamp along lower, interior setting on the floodplain.	Surface and near-surface sites may be preserved. The oldest sites on the floodplain are likely to be found in these settings (e.g., Gladfelter 1985; Kidder and Fritz 1993).
(5) Contemporary floodplain, convexly shaped, with meander scars of an older river course and geomorphic features of the currently meandering channel.	The location and age of sites are directly related to the time depth of geomorphic activity. Sites in situ on the surface are rare; depth of burial is a function of rates of sedimentation at a particular depositional setting; sites inside of a meander loop are younger than the expansion of that loop; sites outside of a meander loop may be of any age contemporaneous with or younger than the contextual matrix (e.g., Gardner and Donahue 1985; Hajic 1993; Johnson and Logan 1990; Kidder 1996; Kidder and Saucier 1991; Kolb and Boszhardt 1999; Phillips and Gladfelter 1983; Rogers 1987; Van Nest and Vogel 1999).
(6) Infilled scar of a meander cut-off and degraded suite of point bars.	Sites within the cut-off will post-date alluviation and if buried, be at shallow depths. Sites inside of the meander scar cannot be older than its expansion; sites may be preserved outside of it in vertical accretion sediment (e.g., Heinrich 1991).

Table 4.1. Alluvial Contexts of Archaeological Material Continued

(7) Oxbow lake in a meander cut-off. Clay plugs at both ends.	Sites in spatial association with the lake can be of any age post-dating its formation. Shallowly buried sites may be preserved in levees or a suite of point bars (e.g., Autin et al. 1991:561f; Kidder and Fritz 1993).
(8) Point bars formed on the inside (convex) bank of a meander loop separated by swales.	Sites may be found on point bars, or in swales between point bars. The farther the point bar is from the edge of the channel, the more deeply the site is likely to be buried within vertical accretion sediment in swales. No site can be older than the expansion of the meander loop (e.g., Brooks and Sassaman 1990).
(9) Natural levee formed on the outside (concave) bank of a meander loop. Natural levees may form on both sides of an active channel that is not meandering.	Sites preserved on a levee of an active channel are likely to be nearly contemporaneous with the active channel or more recent in age. Burial at depth is unlikely (e.g., Fortier et al. 1991).
(10) Crevasse splay formed at a breech in a natural levee.	Occupation of this depositional environment is likely to be brief and threatened by high-magnitude discharge events while the crevasse is active. This locale may be attractive for occupation when the channel becomes inactive (e.g., Kidder and Saucier 1991; Stafford et al. 1992).
(11) Yazoo-type river flowing in the lower, interior margin of the floodplain at the base of the bluff. The discharge of this river derives from a drainage basin on the upland, not from the major river. The smaller size of this channel indicates that it conveys a lower discharge than the major river.	Sites older than the meandering of the Yazoo river may survive beyond its meander belt in vertical accretion sediments of the major river (e.g., Kidder 1996; MaGahey 1993; Weinstein 1981; see Phillips 1970 for a classic study).
(12) Younger body of alluvial valley fill containing paleochannels that were buried as the river continued to aggrade. The alluvium is comprised predominantly of lateral accretion deposits (channel lag, channel bars, point bars), topped by vertical accretion sediment deposited at flood stages (Q_{ob}). Modern soils on this floodplain are young Entisols, Vertisols, Histosols, and Mollisols.	Lateral accretion, intrachannel deposits are not likely to have been occupied while a channel was active, or to have survived.

[1] See Figure 4.2 for the location of the numbers.

The differentiation of alluvial facies relies on an interpretation of bedding structure and texture and inclusions within a sediment. The sedimentology can be complex, and proper interpretation usually requires investigation by borings and backhoe trenches beyond the actual archaeological site. Lateral accretion deposits include sediments that form as channel lag and bars: point bars, channel side bars, mid-channel bars, and longitudinal and transverse bars. Channel lag sediments are uncommon in channels with a high suspended load. Vertical accretion facies proximal to the channel are levee, swale, and crevasse splay sediments (Farrell 1987). Away from the channel, floodbasin facies aggrade in depressions, commonly near the interior edge of the floodplain.

Vertical accretion also characterizes oxbow lakes and plugs in abandoned channels (e.g., Guccione et al. 1988). Informative discussions of alluvial facies are found in Brakenridge (1988) and Brown (1997, table 1.1). Miall (1996) provides sedimentological details of fluvial sediments and an extensive list of citations.

Archaeological investigation at one site very likely is in the matrix of only one facies. Consequently, the sedimentary stratigraphy at the site level cannot be used to infer basinwide or regional paleohydrogeomorphic conditions or events. On the other hand, alluvial stratigraphies recorded at many archaeological sites in a particular basin or region are invaluable for inferences about hydroclimatic conditions in the past (e.g., Blum and Valastro 1992).

Fluvial Responses to Climate in the Upper Mississippi Valley

Floods bury and preserve as well as destroy the archaeological record, which means that we are presented with a fragmented picture of past occupations and only traces of previous geomorphic dynamics. The flood in 1993 of the Upper Mississippi Basin, by some measures the worst natural disaster in American history, inundated more than 3,100 miles of floodplain in the Midwest. The archaeological resurvey in four states of selected areas with known prehistoric sites showed that after the flood, nearly one-quarter of the known sites were affected by bank erosion or buried by alluvium (Changnon 1996, with references). Reconstruction of past hydrogeomorphic activity in a floodplain is a critical element for understanding its prehistoric utilization. Evidence for paleofloods can be used as a surrogate measure of past hydroclimatology, and there is a plethora of hydrogeomorphic studies of floods and paleofloods and interpretation of these events in the alluvial stratigraphic record (e.g., Baker et al. 1988; Beven and Carling 1989; Mayer and Nash 1987). Many aspects of the subsequent discussion can be pursued further in these publications.

In the Midwest, flooding occurs because of snowmelt in the spring (a primary factor), summer convectional storms, hurricanes, and frontal systems. These and other weather conditions constitute the regional climate that is the synthesis of the variability in magnitude and frequency of precipitation events and temperature conditions. There is a correlation between precipitation and annual maximum floods with both the spring and summer modes in large basins (floods of the greatest magnitude coincide with snowmelt), while in small basins there is correlation only with the summer precipitation mode (Knox et al. 1975). From this perspective, an increase in alluviation need not signal a wetter climate; it can be due to change in the weather, depending upon the length of the interval of time over which the change in weather occurred.

Reconstruction of paleohydroclimatic activity must be attended by a timescale in order to make a proper assessment. The alluvial stratigraphic record is the net result of a host of events, episodes, phases, and periods that have been filtered by time. The older and longer the interval of time that it encompasses, the less representative of short-lived inputs that record is likely to be (i.e., weather events, the "Joseph" episodes of Hirschboek 1988), and it is precisely the scale of these episodes in actual reality to which aspects of human activity are likely to be attuned and which should be of interest archaeologically.

The causal linkages between climatic variability and vegetation, sediment yields, and fluvial responses have been demonstrated best by Knox and his co-workers (Knox et al. 1975; Knox 1979). This important work established the foundation for interpretations of alluvial, gradational sequences in the Midwest and Upper Mississippi Valley (e.g., Knox 1985, 1988). Statistically significant relationships exist between large-scale atmospheric circulation patterns and flooding. In the Midwest, an increase in the occurrence of storms and floods is associated with a meridional (i.e., longitudinal) atmospheric circulation pattern that brings moist air masses from the Gulf of Mexico into the Mississippi Valley. Floods of geomorphic significance are associated with these air masses. The relationship between hydroclimatic conditions and hydrogeomorphic responses has been affirmed by numerous studies (e.g., Baker et al. 1996; Hayden 1988).

Data show that there is a correlation of anomalies in atmospheric circulation and monthly deviations from the average number of floods with sediment yields (Knox 1979). Both short-term (annular) and longer term (millennial) circulation anomalies and their persistence affect the magnitude and frequency of sediment and water yields, as well as their seasonal concentration. Even modest changes in climate can impact hydrogeomorphic behavior (Knox 1984). It has been shown that over historic, decadal, or longer periods the frequencies of flood magnitudes compare to changes in patterns of large-scale atmospheric circulation (Knox 1984). Higher frequencies of large floods are associated with cooler periods, probably due to an increase in snowmelt. Only a modest difference of 1.2° C between the warmest and coldest periods characterized four intervals of increased flood frequencies, demonstrating that "minor changes of temperature at the mean annual scale can be associated with relatively important changes in magnitudes of low probability floods" (Knox 1984:323). Notably, significant changes in vegetation did not occur during these periods. It is apparent also that short-term climatic changes impact hydrogeomorphic records (Kochel and Miller 1997).

In the Holocene, minor changes in the climate of the Upper Mississippi Valley, changes of an even lesser magnitude than predicted by global circulation models (GCM) for an increased greenhouse effect, triggered significant "abrupt adjustments" in the magnitude and frequency of floods (Knox 1993). During the warmer, drier Altithermal period about 5,000–3,300 years B.P., floods of greatest magnitude had a recurrence interval (RI) of about 50 years. During the subsequent cooler and wetter conditions after about 3,300 years B.P., floods that today have an RI of about 500 years were much more frequent. Even larger floods occurred during the transition from the Medieval warm phase to the subsequent "Little Ice Age" between about A.D. 1250 and 1450. Once again, it is significant that these hydrogeomorphic changes correlate with just modest changes in mean annual temperature of 1–2° C and a decrease in mean annual precipitation of ≤ 10–20 percent (Knox 1993).

Reconstructions of past climates most often use summary statistics, that is, changes in mean annual precipitation and temperature as measured against some historical norm. This is a gross screen to hold the archaeological record against because human behavior takes into account the contemporaneous hydroclimatic patterns, not conditions averaged over a protracted interval of time (e.g., Bamforth 1990). Gross descriptors such as mean annual precipitation are not good predictors of water and sediment yields. Short-term anomalies, seasonality, more systematic variations such as El Niño and La Niña, and local landscape factors all can be more important.

Gradational Sequences and Climate

The classic "geographical" cycle conceived by William Morris Davis is a cycle of gradation encompassing very large intervals of geologic time called stages—youth, maturity, old age, and rejuvenation—through which a landscape was thought to have evolved. Its temporal perspective is beyond the reach of archaeology.

Within the time frame of human prehistory, however, alluvial gradational sequences are of great importance because they package archaeological materials. This gradation is the net result of degradational (incision, or downcutting, and denudation, or subareal erosion) and aggradational (alluviation, colluviation) geomorphic processes that modify the landscape. The record is a succession of deposits and hiati, which are temporal interruptions in the depositional succession. Modification of the landscape at this perspective is recorded by bodies of alluvium that may comprise signatures of the alluvial stratigraphic record (Salvador 1994, with references).

The succession of alluvial units and the unconformities that bound them comprise a gradational sequence. Many of the references cited in this chapter are to studies that link gradational sequences in a particular drainage system to climate. The supposition is that the amount, and perhaps type, of sediment and water transported by the river ultimately are a function of the precipitation introduced to the system. In climatology, patterns of precipitation at a place are viewed as being either stochastic (i.e., chance occurrences at a particular location) or deterministic, meaning there is a causal relationship between the pattern of precipitation and atmospheric dynamics (Hirschboeck 1988). The majority of contemporary hydroclimatic studies are stochastic in character and of limited archaeological appeal because an assumption of randomness for hydrologic events undermines interpretations of prehistoric behaviors and of the climatic environment. A deterministic framework, on the other hand, allows relationships to be established between patterns of climate and precipitation events, stream discharge and drainage basin properties. These links permit inferences about climate in the past, based upon alluvial sequences stored in a drainage system.

Most of the alluvial successions in the central United States have been recorded in conjunction with archaeological investigations (e.g., Caran and Baumgardner 1990). This information, as well as research in other areas (e.g., Brooks et al. 1986; Walker et al. 1997), has contributed significantly to reconstructions of Holocene environments, which illustrates one aspect of the value of archaeology to earth and environmental sciences. There are synthetic discussions of alluvial sequences in the Midwest (Baker et al. 1996; Bettis and Hajic 1995; Van Nest and Bettis 1990) and in the northern (Artz 1995), central (Arbogast and Johnson 1998; Johnson and Logan 1990; Johnson and Martin 1987; Mandel 1992, 1995; Martin 1992; May 1989, 1992) and southern (Blum et al. 1994; Ferring 1990, 1995; Holliday 1995; McQueen et al. 1993; Mear 1995; Nordt 1995) regions of the Great Plains and High Plains. These studies recognize multiple phases of aggradation, soil formation, and downcutting in the drainage systems that have been investigated.

Although there is variation of gradation in space and time throughout the Midwest in the early and middle Holocene, there is a regional pattern of flushing of alluvium from smaller drainage basins in conjunction with the construction of alluvial fans and aggradation in larger valleys. The broader, regional pattern is tied to bioclimatic change (Knox 1983), while gradational responses in individual basins can be attributed to nonclimatic causes (e.g., Van Nest 1993). Within a given drainage network, the ages of alluvial fills and periods of soil formation vary diachronically among (and even within) the smaller basins of the system, but there is temporal and spatial synchronicity in a larger, regional context. Alluvium of early and mid-Holocene ages has been evacuated from smaller basins ($\leq$ third order) and stored in larger floodplains and terraces as well as in alluvial fans graded to them. The late Holocene alluvium is preserved in the smaller basins, where in a few cases it buries the older alluvium, and on the surface of floodplains of larger systems.

Spatial variation of the temporal gradational pattern in Kansas and neighboring areas in Nebraska, Missouri, and Oklahoma illustrates the complexity of hydroclimatic systems and hydrogeomorphic responses (e.g., Johnson and Martin 1987). The implication of this pattern for the preservation of archaeological sites of a particular age is clear (for particularly good examples see Bettis and Hajic 1995; Blum et al. 1992; Johnson and Logan 1990; Johnson and Martin 1987; Mandel 1992, 1995, 1999). Waters and Nordt (1995) in their study of the Brazos River in Texas demonstrated how gradational complexity in an alluvial sequence covering the past 18,000 years can be the result of different factors acting individually, or in concert. Of obvious importance is the effect of climatic inputs on water and sediment yields and the storage of alluvium in the drainage basin as a result of their changing proportions.

Over the past decade or so these and other studies have shown that gradational sequences may be regionally synchronous or asynchronous, both within and among drainage basins. Preservation of the archaeological record therefore will vary in the same way. In a given case, an understanding of the gradational history is requisite for an interpretation of the archaeology. This notion no longer is a hypothesis; it is an axiom for the design and interpretation of archaeological surveys and the reconstruction of prehistoric settlement patterns. When differences in spatial and temporal patterns of gradation are recognized in a drainage system, explanations must be sought that can include cultural as well as noncultural factors. Some authors, for example, have attributed accelerated erosion in pre-Columbian time to land-use practices rather than to a change in the climate (e.g., Denevan 1992).

Alluvium, Soil, and Archaeology

Soil will develop in alluvium that remains an exposed surface for a prolonged time. The pedogenesis may continue if the rate of soil formation is greater than the rate of alluviation. Where an alluvial surface is available for exploitation and occupation for a long time, archaeological sites of different periods may be found at the top of the soil profile. In the case where pedogenesis keeps pace with alluviation, multiple phases of prehistoric occupation of the alluvial surface will leave artifacts at various depths in a soil profile (see Ferring 1986; also Waters 1992, fig. 2.34). When the soil horizon becomes buried, it is a paleosol, and it may denote a time-transgressive paleosurface with which artifacts of various ages might be associated. Soil orders that commonly occur in alluvial settings are Entisols, Vertisols, Histosols, and perhaps Mollisols.

A soil developed in and buried by alluvium denotes an interruption of deposition, or hiatus. Depending upon the length of time of the hiatus, the frequency of occupation of that surface, and the rate of sedimentation, an assemblage or assemblages of artifacts on or in an alluvial soil may be contemporaneous or mixed in age. Holliday (1992) discusses the affects of varying rates of sedimentation and pedogenesis at the early to mid-Holocene sites of Wilson-Leonard and Lubbock Lake in the Great Plains of Texas, and the Cherokee Sewer site in western Iowa.

Because pedogenesis is a slow process and because it encompasses an interval of time that may include erosion or deposition on a floodplain, the relative rates of alluviation and soil formation determine the extent of development of the A and B soil horizons (i.e., solum) and the interpretation of archaeological material within them. Follmer (1982) described three circumstances where the relative rates of alluviation and pedogenesis impact soil properties: (a) slow alluviation, which allows upward accretion and development of an overthickened B horizon; (b) alluviation at a moderate rate, in which case the faster, overthickening of the A horizon out-paces development of the B horizon—the thickness of which, then, is comparatively unchanged; (c) burial by rapid deposition with arrested soil formation and creation of a buried paleosol. The time-transgressiveness of the top of the alluvial soil decreases as the rate of burial increases and, commensurately, the rate of soil formation is retarded (see the informative illustration in Waters 1992, fig. 2.34).

In geomorphology, the notion of stability in a landscape is that of a landform surface that is not undergoing degradation or aggradation, and that the surface may be characterized by soil formation (Holliday 1992). This notion is framed from the perspective of the geomorphic evolution of a landscape in geologic time encompassing phases of net aggradation, net degradation, and stability and pedogenesis. From a pedological perspective, however, a surface is not "stable" (Johnson 1990) because pedogenesis is dynamic (e.g., Johnson et al. 1990) as opposed to static or stable. The surface experiences upbuilding and, as a biomantle, mixing (Johnson 1990; Johnson and Watson-Stegner 1990), both of which disturb artifactual contents. If the parent material is alluvium, likely additions of sediment further compromise the notion of stability.

The Usefulness of Alluvial Soils in Archaeology

The temporal and spatial scales of our observations in both archaeology and pedology have been seen as comparable as well as compatible at the site and regional levels (Holliday et al. 1993). Archaeologists and pedologists observe and record field information at the same scales and sometimes for the same objective when the concern is site formation processes. However, at both the archaeological site and regional levels the intervals encompassed by pedogenesis and by human habitation may be markedly different, which is certainly the case in the archaeology of noncomplex societies of prehistory. The former greatly exceeds the latter so that the pedogenic time scale holds little archaeological usefulness (Cremens and Hart 1995), but the spatial scales of soil and habitation can remain consonant and archaeologically relevant.

Alluvial soils occur on floodplains, terraces (raised, abandoned floodplains), and fans (e.g., Bettis and Hajic 1995; Holliday 1987; Stafford et al. 1992). Alluvial pedology (the morphology, classification, and genesis of soil in alluvium) is important archaeologically for four reasons, discussed briefly below: reconstruction of site formation processes (e.g., Ferring 1992; Larson 1992); stratigraphy and correlation (e.g., Bettis 1992; Blum and Valastro 1992; Holliday 1987; Johnson and Logan 1990; Mandel 1992); paleoenvironmental reconstruction (e.g., Picha and Gregg 1993); and prediction of the locations of undiscovered sites (e.g., Bettis 1992; Blum et al. 1994; Ferring 1992). The relevance of any of these points will vary with the ages of the archaeology, the alluvium and the mosaic of regional paleogeomorphic features and surfaces.

At local and archaeological site scales, pedological information can disclose otherwise unrecognized conditions. Reider and Karlstrom (1987) were able to reconstruct middle Holocene hydrologic circumstances at a site that were atypical of the regional picture (see also Larson 1992). Similarly, the pedogenic records at several sites in the High Plains denoted local hydrologic conditions that were different from the regional pattern of unchanged vegetation throughout the Holocene (Holliday 1987). In other contexts, soil has been used in archaeological studies for recognizing floodplain surfaces of different ages and the pattern of channel-shifting implied by these differences (Benn and Bettis 1999; Frink and Hathaway 1999; Stafford and Creasman 1998), and to distinguish remnants of terraces that are equivalent morphologically but not chronologically. Foss and co-workers (Foss et al. 1995) document a low terrace with buried A horizons and artifacts that at other locations is composed entirely of recent alluvium without evidence of pedogenesis. This circumstance clearly shows that several exposures in the same morphologic feature can preserve quite different gradational histories. Soil and paleosol properties have been used to correlate alluvial terraces that are of different ages and thereby establish an important framework for assessing their archaeological potential (e.g., Holliday 1992).

Holocene soils can be used at a regional scale to erect a chronosequence (e.g., Holliday 1992) and to establish regional correlations (e.g., Johnson and Logan 1990; Mandel 1992). The boundary of a chronostratigraphic unit is synchronous—it is a time line (plane)—but if a soil unit has no chronostrati-graphic designation, it is of little use for archaeological chronology. On the other hand, if a boundary does have a chronostratigraphic designation, its temporal interval is likely to be too great to resolve archaeological questions at the site level. Even when the time line of a soil is "established" by radiocarbon dating, the date is not a finite determination because formation of pedogenic carbon is time-transgressive; the date is an approximation of the mean residence time of the carbon (e.g., Stein 1993).

The correlation of soils also is made difficult because they are likely to be both spatially discontinuous and vertically and laterally variable, such that the signatures of chemical, physical, or morphologic properties are not consistent. But some (e.g., Holliday et al. 1993) observe that the chemical and physical properties of a soil are not appreciably different in archaeological and nonar-chaeological settings, and for this and other reasons soil science provides a scalar bridge between archaeology and the earth sciences. Within the Holo-cene, the pedostratigraphic unit as formally defined (NACOSN 1983) does not lend itself to archaeological applications (Ferring 1992). What is more, Holocene climatic changes, for the most part, were of insufficient intensity or duration to permit the detection of pedogenic responses that would be impor-tant for archaeologists (Holliday et al. 1993).

Research in the Smokey Hill and Pawnee basins in Kansas provides an ex-ample of using paleosols for geomorphic reconstruction (Mandel 1992). Indi-cations are that some phases of soil formation in the Holocene were basinwide while others were not, and in several instances soil formation was uninter-rupted throughout the late Holocene (see Mandel 1992, fig. 2-15). Conse-quently, there is very little interval-by-interval pedogenic correlation among basins. However, spatio-temporal patterns do emerge when small basins and large ones are compared separately.

In the major valley of the Pawnee, gradational stability and a period of soil formation occurred between about 10,000 B.P. and 7,000 B.P., seen also in the Loop River and Lower Kansas River valleys. Gradational stability is absent for the next 2,000 years of the middle Holocene, which is a general regional pat-tern in the Central Plains, and alluvial fans developed in larger drainage sys-tems. In the late Holocene, phases of soil formation occurred in both large and small valleys between 3,000 B.P. and 2,000 B.P., and in the earlier half of the period between 2,000 B.P. and 1,000 B.P. a phase of soil formation in larger val-leys overlapped with pedogenesis that occurred in smaller valleys in the latter half of the same millennium. Therefore, soil formation continued throughout the entire late Holocene, here and elsewhere, during which time in many basins spates of geomorphic instability occurred. This can mean that while the regional hydroclimatic environment of the late Holocene was unchanged, hydrogeomorphic systems experienced asynchronous variations of gradational instability. Sediment stored in larger valleys was reworked by late Holocene channel migration and entrenchment. In spite of the cut-fill cycles in lower order valleys in the late Holocene, there was net storage in these systems. A regional reconstruction such as this is essential for reconstructing prehistoric settlement patterns and for predicting where archaeological sites of a particular period should be found.

The spatial variation in soil types and ages provides a means for assessing the archaeological potential of locations on the floodplain (e.g., Frink and Hathaway 1999; Stafford and Creasman 1998). The progress of pedogenesis on a floodplain depends very much on the magnitude and frequency of its inundation. Slow rates of sedimentation should allow pedogenesis to keep pace with the accretion of alluvium, and envelop archaeological material within the epipedon, which is the soil horizon at the surface (e.g., Larson 1992). Rapid alluviation should preclude development of an epipedon and bury occupations at depths greater than that affected by pedogenesis (e.g., Ferring 1986).

On large floodplains, the comparative rates of soil development should, theoretically, vary spatially. In the floodbasin, for example, compared to the environs of an active channel soil development should continue through time as overbank alluviation progressively raises the elevation, reduces the visibility of archaeology, and reduces the frequency of inundation, assuming that the hydroclimatic regime remains unchanged. Soils in these settings should be older, more deeply developed, and noncumulative or mildly cumulative in character. Artifacts may be buried under or on the surface at these locations depending upon the temporal relationship of the rate of sedimentation and the age of the occupation. Absence of a soil at a floodplain setting may connote either rapid sedimentation or degradation. An informative commentary on the relationship of soil development in alluvium to geomorphic situations is provided by Ferring (1992:2–9).

The use of proper stratigraphic terminology is of particular importance in archaeology because interpretive confusion arises when descriptors are used incorrectly. An alluvial matrix, for example, may retain elements of three different imprints, each with its own descriptive conventions: lithologic stratigraphy of alluvium (geological), ethnostratigraphy (archaeological), and pedostratigraphy (pedological). At a given location on a floodplain, buried artifacts can occur within the contexts of all three taxonomies at the same time. Since each has its own terminology for description, it is important that the correct terms be used. Boundary properties are of special significance in this regard; Stein (1990) and Cremens and Hart (1995) provide more lengthy discussions of this concern.

Commentary and Conclusions

In several publications, Schumm (1988, 1991) discussed the fluvial process-response system in terms of morphologic components, the channel and the floodplain, and the cascading components of water and sediment input-output. He has described at least ten problems that must be considered when engaged in reconstructions, or "extrapolation," a practice also called postdiction or retrodiction. The foregoing observations about alluvium reinforce several of Schumm's conclusions, and highlight interpretive challenges for the reconstruction of past environments or environmental conditions from hydrogeomorphic evidence. Reconstructions must be soundly based if they are to be used to interpret patterns of prehistoric human settlement and exploitation of the environment.

Interpretive Challenges

1. Location within the system. Aggradation and degradation can occur simultaneously in different parts of the same drainage basin and, thus, invalidate extrapolation in space from just one place of observation.

2. Sensitivity. One climatic event may trigger different responses within a drainage basin depending upon prior conditions; a saturated matrix, for example, will reach disequilibrium before an unsaturated one. Consequently, because of prior conditions and nearness to a threshold, the same (climatic) event can trigger major or insignificant responses the evidence for which depends upon one's place of observation.

3. Convergence. Different causes can result in the same response: aggradation results from changes in base level, from change in the precipitation/potential evapotranspiration ratio, or from change in surface cover. Different causes or processes that result in the same effect may compromise interpretation of process based on form alone.

4. Complexity. Geomorphic thresholds can be exceeded because of extrinsic conditions or because of intrinsic adjustments. For example, a change in sediment concentration will occur by bank erosion, by channel scour, and by increased hillslope erosion. When a system may be unable to adjust in a "progressive and systematic fashion, . . . behavior can be episodic with periods of aggradation interrupting degradation. . . . This produces a very complex geo-

Table 4.2. The Meaning of Some Geomorphic Propositions for
Archaeological Interpretation

GEOMORPHIC PROPOSITION	IMPLICATION FOR ARCHAEOLOGY
I. Sedimentary units and the disconformities that bound them may be representative of appreciably different capsules of time.	Alluvial matrices are time-transgressive and so, too, may be the artifactual contents. Alluvial disconformities signify blocks of missing time and archaeology.
II. Contrasts between the inputs (water and sediment of a cascading system) and responses (adjustments by the hydromorphologic system) of the fluvial system increase as the spatial dimension increases.	Preservation of the archaeological record is a function of the sensitivity of a fluvial system to changes in discharge and sediment load. The geomorphic contexts of archaeological sites may be explained by the size of the fluvial system instead of, or in addition to, cultural choices.
III. There is a direct relationship between the size of a drainage system and its reaction and relaxation times and, therefore, the span of time that landforms in the basin represent. It is observed that smaller systems (basins) are the more likely to equilibrate with shorter-term hydrogeomorphic developments, while larger basins require more time. A corollary is, then, that smaller areal units are adjusted to shorter term causes, and larger spatial components of the landscape retain features that require greater lengths of time for development.	Sedimentological evidence for the reconstruction of short-term climatic and environmental change is more likely to be preserved in smaller systems than in larger ones. The maximum age of archaeological material stored in smaller systems is younger than that stored in larger ones.
IV. Components of an alluvial sequence that are due to frequent events of low magnitude can be interpreted at a finer resolution than can components that are the product of infrequent events of great magnitude. This means that aggradation by "low-energy" deposition can be indicative of sustained hydrologic conditions, while aggradation by "high-energy" discharges may connote infrequent, individual events of large magnitude.	The dynamic nature of a past alluvial system must be deciphered if human adjustments (short-term compensations that are part of a cultural system) in prehistoric lifeways are to be distinguished from adaptations (longer term changes of the cultural system itself).
V. Differences between and among alluvial sequences could be interpreted as indicative of their being at different levels of a hydrogeomorphic hierarchy. An extension of this proposition is, then, that similarities of systemic components of gradational units between or among basins implicate comparable temporal and spatial hierarchical rank.	Paleohydrology reconstructed at the setting of an archaeological site can be an indication of that place's position in a geomorphic hierarchy, rather than of paleoenvironmental conditions. Locational elements of prehistoric settlement might associate spatially with elements of a hydrogeomorphic hierarchy.

morphic and stratigraphic record, the details of which cannot be attributed to external influences but rather to the adjustment of the system itself" (Schumm 1988:244f). Such episodic behavior may pertain only to high-energy fluvial systems.

5. Spatial and temporal scales. Complexity within the fluvial system increases as area and scale increase: (a) as time spans become longer, average rates of change decrease; the older the alluvial sequence, the smaller the proportion

of time it represents and the more incomplete the gradational record becomes; (b) there is a direct relationship between the size of a basin and the detail and complexity of the gradational record; a smaller basin retains a smaller proportion of the alluvial history of an area. There are, therefore, inverse relationships between the accuracy of postdiction and the size of the fluvial system, and the length of time over which the extrapolation is made.

All of these maxims are not likely to pertain in a given case or even the cases discussed here, but any one is sufficient to warrant caution when using alluvial information and hydrogeomorphic features for reconstructions. Several "propositions" regarding hierarchy and spatial scale of geomorphic processes that have been formulated by de Boer (1992) complement Schumm's admonitions, and they deserve consideration by archaeologists. The propositions as stated in Table 4.2 are modified from de Boer's original formulations.

Recent Directions

While the role of geomorphology in archaeology perhaps has not changed appreciably since publication of the paper upon which this discussion builds (Gladfelter 1985), the breadth and depth of geomorphological contributions have. Most importantly, a shift of geomorphology into the mainstream of archaeological research has occurred, and as a result several topics now are widely discussed.

It is generally, if not conventionally, recognized and accepted that the spatial pattern of artifacts is a legacy of both cultural and noncultural geomorphic factors, which are linked by the study of site formation processes. Scale—both spatial and temporal—has become recognized as an important factor that affects perceptions and interpretations of the archaeological record and the understanding of hydrogeomorphic systems. There is an increasing awareness of and concern for catastrophic occurrences, and a realization that such events are inherent components of geomorphic systems, and of cultural ones as well. And there is much attention given to the spatial and temporal complexities of the linkage of climate and geomorphic systems. In archaeology, as yet there has not been an evaluation of comparable breadth of the linkages between hydroclimatic systems and culture.

Acknowledgments

I thank the editors of this volume for inviting my participation and for critical comments on an early draft of the paper (Stein), and two anonymous reviewers for recognizing errors of commission and omission. Illustrations were prepared by Ray Brod, Cartography Laboratory, University of Illinois at Chicago.

While this paper was in preparation, a respected colleague and valued friend passed away. Carl L. Hansen and I met as graduate students at the University of Wisconsin, Madison, when Karl Butzer and he were preparing *Desert and River in Nubia* (University of Wisconsin Press, 1968). Carl's persistent inquisitiveness unconstrained by convention, and his keen mind and terrific sense of humor will be remembered.

References Cited

Arbogast, A. F., and W. C. Johnson
1998   Late-Quaternary Landscape Response to Environmental Change in South-Central Kansas. *Annals of the Association of American Geographers* 88:126–145.

Artz, J. A.
1995   Geological Contexts of the Early and Middle Holocene Archaeological Record in North Dakota and Adjoining Areas of the Northern Plains. In *Archaeological Geology of the Archaic Period in North America,* pp. 67–86. Geological Society of America, Special Publication 297. Boulder, Colorado.

Autin, W. J., S. F. Burns, B. J. Miller, R. T. Saucier, and J. I. Snead
1991   Quaternary Geology of the Lower Mississippi Valley. In *The Geology of North America,* Vol. k-2, edited by R. B. Morrison, pp. 547–582. Geological Society of America, Boulder, Colorado.

Baker, R. G., E. A. Bettis III, D. G. Schwert, D. G. Horton, G. A. Chumbley, L. A. Gonzalez, and M. K. Reagan
1996   Holocene Paleoenvironments of Northeast Iowa. *Ecological Monographs* 66:203–234.

Baker, V. R., R. C. Kochel, and P. C. Patton (editors)
1988   *Flood Geomorphology.* John Wiley and Sons, New York.

Bamforth, D. B.
1990   An Empirical Perspective on Little Ice Age Climatic Change on the Great Plains. *Plains Anthropologist* 35:359–366.

Benn, D. W., and E. A. Bettis III
1999   Holocene Landscapes and Prehistoric Settlement Patterns: Upper Mississippi River Valley. Abstracts, 46. 64th Annual Meeting of the Society for American Archaeology, Chicago.

Best, J. L., and C. S. Bristow (editors)
1993   *Braided Rivers.* Special Publication 75. Geological Society of London, London.

Bettis, E. A., III
1992   Soil Morphologic Properties and Weathering Zone Characteristics as Age Indicators in Holocene Alluvium in the Upper Midwest. In *Soils in Archaeology: Landscape Evolution and Human Occupation,* edited by V. T. Holliday, pp. 119–144. Smithsonian Institution Press, Washington, D.C.

Bettis, E. A., III, and E. Hajic
1995   Landscape Development and the Location of Evidence of Archaic Cultures in the Upper Midwest. In *Archaeological Geology of the Archaic Period in North America,*

edited by E. A. Bettis III, pp. 87–114. Geological Society of America, Special Paper 297. Boulder, Colorado.

Beven, K., and P. Carling (editors)
1989   *Floods: Hydrological, Sedimentological and Geomorphological Implications.* John Wiley and Sons, Chichester.

Blum, M. D., J. T. Abbott, and S. Valastro Jr.
1992   Evolution of Landscapes on the Double Mountain Fork of the Brazos River, West Texas: Implications for Preservation and Visibility of the Archaeological Record. *Geoarchaeology: An International Journal* 7:339–370.

Blum, M. D., R. S. Toomey III, and S. Valastro Jr.
1994   Fluvial Response to Late Quaternary Climatic and Environmental Change, Edwards Plateau, Texas. *Palaeogeography, Palaeoclimatology, Palaeoecology* 108:1–21.

Blum, M. D., and S. Valastro Jr.
1992   Quaternary Stratigraphy and Geoarchaeology of the Colorado and Concho Rivers, West Texas. *Geoarchaeology: An International Journal* 7:419–448.

de Boer, D. H.
1992   Hierarchies and Spatial Scale in Process Geomorphology: A Review. *Geomorphology* 4:303–318.

Brakenridge, G. R.
1988   River Flood Regime and Floodplain Stratigraphy. In *Flood Geomorphology,* edited by V. R. Baker, R. C. Kochel, and P. C. Patton, pp. 139–156. John Wiley and Sons, New York.

Brooks, M. J., and K. E. Sassman
1990   Point Bar Geoarchaeology in the Upper Coastal Plain of the Savannah River Valley, South Carolina; a Case Study. In *Archaeological Geology of North America,* edited by N. P. Lasca and J. Donahue, pp. 183–198. Geological Society of America, Centennial Special Vol. 4. Boulder, Colorado.

Brooks, M. J., P. A. Stone, D. J. Colquhoun, and K. B. Steele
1986   Geoarchaeological Research in the Coastal Plain Portion of the Savannah River Valley. *Geoarchaeology: An International Journal* 1:293–307.

Brown, A. G.
1997   *Alluvial Geoarchaeology: Floodplain Archaeology and Environmental Change.* Cambridge University Press, Cambridge.

Caran, S. C., and R. W. Baumgardner Jr.
1990   Quaternary Stratigraphy and Paleoenvironments of the Texas Rolling Plains. *Geological Society of America Bulletin* 102:768–785.

Carling, P., and K. Bevin
1989   The Hydrology, Sedimentology and Geomorphological Implications of Floods: An Overview. In *Floods: Hydrological, Sedimentological and Geomorphological Implications,* edited by K. Bevin and P. Carling, pp. 1–9. John Wiley and Sons, Chichester.

Changnon, S. A.
1996   *The Great Flood of 1993.* Westview Press, Boulder, Colorado.

Church, M.
1978   Palaeohydrological Reconstruction from a Holocene Valley Fill. In *Fluvial Sedimentology,* edited by A. D. Miall, pp. 743–772. Canadian Society of Petroleum Geology Memoir 5. Calgary.

Clark, W. C.
1985   Scales of Climate Impacts. *Climate Change* 7:5–27.

Cremens, D. L., and J. P. Hart

1995   On Chronostratigraphy, Pedostratigraphy and Archaeological Context. In *Pedological Perspectives in Archaeological Research,* edited by M. E. Collins, B. J. Carter, B. G. Gladfelter, and R. J. Southard, pp. 15–33. Special Publication 44. Soil Science Society of America, Madison, Wisconsin.

Denevan, W. M.

1992   The Pristine Myth: the Landscape of the Americas in 1492. *Annals of the Association of American Geographers* 82:369–385.

Ethridge, F. G., and S. A. Schumm

1977   Reconstructing Paleochannel Morphologic and Flow Characteristics: Methodology, Limitations and Assessment. In *Fluvial Sedimentology,* edited by A. D. Miall, pp. 703–721. Canadian Society of Petroleum Geology, Calgary.

Farrell, K. M.

1987   Sedimentology and Facies Architecture of Overbank Deposits of the Mississippi River, False River Region, Louisiana. In *Recent Developments in Fluvial Sedimentology,* edited by F. G. Ethridge, R. M. Flores, and M. D. Harvey, pp.111–120. Special Publication 39. Society of Economic Paleontology and Mineralogy.

Faulkner, D. J.

1998   Spatially Variable Historical Alluviation and Channel Incision in West-Central Wisconsin. *Annals of the Association of American Geographers* 88:666–685.

Ferring, C. R.

1986   Rates of Fluvial Sedimentation: Implications for Archaeological Variability. *Geoarchaeology: An International Journal* 3:259–274.

1990   Archaeological Geology of the Southern Plains. In *Archaeological Geology of North America,* edited by N. P. Lasca and J. Donahue, pp. 253–266. Geological Society of America, Centennial Special Vol. 4. Boulder, Colorado.

1992   Alluvial Pedology and Archaeological Research. In *Soils in Archaeology: Landscape Evolution and Human Occupation,* edited by V. T. Holliday, pp. 1–39. Smithsonian Institution Press, Washington, D.C.

1995   Middle Holocene Environments, Geology and Archaeology in the Southern High Plains. In *Archaeological Geology of the Archaic Period in North America,* edited by A. E. Bettis III, pp. 21–35. Geological Society of America, Special Paper 297. Boulder, Colorado.

Follmer, L. R.

1982   The Geomorphology of the Sangamon Surface: Its Spatial and Temporal Attributes. In *Space and Time in Geomorphology,* edited by C. E. Thorn, pp. 117–146. Allen and Unwin, London.

Fortier, A. C., T. O. Maher, and J. A. Williams

1991   *The Sponemann Site: the Formative Emergent Mississippian Sponemann Phase Occupation.* American Bottom Archaeology, FAI 270 Site Reports. University of Illinois Press, Urbana.

Foss, J. E., R. J. Lewis, and M. E. Timpson

1995   Soils in Alluvial Sequences: Some Archaeological Implications. In *Pedological Perspectives in Archaeological Research,* edited by M. E. Collins, B. J. Carter, B. G. Gladfelter, and R. J. Southard, pp. 1–14. Special Publication No. 44. Soil Science Society of America, Madison, Wisconsin.

Frink, D., and A. Hathaway

1999   Pedomorphic Understandings of River Systems' Behavior through Space and Time:

Key to Managing Cultural Resources. Abstracts, 113. 64th Annual Meeting of the Society for American Archaeology, Chicago.

Fukuoka, Masanobu
1978   The One-Straw Revolution: An Introduction to Natural Farming. Translated by C. Pearce, T. Kurosawa, and L. Korn. Rodale Press, Emmaus.

Gardner, G. D., and J. Donahue
1985   The Little Platte Drainage, Missouri: A Model for Locating Temporal Surfaces in a Fluvial Environment. In Archaeological Sediments in Context, edited by J. K. Stein and W. R. Farrand, pp. 69–89. Institute of Quaternary Studies, Orono, Maine.

Gladfelter, B. G.
1981   Developments and Directions in Geoarchaeology. In Advances in Archaeological Method and Theory, Vol. 4, edited by M. B. Schiffer, pp. 343–364. Academic Press, New York.
1985   On the Interpretation of Archaeological Sites in Alluvial Settings. In Archaeological Sediments in Context, edited by J. K. Stein and W. R. Farrand, pp. 41–49. Institute of Quaternary Studies, Orono, Maine.

Guccione, M. J., R. H. Lafferty III, and L. S. Cummings
1988   Environmental Constraints of Human Settlement in an Evolving Holocene Alluvial System: The Lower Mississippi River. Geoarchaeology: An International Journal 3:65–84.

Guccione, M. J., M. C. Sierzchula, R. H. Lafferty III, and D. Kelley
1998   Site Preservation along an Active Meandering and Avulsing River: The Red River, Arkansas. Geoarchaeology: An International Journal 13:475–500.

Hajic, E. R.
1990   Stratigraphic and Geomorphic Evolution of the Koster Archaeological Site. Research Series, vol. 10. Center for American Archaeology, Kampsville, Illinois.
1993   Geomorphology of the Northern American Bottom as a Context for Archaeology. Illinois Archaeology 5:54–65.

Hassen, H.
1993   Floodplain Landscapes Evolution and Prehistoric Settlement: An Example from the Meredosia Region of the Lower Illinois River Valley. Illinois Archaeology 5:66–78.

Hayden, B. P.
1988   Flood Climates. In Flood Geomorphology, edited by V. R. Baker, R. C. Kochel, and P. C. Patton, pp. 1–26. John Wiley and Sons, New York.

Heinrich, P. V.
1991   A Sedimentological Explanation for the Distribution of Archaeological Sites in a Meander Belt as Stated by the "Relict Channel Rule." Abstract in American Association of Petroleum Geologists 75:1524–1525.

Hirschboeck, K. K.
1988   Flood Hydroclimatology. In Flood Geomorphology, edited by B. R. Baker, R. C. Kochel, and P. C. Patton, pp. 27–49. John Wiley and Sons, New York.

Holliday, V. T.
1987   Geoarchaeology and Late Quaternary Geomorphology of the Middle South Platte River, Northeastern Colorado. Geoarchaeology: An International Journal 2:317–329.
1992   Soil Formation, Time and Archaeology. In Soils in Archaeology: Landscape Evolution and Human Occupation, edited by V. T. Holliday, pp. 101–117. Smithsonian Institution Press, Washington, D.C.

1995   *Stratigraphy and Paleoenvironments of Late Quaternary Valley Fills on the Southern High Plains.* Geological Society of America, Memoir 186. Boulder, Colorado.

Holliday, V. T., C. R. Ferring, and P. Goldberg

1993   The Scale of Soil Investigations in Archaeology. In *Effects of Scale on Archaeological and Geoscientific Perspectives,* edited by J. K. Stein and A. R. Linse, pp. 29–37. Geological Society of America, Special Paper 283. Boulder, Colorado.

Jackson, R. G., II

1981   Sedimentology of Muddy Fine-Grained Channel Deposits in Meandering Streams of the American Middle West. *Journal of Sedimentary Petrology* 51:1169–1192.

Johnson, D. L.

1990   Biomantle Evolution and the Redistribution of Earth Materials and Artifacts. *Soil Science* 149:84–102.

Johnson, D. L., E. A. Keeler, and T. K. Rockwell

1990   Dynamic Pedogenesis: New Views on Some Key Soil Concepts, and a Model for Interpreting Quaternary Soils. *Quaternary Research* 34:306–319.

Johnson, D. L., and D. Watson-Stegner

1990   The Soil-Evolution Model as a Framework for Evaluating Pedoturbation in Archaeological Site Formation. In *Archaeological Geology of North America,* edited by N. P. Lasca and J. Donahue, pp. 541–560. Geological Society of America, Centennial Special Vol. 4. Boulder, Colorado.

Johnson, W. C., and B. Logan

1990   Geoarchaeology of the Kansas River Basin, Central Great Plains. In *Archaeological Geology of North America,* edited by N. P. Lasca and D. L. Donahue, pp. 267–299. Geological Society of America, Centennial Special Vol. 4. Boulder, Colorado.

Johnson, W. C., and C. W. Martin

1987   Holocene Alluvial-Stratigraphic Studies from Kansas and Adjoining States of the East-Central Plains. In *Quaternary Environments of Kansas,* pp. 109–122. Kansas Geological Survey, Guidebook No.5. Lawrence.

Kidder, T. R.

1996   Perspectives on the Geoarchaeology of the Lower Mississippi Valley. *Engineering Geology* 45:305–323.

Kidder, T. R., and G. J. Fritz

1993   Subsistence and Social Change in the Lower Mississippi Valley: The Reno Brake and Osceola Sites, Louisiana. *Journal of Field Archaeology* 20:281–297.

Kidder, T. R., and R. T. Saucier

1991   Archaeological and Geological Evidence for Protohistoric Water Management in Northeast Louisiana. *Geoarchaeology: An International Journal* 6:307–335.

Knox, J. C.

1979   *Hydrogeomorphic Implications of Climate Change.* Department of Geography, Center for Geographic Analysis, Madison (Contract DACW 72-78-C-0025, U.S. Army Coastal Engineering Research Center, Fort Belvoir, Virginia).

1983   Responses of River Systems to Holocene Climates. In *Late Quaternary Environments of the United States,* edited by H. E. Wright Jr., pp. 26–41. University of Minnesota Press, Minneapolis.

1984   Fluvial Responses to Small-Scale Climate Change. In *Developments and Applications of Geomorphology,* edited by J. E. Costa and P. J. Fleisher, pp. 318–342. Springer, New York.

1985   Responses of Floods to Holocene Climatic Change in the Upper Mississippi Valley. *Quaternary Research* 23:287–300.

1988   Climatic Influence on Upper Mississippi Valley Floods. In *Flood Geomorphology,* edited by V. R. Baker, R. C. Kochel, and P. C. Patton, pp. 279–300. John Wiley and Sons, New York.

1993   Large Increases in Flood Magnitude in Response to Modest Changes in Climate. *Nature* 361:430–432.

Knox, J. C., R. J. Bartlein, K. K. Hirschboeck, and R. J. Muckenhirn

1975   *Response of Floods and Sediment Yields to Climatic Variation and Land Use in the Upper Mississippi Valley.* Institute for Environmental Studies Report 52. University of Wisconsin, Madison.

Kochel, R. C.

1988   Geomorphic Impact of Large Floods: Review and New Perspectives on Magnitude and Frequency. In *Flood Geomorphology,* edited by V. R. Baker, R. C. Kochel, and P. C. Patton, pp. 169–186. John Wiley and Sons, New York.

Kochel, R. C., and J. R. Miller

1997   Geomorphic Responses to Short-Term Climatic Change: An Introduction. *Geomorphology* 19:171–173.

Kolb, M. F., and R. F. Boszhardt

1999   Holocene Fluvial Landscapes, Geoarchaeology and Settlement Patterns in the Upper Mississippi Valley. Abstracts, 164. 64th Annual Meeting of the Society for American Archaeology, Chicago.

Kuehn, D. D.

1993   Landforms and Archaeological Site Location in the Little Missouri Badlands: A New Look at Some Well-Established Patterns. *Geoarchaeology: An International Journal* 8:313–332.

Larson, M. L.

1992   Site Formation Processes in the Cody and Early Plains Archaic Levels at the Laddie Creek Site, Wyoming. *Geoarchaeology: An International Journal* 7:103–120.

Lewin, J.

1989   Floods in Fluvial Geomorphology. In *Floods: Hydrological, Sedimentological and Geomorphological Implications,* edited by K. Bevin and P. Carling, pp. 265–284. John Wiley and Sons, Chichester.

MaGahey, S. O.

1993   *Paleo-Indian and Early Archaic Material: Implications of Distribution in Mississippi.* Mississippi Department of Archives and History, Jackson.

Maill, A. D.

1966   *The Geology of Fluvial Sediments: Facies Models, Drainage Basins and Petroleum Geology.* Springer-Verlag, Berlin

Maizels, J. K., and J. Aitken

1991   Palaeohydrological Changes during Deglaciation in Upland Britain: A Case Study from North-East Scotland. In *Temperate Palaeohydrology,* edited by N. L. Starkel, J. Gregory, and J. B. Thornes, pp. 105–146. John Wiley and Sons, Chichester.

Mandel, R. D.

1992   Soils and Holocene Landscape Evolution in Central and Southwestern Kansas: Implications for Archaeological Research. In *Soils in Archaeology: Landscape Evolution and Human Occupation,* edited by V. T. Holliday, pp. 41–100. Smithsonian Institution Press, Washington, D.C.

1995   Geomorphic Controls of the Archaic Record in the Central Great Plains of the United States. In *Archaeological Geology of the Archaic Period in North America,* edited by E. A. Bettis III, pp. 37–66. Geological Society of America, Special Paper 297. Boulder, Colorado.

1999   *Geoarchaeology in the Great Plains.* University of Oklahoma Press, Norman.

Martin, C. W.

1992   Late Holocene Alluvial Chronology and Climate Change in the Central Great Plains. *Quaternary Research* 37:315–322.

May, D. W.

1989   Holocene Alluvial Fills in the South Loup River Valley, Nebraska. *Quaternary Research* 32:117–120.

1992   Late Holocene Valley-Bottom Aggradation and Erosion in the South Loup River Valley, Nebraska. *Physical Geography* 13:115–132.

Mayer, L., and D. Nash (editors)

1987   *Catastrophic Flooding.* Allen and Unwin, Boston.

McDowell, P. T., T. Webb III, and P. J. Bartlein

1990   Long-Term Environmental Change. In *The Earth as Transformed by Human Interaction: Global and Regional Changes in the Biosphere over the Past 300 Years,* edited by B. L. Turner, W. C. Clark, R. W. Kates, J. F. Richards, J. T. Mathews, and W. B. Meyer, pp. 143–162. Cambridge University Press, Cambridge.

McQueen, K. C., J. D. Vitek, and B. J. Carter

1993   Paleoflood Analysis of an Alluvial Channel in the South-Central Great Plains: Black Bear Creek, Oklahoma. *Geomorphology* 8:131–146.

Mear, C. E.

1995   Quaternary Geology of the Upper Sabinal River Valley, Uvalde and Bandera Counties, Texas. *Geoarchaeology: An International Journal* 10:457–480.

Miall, A. D.

1996   *The Geology of Fluvial Sediments: Facies Models, Drainage Basins and Petroleum Geology.* Springer-Verlag, Berlin.

NACOSN

1983   North American Stratigraphic Code, North American Commission on Stratigraphic Nomenclature. *American Association of Petroleum Geology Bulletin* 67:841–875.

Nanson, G. C., and J. C. Croke

1992   A Genetic Classification of Floodplains. *Geomorphology* 4:459–486.

Nordt, L. C.

1995   Geoarchaeological Investigations of Henson Creek: A Low-Order Tributary in Central Texas. *Geoarchaeology: An International Journal* 10:205–221.

Phillips, J. L., and B. G. Gladfelter

1983   The Labras Lake Site and the Paleogeographic Setting of the Late Archaic in the American Bottom. In *Archaic Hunters and Gatherers in the American Midwest,* edited by J. L. Phillips and J. A. Brown, pp. 197–218. Academic Press, New York.

Phillips, P.

1970   *Archaeological Survey in the Lower Yazoo Basin, Mississippi, 1949–1955.* Papers of the Peabody Museum of Archaeology and Ethnology, Vol. 60. Harvard University, Cambridge.

Picha, P. R., and M. L. Gregg

1993   Chronostratigraphy of Upper James River Floodplain Sediments: Implications for

Southeastern North Dakota Archaeology. *Geoarchaeology: An International Journal* 8:203–215.

Putnam, D. E.

1994   Vertical Accretion of Flood Deposits and Deeply Stratified Archaeological Site Formation in Central Maine, USA. *Geoarchaeology: An International Journal* 9:467–502.

Reider, R. G., and E. T. Karlstrom

1987   Soils and Stratigraphy of the Laddie Creek Site (48BH345), and Altithermal Occupation in the Big Horn Mountains, Wyoming. *Geoarchaeology: An International Journal* 2:29–47.

Rogers, R. A.

1987   Frequency of Occurrence of Paleoindian Sites in the Neosho River Drainage of Kansas, A Geomorphological Analysis. In *Quaternary Environments of Kansas,* edited by W. C. Johnson, pp. 197–200. Kansas Geological Survey, Guidebook Series 5. Lawrence.

Running, G. L.

1995   Archaeological Geology of the Rustad Quarry Site (32RI775): An Early Archaic Site in Southeastern North Dakota. *Geoarchaeology: An International Journal* 10:183–204.

Salvador, A. (editor)

1994   *International Stratigraphic Guide: A Guide to Stratigraphic Classification, Terminology and Procedure.* Geological Society of America, Boulder, Colorado.

Schumm, S. A.

1968   Speculation Concerning Paleohydologic Controls of Terrestrial Sedimentation. *Geological Society of America Bulletin* 79:1573–1588.

1988   Variability of the Fluvial System in Space and Time. In *Scales and Global Change,* edited by T. Rosswall, R. G. Woodmansee, and P. G. Risser, pp. 225–250. John Wiley and Sons, Chichester.

1991   *To Interpret the Earth: Ten Ways to Be Wrong.* Cambridge University Press, Cambridge.

Stafford, C. R.

1995   Geoarchaeological Perspectives on Paleolandscapes and Regional Subsurface Archaeology. *Journal of Archaeological Method and Theory* 2:69–104.

Stafford, C. R., and S. Creasman

1998   The Hidden Record: Soil-Geomorphic Landscapes and Settlement Archaeology in the Middle Ohio River Valley. Abstracts, 282. 63rd Annual Meeting of the Society for American Archaeology, Seattle.

Stafford, C. R., D. S. Leigh, and D. L. Asch

1992   Prehistoric Settlement and Landscape Change on Alluvial Fans in the Upper Mississippi River Valley. *Geoarchaeology: An International Journal* 7:287–314.

Stein, J. K.

1990   Archaeological Stratigraphy. In *Archaeological Geology of North America,* edited by N. P. Lasca and J. Donahue, pp. 513–523. Geological Society of America, Centennial Special Vol. 4. Boulder, Colorado.

1993   Scale in Archaeology, Geosciences and Geoarchaeology. In *Effects of Scale on Archaeological and Geoscientific Perspectives,* edited by J. K. Stein and A. R. Linse, pp. 1–10. Geological Society of America, Special Paper 283. Boulder, Colorado.

Stein, J. K., and A. R. Linse (editors)

1993   *Effects of Scale on Archaeological and Geoscientific Perspectives.* Geological Society of America, Special Paper 283. Boulder, Colorado.

Styles, T. R.
1985   *Holocene and Late Pleistocene Geology of the Napolean Hollow Site in the Lower Illinois Valley.* Kampsville Archeological Center, Research Series, vol. 5. Center for American Archaeology, Kampsville, Illinois.

Thornthwaite, C. W.
1948   An Approach Toward a Rational Classification of Climate. *Geographical Review* January:55–94.

Van Nest, J.
1993   Geoarchaeology of Dissected Loess Uplands in Western Illinois. *Geoarchaeology: An International Journal* 8:281–311.

Van Nest, J., and E. A. Bettis III
1990   Postglacial Response of a Stream in Central Iowa to Changes in Climate and Drainage Basin Factors. *Quaternary Research* 33:73–85.

Van Nest, J., and G. A. J. Vogel
1999   Geoarchaeological Record of Holocene Mississippi River Floods in the Sny Bottom of Western Illinois. Abstracts, 291. 64th Annual Meeting of the Society for American Archaeology, Chicago.

Walker, I. J., J. R. Desloges, G. W. Crawford, and G. D. Smith
1997   Floodplain Formation Processes and Archaeological Implications at the Grand Banks Site, Lower Grand River, Southern Ontario. *Geoarchaeology: An International Journal* 12:865–887.

Waters, M. R.
1992   *Principles of Geoarchaeology: A North American Perspective.* The University of Arizona Press, Tucson.

Waters, M. R., and L. C. Nordt
1995   Late Quaternary Floodplain History of the Brazos River in East-Central Texas. *Quaternary Research* 43:311–319.

Weinstein, R. A.
1981   Meandering Rivers and Shifting Villages: A Prehistoric Settlement Model in the Upper Steele Bayou Basin. *Southeastern Archaeological Conference Bulletin* 24:37–41.

Wharton, G.
1995   The Channel-Geometry Method: Guidelines and Applications. *Earth Surface Processes and Landforms* 20:649–660.

Williams, G. P.
1984   Paleohydrologic Equations for Rivers. In *Developments and Applications of Geomorphology,* edited by J. E. Costa and P. J. Fleisher, pp. 343–367. Springer-Verlag, Heidelberg.

Willis, B. J.
1989   Palaeochannel Reconstruction from Point Bar Deposits: A Three Dimensional Perspective. *Sedimentology* 36:757–766.

5

Archaeological Sediments in Lake Margin Environments

Craig S. Feibel

The lake margin setting is a highly diverse and dynamic environment. It is a transitional zone where small fluctuations in environmental parameters are often recorded by shifts in sedimentary pattern. These shifts can be particularly dramatic where facies changes alternate between subaerial and subaqueous settings. Sediments and depositional features of the lake itself may preserve a detailed record of environmental characteristics, while the subaerial component of the lake margin setting may accumulate an archive of human activities and their context. The presence of water and, commonly, of diverse and abundant food resources, makes lake margins a focal area for human foraging and settlement. The character of these sediments records details of the depositional environment as well as of the events that led to burial and preservation of an archaeological assemblage.

This chapter will examine a few of the characteristics that make lake margins important components of the archaeological record by looking at the characteristics of lake systems and lake margins, the types of sediments that tend to accumulate in and around them, and the ways in which archaeological evidence can be incorporated into this accumulation. Several examples from on-going research will be used to illustrate how important investigation of lake margin sediments can be to a fuller understanding of the archaeological record.

Lakes, Lake Margins, and Lake Margin Sites

The characteristics of lakes and lake margins, and in particular their high degree of variability, have a strong influence on the environments, processes, sediments, and sites associated with them. Lakes are large inland bodies of standing water. "Large" is a user-defined variable here, usually taken to mean

"bigger than a pond," and typically (though not always) deep enough to pro-
hibit rooting of emergent vegetation in some areas. Lakes vary tremendously
in size. As measured by surface area, they range from the enormous Caspian
Sea (covering nearly half a million sq km) to small features with surfaces of
only a few tens to hundreds of square meters. Smaller examples are by far the
more numerous. The wide range in size of lakes is mirrored in the age distribution of these features, with a few very ancient examples (such as the Miocene
origins of Lake Baikal; Williams et al. 1997), and many much younger features.
Lakes are most numerous in high-latitude and high-elevation (glaciated) regions, and most extant lakes formed subsequent to the last glacial maximum
(ca. 18 ka). The overall youth of the majority of lakes should not be surprising,
as these features are sediment traps, and in any but the most mature terrains
have a high sediment influx. Thus they tend to fill in rapidly. This characteristic is of importance from the archaeological perspective, as it often produces
conditions of rapid burial and preservation for sites.

One of the most fundamental differences in character separates those lakes
that are hydrologically open (exorheic), with an outlet of some sort, from those
which are hydrologically closed (endorheic), lacking an outlet. The difference
has implications for the stability of the lake surface (lake level), as well as for
the character of both the waters and the sediments in the system. Exorheic
systems tend to remain freshwater in character, with little concentration of
solutes beyond that of the influent streams. The dilute nature of these waters
seldom produces significant chemical sedimentation and may foster dissolution of some mineral phases. These lakes also tend to have stable surfaces, or at
least a stable maximum level with short-term drops resulting from insufficient
influx from source areas. Endorheic systems commonly have concentrated waters, as evaporation leaves behind solutes brought in by runoff or groundwater,
resulting in a saline or alkaline character of the waters. This often results in distinctive suites of chemical precipitates (Eugster and Hardie 1978). These systems are also highly unstable, and lake levels fluctuate with the seasonality of
the catchment water supply. As a result, these lakes may preserve excellent and
detailed records of local climatic history.

The form of lakes can also vary tremendously, from the long, linear, and
deep rift valley lakes like Baikal and Tanganyika to broad and shallow pans
such as those found in the Great Basin of North America. Of particular significance here is the topographic gradient across the shoreline. Steep gradient
margins may concentrate wave energy, but respond slowly to lake level changes
and sedimentation. Low gradient shorelines can dissipate wave energy, but
even small changes in lake level or inputs of sediment may result in dramatic

lateral movement of the shore. Another important aspect of lake surface is its shape and relationship to prevailing winds. Winds often determine how currents move sediment around within a lake. In addition, the linear measure of lake surface across which prevailing winds blow, the fetch, determines the strength of onshore waves. Commonly the lake margin nearest the source of winds will have a relatively low energy setting, while the margin facing the oncoming winds will be a much higher energy beach.

Lake Margin Environments

The diversity of settings along lake margins allows for a high degree of variability in the sediments that accumulate there. A few common examples of lake margin environments are illustrated in Figure 5.1. The distribution of these environments is largely determined by the underlying geology, wind and wave patterns, sediment supply, and vegetation development. A simple split into high-energy and low-energy environments reveals the dominant trends of coarse sediment and better sorting in the high-energy situations, and of finer sediments and poorer sorting in lower energy settings. This is often the most straightforward relationship to be extracted from a sequence of lake margin sediments. Beyond this, the details of sediment composition, primary structures, and biotic components record many indicators of the precise setting. Each recognizable package of sediment, with its characteristic particle size, colors, structures, and fossils, comprises a sedimentary facies. Each facies records a discrete environment, and thus the ability to distinguish fine-scale differences in sedimentary facies determines the potential for reconstructing detailed differences in lake margin environments. A lake margin sequence is often characterized by fairly rapid facies shifts, which reflect spatial and temporal changes in setting. Detailed three-dimensional analysis of facies changes can thus be used to record changes in lake margin environments across a landscape and through time. This spatial and temporal information is of particular importance in understanding either a single archaeological occurrence or a series of accumulations.

The most important parameter determining the character of a lake margin is sediment type. There are a number of useful reviews of the characteristics of lacustrine sediments from the geological perspective (Collinson 1978; Kelts 1988; Sly 1978; Talbot and Allen 1996). Only a few general aspects will be touched upon here, as they relate to the landforms and depositional features of lakes (Fig. 5.1). Bedrock shorelines express a form determined by geological heritage, be it faulting, fluvial erosion, or glacial scouring. Even relatively nonresistant

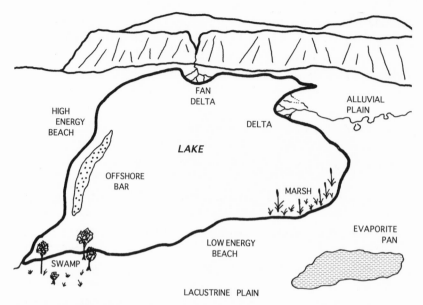

Figure 5.1. Examples of typical lake margin environments that occur in association with archaeological sites.

bedrock responds only slowly to lake processes. Wave-cut benches, however, such as those of pluvial Lake Bonneville (Currey 1980), may be prominent features preserved in present-day landscapes. Where local relief is high, particularly in arid settings, alluvial fans may verge on lake margins. This produces a feature known as a fan delta, with gravels and even boulder conglomerates interfingering with lacustrine sediments. These conglomerates produce a relatively steep shoreface. The coarser components tend not to move far from the point where waning streamflow (or gravity) dropped them, while the finer components can be reworked along shore or offshore.

Perhaps the most typical sediment found in lake margin settings is sand. The availability of sand-sized material and even a minimal amount of wave energy will quickly sort a clean sandy beach and move out finer components. The sands can maintain a moderately steep shoreface, and the combination of particle size and sorting usually leaves them well drained. Sandy beaches are very stable features, with only the slow increase in maturity of the sands marking the passage of time. Storm events, however, may rearrange beach components, in particular piling up sands in an onshore beach ridge that can remain as a prominent feature on the landscape. Sandy margins are commonly devoid of vegetation in the active shoreface, but may become vegetated where stable.

Where wind energy is sufficient, sand supply at the beach face may enable the development of eolian dunes. As the physical energy of the environment decreases, it becomes possible for smaller and smaller particles to accumulate, and muddy lake margins develop. Most typically this indicates minimal wind and wave energy, as in a sheltered beach or bay, but prolific emergent vegetation may also act to damp out wind and wave energy. Muddy shorelines are generally very low gradient and poorly drained.

The characteristic features of lake margins make them very attractive for human activities and even settlement. Water availability is probably the single most important factor, but most lake margins also present a wide range of other available resources, from shellfish to tubers, as well as potential access to water-borne transport. The type of activity undertaken, as well as its frequency and duration, will determine the sorts of archaeological materials and signatures left in the lake margin setting. The subsequent evolution of the lake margin will determine whether those traces are disturbed or simply covered, and then buried and preserved. Groundwater and diagenetic history may also affect the archaeological record. For example, anoxic conditions resulting from a high groundwater table may allow long-term preservation of otherwise perishable materials (e.g., wood) in a wet site. Lake margin archaeological components range from isolated tool discards and butchery remains to boats and structural components as complex as villages.

Problems of Scale

Before approaching specific aspects of sediments in lake margin settings, it is useful to consider how elements of scale can influence our understanding. The impact of scale must be considered as it affects three areas of interest here: the scale of lakes and lake margin environments, the scale of the processes that act there, and the scale of the sites through which we try to reconstruct an archaeological context (Stein and Linse 1993). Using the concept of spatial-temporal scales (Delcourt and Delcourt 1991), it is possible to visualize the effects of differing scales of analysis on archaeological problems in lake margin settings (Fig. 5.2). The spatial and temporal scales of a lake will exceed, often greatly, the scale of an individual site. The lake may respond to processes of even larger scale, such as global-scale climatic cycles, and thus the integrated record of a lake's history may provide important links to the larger world. These links may have important implications for the context of the site, such as defining its age, or its climatic setting. Thus the record of the lake, even beyond the bounds of the site under investigation, may be critical to a broader understanding.

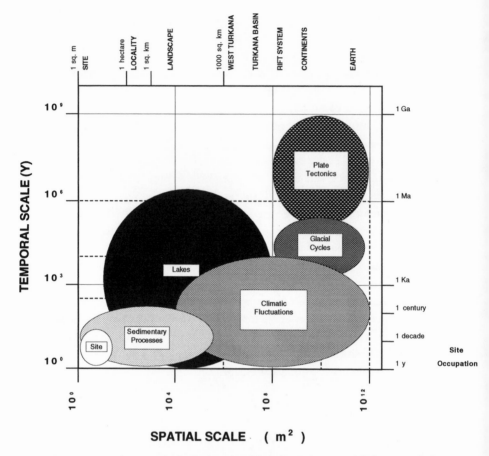

Figure 5.2. Spatial-temporal relationships (modeled after Delcourt and Delcourt 1991). Axes are time (in years) and space (in square meters). Individual fields indicated cover the relationships between lakes, large-scale controlling factors (plate tectonics, glacial cycles, climatic fluctuations), and smaller scale sedimentary processes.

Within the spatial and temporal bounds of the site, the processes at play are generally smaller scale: wind and waves, erosion, and deposition. These - processes may be reflected in the character of the sediments at the outcrop, profile, hand specimen, and even microscopic scale. The critical point is to be certain to match the scale of the evidence and the processes it reflects to the questions at hand. It is usually necessary to go beyond the site and its accumulation to get many important answers, whether they be revealed through a microscopic examination of a carbonate mud or through a large-scale analysis of cyclicity in a deepwater core. Just as an individual artifact may be virtually worthless without the details of its in situ context, an entire site loses much of its potential value when viewed only within site boundaries.

Lake Margin Sediments

From the perspective of particle genesis, the sediments that accumulate in lake margin settings can be considered in terms of two primary sediment types: those produced elsewhere and carried onto the site (allochthonous), and those produced in situ, on the site (autochthonous). The first type consists mainly of detrital clastics, particles (clasts) produced by the breakdown of pre-existing rocks (detritus). A full understanding of the origin and history of this type of material requires a survey of its provenance, the sediment source areas. Provenance studies can yield important information on transport patterns, changing drainage networks, and landscape evolution. Detrital clastics commonly make up the bulk of lake margin sediments in tectonically active terranes, glaciated regions, and mature landscapes. The characteristics and composition of detrital clastic particles often record aspects of depositional process and maturation, because particle surfaces evolve and the proportion of more stable phases (e.g., quartz) increases.

The second major type of sediment in lake margin settings is produced in situ, either chemically or biochemically. Common chemical sediments include salts and carbonates, and they may range from clay-sized particles to large crystals, nodules, and encrustations. Bioclasts include an extremely wide range of particles, most commonly of calcareous (mollusc shells and ostracod valves), siliceous (diatom frustules), and carbonaceous (plant matter) composition. Coquinas, weakly indurated deposits dominated by complete or fragmentary calcareous bioclasts, are common in lake margin settings. Bioclastic materials offer the additional complication of being subject to the usual physical transport by currents and flows, as well as to movement by the organism's locomotory powers, to floating, or to transport by consuming or collecting organisms, even humans. While many physical sedimentologists tend to think primarily in terms of sediment transport, it is important to remember that much of the bioclastic component of a site may have formed in situ or reached the site under its own power. A further complication arises with the human introduction of particles to a site. Manuports, flakes, food refuse, and construction materials all join the natural sediment accumulation, to be buried, modified, or redistributed on site as anthropogenic components.

There are many ways to look at the composition of sediments from lake margin settings (e.g., Gale and Hoare 1991; Lewis and McConchie 1994). Each different approach yields information on slightly different aspects of the formation, transport, deposition, and modification of the particles. Thus, a diversity of investigative approaches yields a robust data set and helps avoid many of the pitfalls inherent in any single approach.

Processes of Deposition and Modification

A transitional environment such as a lake margin produces a complex pattern of sedimentation and sediment modification as conditions change. In this setting three types of transitions often leave their signatures in the rock record: (1) the successive shifting of ambient erosional, transport, and depositional processes, (2) the geologically abrupt and often catastrophic effect of large-scale events, and (3) the often subtle but critical switch from subaqueous to subaerial conditions. Furthermore, the effect of time in both subaqueous and subaerial environments may act to allow post-depositional modification including dissolution, cementation, and soil formation (pedogenesis).

Ambient Processes

Water is the primary agent of sediment erosion, transport, and deposition in the lake margin setting. The action of water is manifest in two dominant modes: the effects of waves and currents within the standing body of water, and the effects of unidirectional flow in rivers, deltas, and runnels at the lake margin. The processes most unique to the lake margin environment are those resulting from the waves and currents which redistribute portions of the water body. Waves have a distinctive pattern of energy flow, moving onshore and then retreating offshore. This oscillating flow can produce distinctly symmetrical ripple marks with little net movement of sediment when waves flow directly onshore, or if flow is oblique to the shoreline, can result in complex asymmetrical ripples and significant along-shore transport. The repetitive nature of wave action tends to produce a high degree of sediment sorting, and over long periods of time will result in increased sediment maturity and clast roundness. Since lakes exhibit essentially no tidal effects, the wave range is determined by variation in wind intensity and fluctuations in lake level. Larger patterns of circulation within a lake may result in redistribution of sediment along shore.

Rivers, deltas, and runnels all act as point sources of sediment to the lake system and may distribute sediment out into the lake body as well as onto the lake margin. They have their own features of sediment character, which may be reflected in localized subenvironments within the lake margin setting. As these are often the dominant sources of sediment supply to the lake margin setting, they are an important component of the overall picture.

Although the primary depositional processes associated with the lake margin setting are processes driven by water, eolian effects are also quite common. Two aspects of eolian influence will be considered here: the transport and redeposition of beach sand in dune settings and the influx of eolian dust. Since lake margins are often exposed to strong winds and an unvegetated sediment source is readily available at the shore face, eolian transport of sands and redeposition in a dune field on the landward side of the beach is a common occurrence. The intensity of the winds, the volume of available sand, and the type of onshore vegetation will generally determine the extent of the dune field, but in favorable circumstances the dunes may be considerable. Such dune systems can be important burial sites for archaeological occurrences. Regional patterns of winds and eolian transport may contribute a significant component of dust, some of which may have been transported long distances, to the lake margin setting. This may accumulate onshore, in a dune environment, or be winnowed offshore into the fine-grained lacustrine sequence. Eolian contributions are often difficult to measure, but given the effectiveness of lakes as sediment traps, may be considerable.

Events

Within the spatial and temporal perspective of lake margin settings, many processes are widespread and relatively continuous in operation. Examples would be the winnowing and redistribution of sediment by wave action, and the settling of fine particles out of suspension. But often an important component of the sedimentary record of lake margins is the localized, episodic component produced by geological or meteorological events. For lake margin settings, the most prominent of these is the storm accumulation. Storms are episodic catastrophes, bringing unusually high wave energy to bear on the lake margin. They may have important erosional effects, but most typically they result in the accretion of a storm layer on the beach face, or of a beach ridge some distance above the fairweather waterline. In systems where the overall accumulation rate at the shoreline is slow, storm deposits may dominate the sequence. Other types of episodic events may result in the inundation or exposure of stretches of lake margin, and they are treated below.

Fluctuating Exposure

The most fundamental shift in a lake margin setting is the transition between subaerial and subaqueous character, and yet this change is not always easy to identify. This transition is accompanied by significant changes in depositional and post-depositional processes, but the degree to which these are developed in the sedimentary record will vary. Recognizable features will depend upon the rate and character of the transition (fast or slow, low-energy or high-energy) as well as the duration of the successive environments. Fluctuating exposure can leave very distinctive evidence in the sedimentary record. Exposure of offshore muds may be followed by incipient soil formation, and a suite of pedogenic characteristics. Brief inundation may leave laminated muds, undisturbed aquatic fossils, and shallow-water primary structures. Sediments often have a multiphase history, with some aspects of the sedimentary particles and their fabric reflecting primary depositional processes, and others reflecting the effects of post-depositional modification. Lake-level changes, and alternating submergence and exposure events, often act to intensify post-depositional effects. Because changes of this nature are fairly typical of the lake margin setting, all of the available evidence needs to be evaluated for the possibility of fluctuations of this sort.

A Fluctuating Lake Margin at Gesher Benot Ya'aqov, Israel

The Acheulean site of Gesher Benot Ya'aqov (GBY), located today on the banks of the Jordan River in the Dead Sea Rift of Israel, presents a useful record of variability in lake margin sediments. Recent work at the site (Goren-Inbar et al. 1992, 2000) has recovered a rich assemblage of lithic artifacts, fossil bones, and an associated faunal and floral assemblage. At the time of accumulation, the site lay on the margin of the paleo-Lake Hula, with a nearby stream supplying sediment and raw material for the human occupants of the site.

Strata at GBY have been tilted by subsequent activity on the Dead Sea Rift faults. A series of six geological trenches (Fig. 5.3) were excavated to supplement exposures on the banks of the Jordan River and in the archaeological areas, and allowed the establishment of a composite section. This composite totals some 34 m of sediments, with at least nine occupation levels, some of them complexes (Fig. 5.4). The bulk of the sedimentary succession is fine grained, with both organic-rich and carbonate-rich muds of autochthonous origin. The sequence also contains prominent strata in which gravels, molluscan sands, and coquinas predominate. The archaeological materials, as well as a rich vertebrate fauna, are found in association with both types of deposits, and the sediments themselves give important clues about the circumstances of accumulation and burial on the site.

Artifacts and bones occur in three associations (Fig. 5.5). The first is on top of storm-generated beach strata (e.g., Layer II-6). In this setting, an accretionary unit of about 10–20 cm of sands, gravelly sands, or molluscan sands records a storm event, which plastered coarse sediments from the beach and

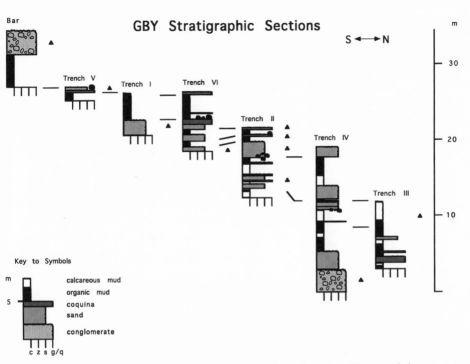

Figure 5.3. Stratigraphic sections from Gesher Benot Ya'aqov, Israel. Particle size and character is represented on the horizontal axis (c = clay, z = silt, s = sand, x = gravel/coquina) and with patterns.

near-shore environment onto the shore face. This then became a stable surface for some interval of time, and an accumulation of stones and bones built up on its surface. A subsequent storm unit may incorporate some of the archaeological materials into the storm bed, but most remains in a discrete horizon between sterile beds. The stability of these storm beds on the beach face is attested to by the high degree of abrasion and polish on fragmented molluscs and by the sorting of the detrital clastics. The freshness of most of the artifact edges implies that they accumulated well above the strand line, on the upper beach face.

In the second type of association (e.g., Layer V-5), artifacts and bones are concentrated at the interface between fine-grained offshore muds and a mollusc coquina. In this situation the muds were deposited offshore, and a brief drop in lake level produced a land surface on which artifacts and bones accumulated. A rise in lake level accompanied by storm concentration of offshore molluscs buried the archaeological accumulation, and in the process incorporated some of the material into the coquina. This was a short-term and discrete

Stratigraphic Sequence at
Gesher Benot Ya'aqov, Israel

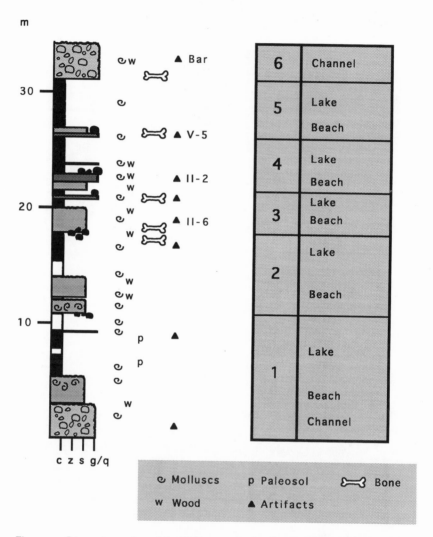

Figure 5.4. Composite section of the GBY sequence, showing the important archaeological levels as well as the pronounced cyclicity of the sequence (c = clay, z = silt, s = sand, x = gravel/coquina).

Archaeological Associations at Gesher Benot Ya'aqov

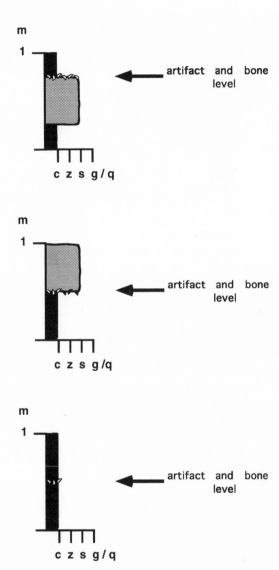

Figure 5.5. Facies sequences in which artifacts and bones occur at GBY (c = clay, z = silt, s = sand, g/t = gravel/coquina).

event burying the archaeological level in a transgression as is reflected in the unbroken and unabraded character of the bulk of the molluscan material.

In the third association, scattered artifacts or bones occur within the offshore muds. In this situation, the archaeological materials (e.g., Layer III-2) record short-term regressions, when offshore muds became land surfaces on which cultural debris accumulated. In some of these cases, incipient soil features are visible at the artifact-bearing horizon, but in others the materials are the only clue to a brief episode of exposure. Only rarely was exposure prolonged enough to overprint the lacustrine muds with soil characteristics, such as soil structure and the leaching of carbonate from the highly calcareous parent material.

Analysis of the sediments (Fig. 5.6) demonstrates rapid shifts in abundance of carbonate and organics, typical of a fluctuating lake margin setting. In the case of the GBY sediments, carbonate and organic material vary inversely, and the detrital component is quite small. These sedimentological analyses do not provide a complete picture of accumulation history at the site, however. One significant component is absent from the picture—the anthropogenic contribution of artifacts, bones, and manuports. As they occur concentrated within occupation horizons (interfaces), they escape the standard sedimentological characterization focused on layers. And as the components of this assemblage are excavated and removed by archaeologists, their contribution as sedimentary clasts to the overall picture must be reconstituted from an analysis of them as particles. Since some of the artifact-rich strata at GBY consist largely of anthropogenic materials, this can be a very important component of the overall sedimentary history.

The detrital clastic component at GBY provides clues to another aspect of palaeogeography—the relationship of the site to sediment source areas. Today the site is situated on the banks of the south-flowing Jordan River. But detrital sediments, including some of the larger clasts used as raw material for stone-tool production, point to dramatic changes in this rift valley setting over time. Although the bulk of the detrital component is basaltic lava, there is a minor but consistent component of limestone and chert, including material identifiable as being Eocene in age (Goren-Inbar et al. 1992). The most likely source for these clasts is in the limestones of the Safad Mountains, west of the site. Such clasts presently reach the Jordan River via a tributary, the Rosh Pinna stream, which traverses a deep gorge to join the Jordan *south* of GBY. Thus, the only possible route for these clasts, from cobble through sand-sized material, is for this section of the Jordan River to have been flowing *north* at the time the site formed, ca. 780 ka (Verosub et al. 1998). Thus a few limestone and chert clasts can rewrite the history of an entire river.

In addition to the details of accumulation of the artifact-bearing strata, the sedimentary sequence at GBY displays some larger scale patterns that are also of significance to the history of the site. The composite stratigraphic column, and analysis of the sediment components, fossils, and other proxy records, all

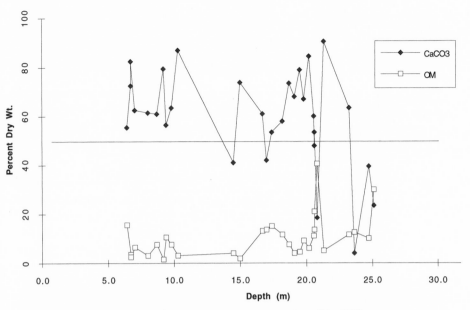

Figure 5.6. Analytical data for sediment composition in a portion of the GBY sequence. Most of the sediments are predominantly carbonate, including both fine-grained micrite precipitated biochemically in the lake and mollusc shells accumulated near shore. Organic matter content is high in these sediments, reflecting the preservation in anoxic conditions of this wet site.

document a strong cyclical pattern to the GBY sequence. A series of five short-order cycles of changing lacustrine facies is nested within a longer period record of lacustrine-alluvial fluctuation. These records all relate to changes in lake level, sediment type, and water chemistry. Such a cyclical pattern most likely relates to control by a large-scale periodic signal in climate, and in this case is most likely attributable to the ca. 20,000-year and 100,000-year Milankovitch cycles of global climate (Feibel et al. 1998). Recognition of the larger scale patterning in the sedimentary record at GBY can thus supply important evidence for the relative and even absolute time frames for the sedimentary and archaeological records.

High-Energy Shorelines of West Turkana, Kenya

The early Pleistocene history of the Turkana Basin in northern Kenya includes a rich record of lake margin settings associated with precursors of present-day Lake Turkana (Brown and Feibel 1991; Feibel et al. 1991). Archaeological sites

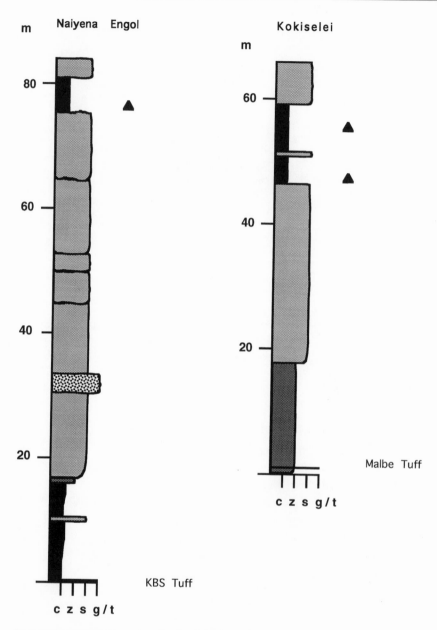

Figure 5.7. Stratigraphic sections for the Kokiselei and Naiyena Engol archaeological sites in West Turkana, Kenya (c = clay, z = silt, s = sand, g/t = gravel/tuff). Archaeological sites are indicated by triangles.

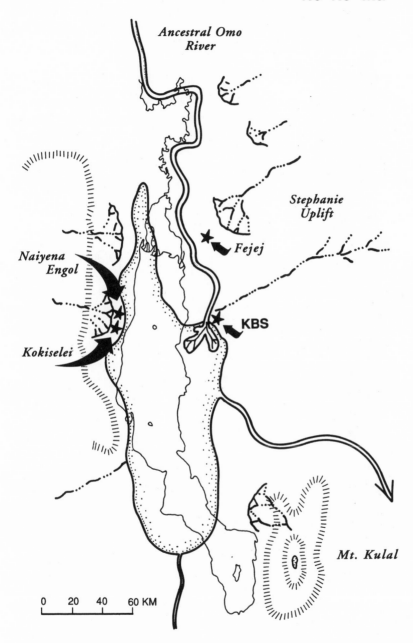

Figure 5.8. Paleogeographic setting of the West Turkana archaeological sites at ca. 1.8–1.9 Ma.

on the western shore of an ancient lake at 1.7 Ma (termed the Lorenyang Lake) provide a record of early hominid activities along a high-energy shoreline. They are of particular interest as they are the only sites at which early hominid activities in this region are directly associated with lake margins (Rogers et al. 1994). Two site complexes, Kokiselei and Naiyena Engol (Kibunjia et al. 1992), occur in nearly identical stratigraphic settings (Fig. 5.7). Both occur in the fine-grained interval that overlies a thick package of beach sands, gravels, and coquinas. The character of the beach sediments provides important clues to the overall depositional system, in particular to sediment sources and transport processes. The beach sands are predominantly quartzo-feldspathic, while pebbles and cobbles are almost entirely volcanic in character. These sands are distributed as a laterally extensive package that can be traced over some 8 km between the site complexes. The sands occur in thick beds often showing high-angle shoreface depositional dips to the east. Conglomerates have similar characteristics, with high-angle primary dips. The cobbles and pebbles show the flattening characteristic of beach gravel clasts. Their distribution, however, is much more restricted, and they occur in lenticular bodies several meters thick and several hundred meters in lateral extent. The lithological differences between sands and gravels reflect two source areas contributing detrital material. The quartzo-feldspathic sources are in the metamorphic terrane more than 100 km to the south. Volcanics derive from the mountains on the rift margin just a few kilometers to the west.

These beach strata reflect long-term stability of the lake shore, as subsidence in this rift valley setting kept pace with sediment supply from longshore drift and rift-margin streams. The beach sands were transported to the lake margin by large rivers located south of the sites (Fig. 5.8) and then reworked along the coastline as winds struck the north-south shoreline obliquely from the southeast (Feibel 1988).

Several archaeological occurrences are documented from massive sandstones at the top of the beach complex, which may represent a dune setting, or simply reworked beach sands. Most of the archaeological sites, however, are situated within mudstones of a lacustrine plain environment, adjacent to the high-energy beaches. With the paucity of direct indicators, it is difficult to determine if these mudstones were deposited during short-term lacustrine transgressions, or as overbank material from the rift-margin streams. One such transgression is clearly marked in the Kokiselei section (Fig. 5.8) by a rich molluscan fauna. In other levels, the mudstones preserve a variety of weakly developed soil features, as well as some markers of swampy conditions, such as opercula of the aquatic pulmonate snail *Pila ovata*.

In the case of the West Turkana archaeological sites, characteristics of the sedimentary particles provide important clues to the surrounding landscape and to the processes affecting sediment transport and accumulation. It is clear that there are a variety of lake margin subenvironments here, but it is difficult to be more precise in situating these early hominid activities.

Other Examples

The important Palaeolithic sites of Olduvai Gorge, Tanzania, are nearly all associated with lake margin settings (Hay 1976; Leakey 1971). In the case of the Olduvai paleolake, the endorheic system fostered chemical concentration of the lake waters, resulting in, among other things, the precipitation of chert nodules that would ultimately become raw material for lithic tool production. The abundance of archaeological sites at Olduvai provides examples from nearly all aspects of lake margin settings (Hay 1971). The well-known site of FLK *Zinjanthropus,* in which abundant artifacts and fossils were found in close association, lies on a lacustrine claystone that has been weakly overprinted with pedogenic features (Hay 1976). In an unusual example, Mary Leakey has suggested that the pits discovered at site JK are in many ways similar to present-day salt workings, such as those on the margin of the soda lake at Magado, Kenya (Leakey 1994).

The Olorgesailie Lake Basin in Kenya preserves a suite of Palaeolithic archaeological sites (Isaac 1977). While early studies focused on hand-axe-rich accumulations in association with stream channels, more recent work (Potts 1989, 1994; Potts et al. 1999) has investigated lower density occurrences in lake-margin paleosols. The rich aquatic record of the ancient Olorgesailie Lake (Owen and Renault 1981, 2000) provides an environmental context into which the pattern of early hominid activities can be placed. The Olorgesailie Lake fluctuated between open- and closed-basin conditions, with both sedimentary and biotic indicators tracking these changes.

A large body of literature on lake margin sites focuses on the unusual aspects of preservation afforded by wet sites—those which have been waterlogged since the time of deposition (Purdy 1988). The early Epipalaeolithic site of Ohalo II (Kislev et al. 1992), in the Lake Kinneret Basin of Israel, is a good example. Among the preserved materials here are a rich faunal and floral record that includes cereal grains and fruits. This site was on the shore of the late Pleistocene Lake Lisan, which filled much of the Dead Sea Rift at its maximum extent (Begin et al. 1974). This is an example of one of the late Pleistocene "mega-lakes" (others include lakes Bonneville and Chad) whose sedimentary records provide context for later human activities in many parts of the world. In the New World, occupation sites are well documented from lake margins of the Great Plains (Holliday 1985) as well.

Summary: Lake Margin Sediments as Archives in Archaeological Contexts

The essence of the lake margin setting is the interface between a body of standing water and the adjacent terrestrial environment. The sedimentary particles here, as well as the characteristics of the strata and facies they comprise, lend themselves to analyses with important implications for archaeological sites and their contents. In virtually all cases, archaeological sites are emplaced in or on terrestrial facies, but they may be buried by lacustrine deposits. Upward reworking in the burial process, or simply the association with lacustrine facies may give the erroneous impression of accumulation of the archaeological materials within the lake itself. Understanding the process of accumulation and burial of archaeological materials requires a detailed understanding of the depositional history of the site. In addition, the sedimentary particles on a site may preserve significant information regarding the environmental context of the site, from details of the local landscape to regional paleogeographic patterns and climatic parameters.

References Cited

Begin, Z. B., A. Ehrlich, and Y. Nathan
1974   *Lake Lisan: The Pleistocene Precursor of the Dead Sea.* Israel Geological Survey Bulletin 63. Jerusalem.
Brown, F. H., and C. S. Feibel
1991   Stratigraphy, Depositional Environments and Paleogeography of the Koobi Fora Formation. In *Koobi Fora Research Project,* vol. 3, *Stratigraphy, Artiodactyls and Paleoenvironments,* edited by J. M. Harris, pp. 1–30. Clarendon Press, Oxford.
Collinson, J. D.
1978   Lakes. In *Sedimentary Environments and Facies,* edited by H. G. Reading, pp. 61–79. Elsevier, New York.
Currey, D. R.
1980   Coastal Geomorphology of Great Salt Lake and Vicinity. In *Great Salt Lake: A Scientific, Historical and Economic Overview,* edited by J. W. Gwynn, pp. 69–82. Utah Geological and Mineral Survey Bulletin 116. Salt Lake City.
Delcourt, H. R., and P. A. Delcourt
1991   *Quaternary Ecology: A Paleoecological Perspective.* Chapman and Hall, London.
Eugster, H. P., and L. A. Hardie
1978   Saline Lakes. In *Lakes: Chemistry, Geology, Physics,* edited by A. Lerman, pp. 237–293. Springer-Verlag, New York.

Feibel, C. S.
1988   Paleoenvironments from the Koobi Fora Formation, Turkana Basin, Northern Kenya. Unpublished Ph.D. dissertation. Department of Geology and Geophysics, University of Utah, Salt Lake City.

Feibel, C. S., N. Goren-Inbar, K. L. Verosub, and I. Saragusti
1998   Gesher Benot Ya'aqov, Israel: New Evidence for its Stratigraphic and Sedimentologic Context. *Journal of Human Evolution* 34(3):A7.

Feibel, C. S., J. M. Harris, and F. H. Brown
1991   Palaeoenvironmental Context for the Late Neogene of the Turkana Basin. In *Koobi Fora Research Project*, vol. 3, *Stratigraphy, Artiodactyls and Paleoenvironments*, edited by J. M. Harris, pp. 321–370. Clarendon Press, Oxford.

Gale, S. J., and P. G. Hoare
1991   *Quaternary Sediments*. Halsted Press, New York.

Goren-Inbar, N., S. Belitzky, K. Verosub, E. Werker, M. Kislev, A. Heimann, I. Carmi, and A. Rosenfeld
1992   New Discoveries at the Middle Pleistocene Acheulean Site of Gesher Benot Ya'aqov, Israel. *Quaternary Research* 38:117–128.

Goren-Inbar, N., C. S. Feibel, K. L. Verosub, Y. Melamed, M. E. Kislev, E. Tchernov, and I. Saragusti
2000   Pleistocene Milestones on the Out-of-Africa Corridor at Gesher Benot Ya'aqov, Israel. *Science* 289:944–947.

Hay, R. L.
1971   Geologic Background of Beds I and II: Stratigraphic Summary. In *Olduvai Gorge*, vol. 3, *Excavations in Beds I and II, 1960–1963*, edited by M. D. Leakey, pp. 9–18. Cambridge University Press, Cambridge.
1976   *Geology of the Olduvai Gorge*. University of California Press, Berkeley.

Holliday, V. T.
1985   Archaeological Geology of the Lubbock Lake Site, Southern High Plains of Texas. *Geological Society of America Bulletin* 96:1483–1492.

Isaac, G. L.
1977   *Olorgesailie: Archeological Studies of a Middle Pleistocene Lake Basin in Kenya*. University of Chicago Press, Chicago.

Kelts, K.
1988   Environments of Deposition of Lacustrine Petroleum Source Rocks: An Introduction. In *Lacustrine Petroleum Source Rocks*, edited by A. J. Fleet, K. Kelts, and M. R. Talbot, pp. 3–26. Geological Society Special Publication 40. Blackwell, Oxford.

Kibunjia, M., H. Roche, F. H. Brown, and R. E. Leakey
1992   Pliocene and Pleistocene Archeological Sites West of Lake Turkana, Kenya. *Journal of Human Evolution* 23:431–438.

Kislev, M. E., D. Nadel, and I. Carmi
1992   Epipalaeolithic (19,000 B.P.) Cereal and Fruit Diet at Ohalo II, Sea of Galilee, Israel. *Review of Palaeobotany and Palynology* 73:161–166.

Leakey, M. D.
1971   *Olduvai Gorge*, vol. 3, *Excavations in Beds I and II, 1960–1963*. Cambridge University Press, Cambridge.
1994   Bed III, Site JK (Juma's Korongo). In *Olduvai Gorge*, vol. 5, *Excavations in Beds III, IV and the Masek Beds, 1968–1971*, edited by M. D. Leakey, and D. A. Roe, pp. 15–35. Cambridge University Press, Cambridge.

Lewis, D. W., and D. McConchie
1994   *Analytical Sedimentology.* Chapman and Hall, New York.

Owen, R. B., and R. W. Renaut
1981   Palaeoenvironments and Sedimentology of the Middle Pleistocene Olorgesailie For-
         mation, Southern Kenya Rift Valley. *Palaeoecology of Africa* 13:147–174.
2000   Spatial and Temporal Facies Variations in the Pleistocene Olorgesailie Formation,
         Southern Kenya Rift Valley. In *Lake Basins through Space and Time,* edited by E. H.
         Gierlowski-Kordesch and K. R. Kelts, pp. 553–560. American Association of Petro-
         leum Geologists, Tulsa, Oklahoma.

Potts, R.
1989   Olorgesailie: New Excavations and Findings in Early and Middle Pleistocene Con-
         texts, Southern Kenya Rift Valley. *Journal of Human Evolution* 18:477–484.
1994   Variables versus Models of Early Pleistocene Hominid Land Use. *Journal of Human
         Evolution* 27:7–24.

Potts, R., A. K. Behrensmeyer, and P. Ditchfield
1999   Paleolandscape Variation and Early Pleistocene Hominid Activities: Members 1 and
         7, Olorgesailie Formation, Kenya. *Journal of Human Evolution* 37:747–788.

Purdy, B. A. (editor)
1988   *Wet Site Archaeology.* Telford Press, Caldwell, New Jersey.

Rogers, M. J., J. W. K. Harris, and C. S. Feibel
1994   Changing Patterns of Land Use by Plio-Pleistocene Hominids in the Lake Turkana
         Basin. *Journal of Human Evolution* 27:139–158.

Sly, P. G.
1978   Sedimentary Processes in Lakes. In *Lakes: Chemistry, Geology, Physics,* edited by
         A. Lerman, pp. 65–89. Springer-Verlag, New York.

Stein, J. K., and A. R. Linse (editors)
1993   *Effects of Scale on Archaeological and Geoscientific Perspectives.* Geological Society of
         America, Special Paper 283. Boulder, Colorado.

Talbot, M. R., and P. A. Allen
1996   Lakes. In *Sedimentary Environments: Processes, Facies and Stratigraphy,* edited by
         H. G. Reading, pp. 83–124. Blackwell Science, Oxford.

Verosub, K. L., N. Goren-Inbar, C. S. Feibel, and I. Saragusti
1998   Location of the Matuyama/Brunhes Boundary in the Gesher Benot Ya'aqov Archae-
         ological Site, Israel. *Journal of Human Evolution* 34(3):A22.

Williams, D. F., J. Peck, E. B. Karabanov, A. A. Prokopenko, V. Kravchinsky, J. King, and
M. I. Kuzmin
1997   Lake Baikal Record of Continental Climatic Response to Orbital Insolation during
         the Past 5 Million Years. *Science* 278:1114–1117.

6

Archaeological Sediments in Coastal Environments

Lisa E. Wells

The coastline, the interface between land and ocean, juxtaposes fertile agricultural lands and marine protein resources with trade facilitated by marine transport. These subsistence and economic advantages have made settlement in coastal zones attractive since the onset of sedentism. As such, the archaeological record in coastal zones is rich and abundant. The coastline is also one of the most dynamic landscape elements, with relative sea level, wave and tide energy, and sediment flux varying on time scales from seconds to millennia. People living in coastal zones have to adapt their lifestyles to the transitory nature of this environment. Geomorphologic and settlement pattern evolution along with stratigraphic records of changing sedimentation styles and environments all reflect the dynamism found along the coastline. Appropriate interpretation of the archaeological record in coastal zones must include an understanding of the dynamic evolution of the coastal landscape.

Three primary factors control the nature and evolution of the coastal zone: relative sea level, energy flux (waves, tides, currents), and sediment flux. Changes in relative sea level can be forced by either changes in the elevation of the land surface (tectonics and isostasy) or by changes in the elevation of the ocean surface (eustasy). Changes in energy flux to the shoreline are controlled by climate (wave generation and current strength and direction) and geography (tidal range and relative importance). Additionally, the tectonic environment and geographic setting will influence the frequency and magnitude of tsunamis and their relative importance to coastal sedimentation. Finally, the nature (grain size and lithology) and rate of sedimentation result from local climatic controls, the geographic and tectonic setting, and the coastal energy regime. Clearly, these factors are not independent and changes in one set of controlling variables will influence the others.

Even in the most stable environment, coastal landforms and geography evolve through time as sediment accumulates or shorelines erode. The nature of erosion or sedimentation is a result of energy flux to the coastline. Coasts are classified into two broad types that describe the dominant energy available to reshape the coastline. *Open coasts* are those exposed to the full impact of short-period wind-driven waves. These coasts are commonly high-energy environments typified by beaches or rocky shorelines. The sediments that accumulate along open coasts are relatively coarse grained and the organic fraction is either large woody debris or carbonate particles. Open coastlines are more likely to be erosive in nature than are protected coastlines. In contrast, *protected coastlines* are located in environments where wind waves are highly attenuated by refraction and tidal energy dominates both sedimentation and landform development. These coasts are commonly low-energy environments typified by estuaries and tidal marshes. The sediments that accumulate along protected coasts are relatively fine grained, and peat is common. The nature of the sedimentary substrate and the amount of energy impinging upon the shoreline also exert strong controls on the nature and distribution of biological resources. Open coasts and protected coasts may exist side by side—for example, the coastal headlands and beaches along the San Francisco shoreline outside the Golden Gate are open coasts while the salt marshes along the shoreline inside the Golden Gate are protected coasts. This first-level classification provides a context for understanding the nature of sedimentation within and around an archaeological site, the availability of biologic resources, and the ease of boat access to the site.

Evolution of the coastline occurs at time scales relevant both to the primary occupation of the site and to its post-occupational transformation. Coastal occupants must deal with oceanographic changes resulting from storms and hurricanes, tsunamis, or oceanographic phenomena like El Niño. The periodicity of these phenomena is dependent upon local geography and may have a significant impact on the choice of settlement location. Both interannual and seasonal changes in the resource base require flexibility in subsistence adaptations. At longer time scales, the relative sea level rise or fall will result in spatial shifts in the physical location of resources and the attendant submergence or stranding of coastal sites. The coastline is always responding to the changing oceanographic conditions.

A paleoenvironmental analysis is fundamental to interpretations of the archaeology of any coastal landscape. These studies should include analysis of sediments from within and around the site as well as the geomorphologic and paleogeographic context of the site(s). This chapter will provide the reader with an introduction to the methods and concepts fundamental to these analyses

with specific examples illustrating the strengths of integrating geoarchaeological analyses into an archaeological study.

Processes Controlling Sediment Distribution: A Nearshore Oceanography Primer

Long-Period Changes in Relative Sea Level

Sea level rises and falls in response to a combination of eustatic, isostatic, and
tectonic processes. Eustatic processes are driven by changes in the volume of
water in the ocean. Eustatic sea level change has fluctuated with the glacial cycles of the Quaternary period as water has cycled back and forth from the ice
caps to the oceans (Fig. 6.1; Fairbanks 1989). At the last glacial maximum (ca. 18
ka) eustatic sea level reached a low stand between 90 and 150 m below modern
sea level (Pirazzoli 1996; Stanley 1995). From ca. 18 ka until ca. 8 ka sea level rose
rapidly as the bulk of the ice caps melted, with a period of slowing between 10
and 11 ka during the short glacial resurgence known as the Younger Dryas event.
Around 8 ka eustatic sea level began to stabilize and the rate of sea level change
slowed dramatically (Fairbanks 1989). When the ice caps melted there was a
large redistribution of the mass of water on the surface of the Earth and the
solid mass of the Earth redistributed itself to maintain isostatic (gravitational)
equilibrium. Isostatic compensation has resulted in very different local sea level
histories depending on location relative to the ice sheets and ocean basins
(Bloom 1983; Clark et al. 1978; Clark and Lingle 1979; Tushingham and Peltier
1992). Glacial margins rebounded and emerged as the weight of the ice was removed, while tropical regions subsided in response to the increased water mass
in the ocean basin and on continental shelves (Tushingham and Peltier 1992).

Tectonic processes are generated by internal stress within the solid earth.
These processes change the level of the land surface relative to the ocean surface. At the time scales of interest to archaeology, we are concerned with the
rise or fall of the land surface in response to near-surface faulting or folding.
Coastlines coincident with subduction zones or collision margins (for example, much of the Pacific or Mediterranean coasts) are tectonically active environments. Vertical motion may be gradual or catastrophic depending on the
regional tectonic forces.

At a practical level, we use geological indicators to interpret the motion
(vertical and/or horizontal) of the shoreline through time, and from these we
reconstruct a relative sea level curve that integrates a combination of all of
these processes. Deconvolving the relative impacts of eustasy, isostasy, and

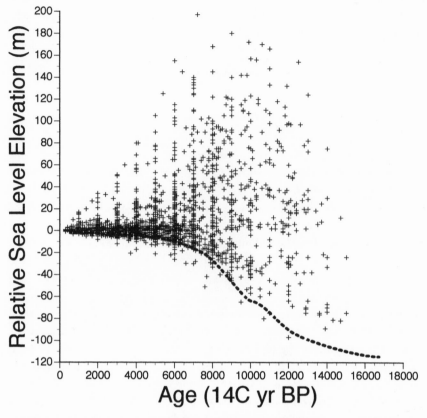

Figure 6.1. Sea level data for the late Quaternary. Crosses indicate relative sea level positions compiled by Tushingham and Peltier (1993). Dashed line is a simplified version of Fairbanks's (1989) proposed glacio-eustatic sea level curve. Data plotting above the eustatic sea level curve are from emergent coasts, while those plotting below the curve are from submerged coasts. The dramatic increase in nearshore sedimentation that began after the rate of sea level rise slowed, ca. 8 ka, is reflected in the increased number of data points at this time.

tectonics is a complicated task, generally beyond the scope of an archaeological investigation. For most archaeological purposes, establishing the nature of relative sea level change at a place is sufficient.

Short-Period Changes in Nearshore Oceanography

Nearshore oceanography includes all those processes that move water and sediment in the littoral zone: waves, tides, tsunamis, and littoral drift. The relative impact and importance of each process results from the local and basinal geography, climate, and tectonic setting.

Short-period waves are generated by wind stress on the ocean surface. Wave size is directly related to the length of time the wind blows and the size of the area (fetch) the wind blows across. Waves within the fetch ("sea") are short-period choppy waves; waves that travel out of the fetch ("swell") are smooth long-period waves. There is no net movement of water by waves in the deep ocean, only when waves shoal (at depths approximately equal to one-quarter the wave length) and break (when the height:length ratio reaches 1:7) in the coastal zone is there a net shoreward or longshore movement of water or sediment by waves. Sediment can be entrained and transported by any process that results in the net motion of water at the sediment/water interface.

When waves enter the coastal zone at an angle, as they usually do, they generate a net motion of water parallel to the coastline known as littoral drift. Littoral drift occurs both when the waves are generated at an angle to the regional trend of the shoreline as well as when waves interact with the smaller scale perturbations of coastal geography. The result is net sediment transport down current with the direction of wave movement. This sediment will become trapped in embayments and may form large progradational complexes. In the regions where sediment accumulates, the coastline will eventually become swash-aligned (parallel to the crests of the predominant waves) thus minimizing littoral drift through time. The resulting form of the coastline and shape of the paleobeaches can be used to interpret changes in wave direction through time (Mason and Jordan 1993; Wells 1996; Zenkovich 1967).

Tides are generated by the gravitational pull of the moon and sun on the Earth. A large bulge of water is pulled away from the earth and toward the moon and a centrifugally forced bulge is located on the opposite side of the Earth. These two bulges can be conceived of as a wave under which the Earth rotates, therefore passing by any location approximately twice per day (every 12 hr 25 min; half the lunar day). The magnitude of the tides at location is a geographic issue, as the tidal waves interact and flow around a basin. Tidal range varies from effectively zero to as high as 12 m (via amplification in narrow funnel-shaped estuaries). The volume of water that is moved into or out of a region during the tidal cycle is referred to as the tidal prism. Strong tidal currents are generated where tidal prism is large. Tidal currents, sediment transport, and erosion peaks at mid-tide, and sediment deposition peaks at slack water (Stoddart et al. 1989). Mudflats, tidal marshes, and mangrove swamps are restricted to protected embayments where tidal energy dominates over wind waves. These are phenomenally productive ecosystems important to the subsistence base of many prehistoric societies (Lightfoot 1997; Pozorski and Pozorski 1987).

Tsunamis are long-period waves generated by submarine earthquakes,

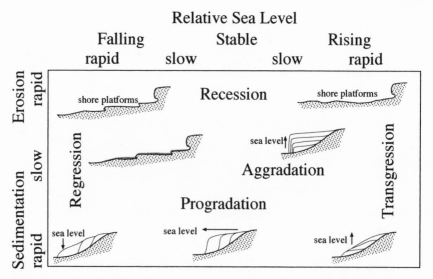

Figure 6.2. Relationships between changes in relative sea level or sediment flux and the resulting geomorphology and depositional facies architecture in coastal environments (adapted from Curray et al. 1967 and Posamentier et al. 1988).

landslides, or volcanic eruptions (Kajiura and Shuto 1990). A sudden, catastrophic motion of the ocean floor will deform the water surface to form a set of very long-period waves (lengths as great as 150 miles; periods of 10 minutes or more). When these waves shoal on gradually sloping coasts their energy is dispersed over a large area, and the waves are often inconsequential. However, when they shoal on a steep coast they can become enormous and destructive; whole communities have been swept away by modern (1998 in New Guinea) or ancient (A.D. 365 in Crete and the Mediterranean; Higgins and Higgins 1996) tsunamis. Tsunamis occur most frequently in tectonically active basins, and they are therefore more common in the Pacific Ocean or Mediterranean Sea than in the Atlantic Ocean. While relatively infrequent, the potential magnitude of their impacts to archaeological sites is large.

A Model for Coastal Evolution

Curray (1964) summarized coastal processes into a predictive model of shoreline evolution (Fig. 6.2; Posamentier et al. 1988). This model results in a five-fold classification that describes the relative motion of the shoreline through time: (1) progradational coasts grow seaward as a result of sedimentation; (2) transgressive coasts are submerged as a result of relative sea level rise; (3) recessive coasts erode landward; (4) regressive coasts emerge as relative sea level falls; and (5) aggradational coasts grow vertically when the rates of sea level rise and sedimentation are roughly equal. The erosive boundary at the base of a package of coastal sediment represents the surface across which sea level once transgressed; the erosive boundary at the top of a package of coastal sediment represents terrestrial erosion after sea level regressed.

Given that the basic shape of the Holocene eustatic sea-level curve is well established, we can use this model to retrodict the status of the coastline. In areas that were directly adjacent to the ice sheets, isostatic rebound resulted in a relative drop in sea level and regressive or recessive shorelines throughout the Holocene Epoch. For most other regions, a rapid transgression occurred in late Pleistocene and early Holocene time, followed by either recession, aggradation, or progradation dependent upon the sedimentation rate. The point in time that marks the end of transgression is often recorded by a paleoshoreline stranded inland of the modern coast. In erosive environments this paleoshoreline will be marked by a sea cliff cut into bedrock or unconsolidated sediments; in sedimentary environments it will be marked by the change from transgressive to regressive sedimentation.

Coastal Sediments: Recognition and Analysis

Sediment is brought into the coastal zone by rivers or gravitationally eroded from seacliffs (Fig. 6.3). Most sediment accretion occurs in areas proximal to or downcurrent of river mouths. The volume and nature of sediment brought to the coast is a therefore a function of the geology, tectonics, climate, oceanography, and geography of the sediment source area, be it a terrestrial drainage basin or an eroding seacliff. Large drainage basins yield large volumes of fine-grained sediment while short, steep drainage basins yield coarse-grained materials. On those rare coasts where there is no inland fluvial drainage (e.g., atolls or reef islands) the sediment available to the beach will be exclusively biogenic and will have been created in the nearshore zones of that island.

Sediment is moved along the coastline by littoral drift or removed from the coastal zone by onshore winds or oceanic currents. Where atmospheric conditions create stable winds, large volumes of sand- to granule-sized material may be moved onshore. The largest coastal eolian complexes occur where hyperarid conditions, strong persistent onshore winds, and a littoral sand source are coincident (Fig. 6.4). Dissolved salts are also transported onshore by sea breezes and can enhance weathering and soil formation. Silt and clay are transported offshore in suspension and become entrained into oceanic

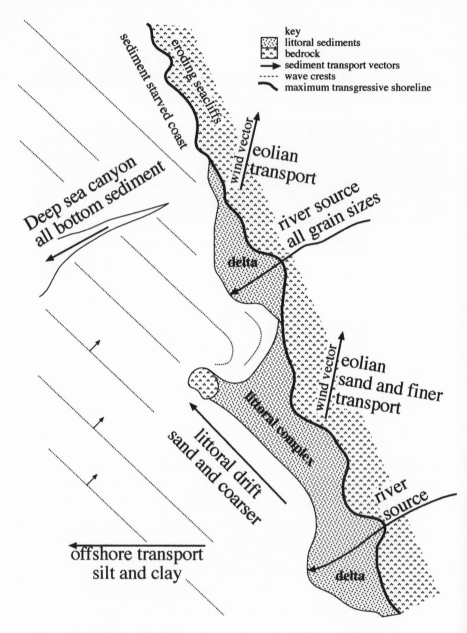

Figure 6.3. Mechanisms of sediment transport into and out of the coastal zone.

Figure 6.4. Shoreline on the north coast of Peru. Wave crests are being refracted around the headland. The beach here is swash-aligned with the wave crests into a classic refraction-aligned beach. Littoral drift direction is to the north (from right to left along the beach). Eolian sand reworked from the shoreline is banked into climbing dunes on the bedrock hills in the background. Seaweed washover has been strewn across the berm on the southern end of the beach. Shore-parallel lineations are the crests of stranded beach ridges.

currents. Coarse-grained sediment generally stays in the littoral zone unless a deep-sea canyon interrupts the littoral drift. Deep-sea canyons can drain large volumes of coastal sediment offshore.

If the rate of sediment delivery outpaces the rate of sediment transport, accretion will occur. If the rate of sedimentation is less than the rate of sediment transport, then the sediment will remain in transit until it reaches some kind of a sink or basin that traps the sediment. Rates and directions of sediment transport vary with wave and tide climate over days, seasons, and centuries. The coastline downcurrent of major sediment traps (embayments, harbors, or sea canyons) will be starved of drifting sediment.

Sediments Deposited by Geological Processes

Sediment grain size is the result of geologic working and sorting of the available sediment population. Sedimentary structures reflect the hydrodynamics of deposition. Post-depositional processes (e.g., bioturbation and weathering) transform the deposits. To interpret the environment of deposition for a given

Table 6.1. Characteristics of Coastal Sediments

BEACHES

Sediment Texture	Well-sorted, well-rounded, polished sand to gravel-sized sediment.
Sedimentary Structures	Bedding planes most commonly dip shoreward, however; landward migrating packages of sediment and washover deposits may dip landward. Planar and cross lamination is common. Clast imbrication is usually shoreward. Coarser and denser sediment is often concentrated in defined beds or along bedding planes. There may be inverse sorting with the coarsest sediment at the highest elevations within the sedimentary sequence.
Beach Rock	Beach rock is intertidal sediment indurated by calcite or aragonite cement deposited in the intertidal zone. It occurs most commonly in arid to tropical regions with an abundance of carbonate in solution. Flaggy in situ beach rock layers dip gently seaward. Large blocks of beach rock may be broken off and reworked in the coast zone. It can be difficult to distinguish beach rock from anthropogenically cemented sediment, however; only beach rock will preserve the sedimentary structures associated with deposition in the coastal zone.
Fossils	Sediment may include broken and reworked shell debris and drift wood. These materials are commonly coarser than the matrix material. In situ shells may occur but are uncommon in the swash zone of the beach.
Soils	Buried soils are uncommon and what soil is present is commonly poorly developed.

DUNES

Sediment Texture	Very well-sorted, well-rounded sand to granule-sized sediment. Deposits of fine-grained dust are uncommon. Grain frosting due to repeated impact is common.
Sedimentary Structures	Tabular strata centimeters to decimeters thick dip upwind while the cross strata between these larger bedding planes generally dip downwind.
Fossils	Any reworked shell material incorporated into dune sediment will have the same sedimentary texture as the non-carbonate sediment.
Soils	Salt crusts are common. Vegetated dune fields will have spotty concentrations of high organic content and finer grained sediment.

ESTUARIES AND TIDAL FLATS (SUBTIDAL DEPOSITION)

Sediment Texture	Poorly to well-sorted sand to clay sediment. Organic content varies over a wide range. Sediment is often saturated.

Table 6.1. Characteristics of Coastal Sediments Continued

Sedimentary Structures	Planar and cross lamination. Where tidal currents are rapid, ripple lamination and larger bedforms may occur. Paleochannels with coarse-grained material in their bases may cross-cut the sediments. Bioturbation may be intense and totally destroy structures.
Fossils	Common plant and shell fossils. Fossils are often in growth position.
Soils	Subtidal sediment is usually anoxic and commonly gray to blue in color. Intertidal sediment will have undergone a variety of redox reactions resulting in a mix of anoxic (gray to blue) and oxidated (orange/red/brown) colorations.
MARSHES	
Sediment Texture	Highly organic sand to clay sediment. Organic contents vary from 10 percent to nearly 100 percent by weight. These low density sediments are commonly saturated.
Sedimentary Structures	Poorly preserved planar to wavy bedding planes. Mud cracks. Bioturbation by roots and some burrowing.
Fossils	Plant macro- and microfossils often comprise the bulk of the sediment. Intertidal micro- and macrofossils of carbonate are less common as the soil is frequently acidic. Fossils from deeper intertidal environments may be washed onto the marsh during storm or extreme high tide events.
Soils	Marsh soils show a variety of colors and textures resulting from redox reactions that occur with the wetting and drying cycles. Sediment color may range from gray/blue to orange/red/brown.
DELTAS	
Sediment Texture	Deltaic sediments are a mixture of nearshore and distal fluvial materials. There will be interbedded packages of beach, dune, estuarine, marsh, and river sediments.
Sedimentary Structures	Small-scale sedimentary structures will be the same as those described for the individual sediment packets. Larger scale structures will include scoured river channels and prograding sediment packets that dip offshore. The sedimentary sequences generally coarsen upward as fluvial deposition replaces nearshore deposition on the delta.
COLLUVIUM	
Sediment Texture	Poorly sorted, subangular to subrounded clay to boulder gravel material. In some environments the finer-grained matrix may be washed away leaving a coarse, angular deposit.
Sedimentary Structures	Poorly developed bedding planes at or near the angle of repose.
Fossils	Rare. At the base of a seacliff beach sediment may fill the interstices between the gravel, and reworked fossils may be

Table 6.1. Characteristics of Coastal Sediments Continued

	deposited in this manner. If colluvium falls into the intertidal zone, barnacles or other intertidal species may occupy the sediments after deposition.
Soils	Usually poorly developed. If deposition is episodic, there may be some reddening and incipient soil formation on bedding planes.
CORAL REEFS	
Sediment Texture	Will be composed of beach, dune, and estuarine sediments with the same textures and structures as those found in other nearshore environments. The difference between reefs and other coastal zones is the abundance of biogenic carbonate clasts. On beaches between a coral reef and a volcanic or continental highland the beach sediment will be a mix of the two sources. On atolls the beach and dunes may be composed exclusively of biogenic sediment. Because of the abundance of carbonate in solution, beach rock is more common in beaches adjacent to reefs than in other environments.
TSUNAMI DEPOSITS	
Sediment Texture	Coarse- to fine-grained sediment. Sediment will be distinctly allochthonous and contrast starkly with the background sediment in the region.
Sedimentary Structures	Washover structures, beds that dip landward, "bathtub ring" deposits in closed depressions, distinct and abrupt changes in sediment texture with clear basal contacts.
Fossils	Allochthonous fossils washed into a region.
Soils	If the sediment is washed into a terrestrial environment, subaerial soil may form on what appears to be a subaqueous deposit.

sedimentary unit we observe its composition, texture, sedimentary structures, and depositional architecture. Ideally, these studies combine field and laboratory analysis as neither approach by itself can fully describe and characterize the sediment (Stein 1992c, 2001; Stein et al. 1992). A variety of texts and manuals provide useful descriptions of the specific techniques (Boggs 1992; Folk 1974; Gale and Hoare 1991; Singer and Janitsky 1986). Typical field descriptions include sediment texture (grain-size distribution), color, sedimentary structures, description of bounding surfaces, soil horizonation, and fossil identification. Typical laboratory analysis may include grain size, organic matter content, mineralogy, microfossil identification, carbonate content, and trace element analysis. This section will describe the nature of sediments deposited in specific environments. A summary of the predominant sediment characteristics for each environment is presented in Table 6.1.

Beaches

Beach sediment is continually washed by wave action and littoral drift. On most beaches wave energy is sufficient to remove silt and clay from the nearshore, leaving sand and gravel behind. Waves and currents are very effective at sorting sediments both vertically on the beach face and along shore. Large storm waves can throw gravel onto the berm well above sea level. Gravel storm berms have been measured with heights up to 13 m above mean sea level (Sunamura 1989). Vertical sorting results from the relationship between wave size and its ability to transport sediment: the coarsest debris is deposited high and the finer sediment low on the beach face. Storm surges and washover may leave coarse sediment and driftwood well inland of the shoreline. In San Francisco Bay, I have observed early historic artifacts incorporated within storm surge deposits. Longshore drift combined with lateral changes in wave energy result in grain-size sorting along the shore (Komar 1998).

Wave action is effective at rounding and polishing the clasts (rock fragments) into shapes ranging from spheres to rods to disks. In coastal Peru resistant beach clasts were a source of raw material for stone tool manufacture (Wells 1988; Wells and Noller 1999). Wave action in the nearshore produces a predictable set of sedimentary structures (Clifton et al. 1971). On the beach face gravel clasts and sediment packages dip gently shoreward. Bar migration yields packages of sediment with planar or cross laminations that dip either onshore or offshore dependent upon the direction of bedform migration. Bedding planes are well defined as wave action is very effective at sorting heavy minerals (e.g., magnetite, ilmenite, amphibole) from less dense carbonate and silicate grains (e.g., quartz, feldspar, calcite).

The high energy environment of beaches yields a low preservation potential for archaeological materials that might have been present within an aggradational sequence. However the frequency of sites on ancient beach berms in Peru (Ortlieb et al. 1993; Richardson 1983; Wells and Noller 1999; Wilson 1988) would suggest that these areas have been common occupational locations throughout prehistory.

Dunes

Sediment reworked by persistent onshore winds is deposited as dunes. Winds are extremely effective at sorting sediment, and the range of grain size in eolian deposits is very narrow, usually medium to fine sand. There may be no textural difference between the source beach sediment and the reworked dune sediment. Asymmetric ripples, the most common eolian bedform, leave a variety of large- and small-scale cross laminations and tabular strata (Hunter

1977). Dune slip faces most commonly dip landward while the tabular packages of climbing strata will dip shoreward.

Coastal dunes support and can be stabilized by salt-tolerant vegetation. This vegetation traps eolian sediment, and facilitates soil formation. Sand dune sediments may, at times, be distinguished from beach sediment by buried soils and higher organic carbon content. Midden soils and artifacts may also be interbedded within the dune sequences (Gilbertson et al. 1999).

Dune sediment can easily be transported into an archaeological site (Akrotiri, Cyprus, Simmons 1999; Tabun Cave, Israel, Jelinek et al. 1974; Farrand 2001). Eolian sand can fill any small depression that forms within a coastal environment. Small, isolated eolian deposits would be recognized as well-sorted, usually unconsolidated, sand to granule-sized material. Well-developed cross stratification may be present, but it is often difficult to observe the sedimentary structures of loose sediment.

Estuaries and Marshes

In protected embayments tidal action predominates over wave action resulting in a unique set of landforms constructed of fine-grained sediment: tidal flats, tidal marshes, mangrove swamps, and tidal channels. Landforms are vertically stratified with respect to tidal range and position. Strong tidal currents produce large subtidal sand bars and box-shaped channels lined with a shell or gravel lag. Weak tidal currents deposit mud and clay on shallow flats. The lower intertidal zone is occupied by mudflats and the upper intertidal zone by salt or brackish marsh.

Distinctive sediments characterize marsh environments. Mudflat sediment is a mix of silt and clay, with high iron content and an in situ molluscan fauna. Tidal marsh peat is a mix of very fine-grained clay and silt with high organic content. Storms wash coarse debris onto the marsh plain. Marshes in tectonically stable environments build up and out, gradually infilling the embayment. Shell mounds constructed on salt marshes surrounding San Francisco Bay, California, may have in part served to lift the settlement above high water (Lightfoot 1997).

Colluvium

Colluvium is not classically considered a part of coastal sedimentation; however, gravitational deposits frequently collect at the base of sea cliffs and within caves along sea cliffs. Wave action undercuts sea cliffs, forming a notch at about mean sea level (Sunamura 1976, 1977). The resulting overhang will eventually become unstable and fail. Depending on the geology of the sea cliff, landslides may also be important sediment sources. The rate of production of colluvial sediment is not constant, and particularly stormy years may result in very high rates of coastal erosion and colluvial sediment flux (Lajoie and Mathieson 1998). Colluvial sediments form a drape at the base of a cliff that is immediately available to coastal processes for reworking. The sediment becomes rounded and finer grained as it is worked down the coast by littoral currents. Where the coast progrades in front of a sea cliff, colluvial deposits will interfinger with beach sediment.

Sea cliff caves are potential rockshelter locations for human habitation (Albert et al. 1999; Barton et al. 1999; Simmons 1999). Once the sea cliff is abandoned due to progradation or regression, colluvial materials will bury both archaeological debris and coastal sediments along the paleoshoreline. Gravitational erosion will continue after the shoreline has receded, but the rate of erosion will decrease when undercutting and oversteepening by waves ceases.

Coral Reefs

Coral reefs are biologically constructed landforms. Their distribution is controlled by water temperature, and therefore, they are more common on the warm western side of the tropical ocean basins than on the cooler eastern side. The reef is built of carbonate precipitated by stony corals and coralline algae, and only small amounts of inorganic or siliciclastic materials are present on the reef. Littoral processes break the precipitated material into clastic sediment that is available for transport and reworking. Sediment transport mechanisms are identical to those that occur on continental shorelines. Atolls are built of storm, beach, and dune sediments surrounding a lagoon. One important difference between coralline and other environments is related to the soluble nature of the substrate and the resulting caves and notches on uplifted islands.

Kirch (1984, 1986) detailed the Holocene history of human migration onto the Pacific islands. The nutrient-depleted soils of coral islands limit the viability of introduced and native organisms as well as the human population that any island can support. Species introduced as part of the subsistence strategy of colonizing people may deplete the natural resources of the island environments.

Sediment Deposited Directly by Humans

For the most part, geological sediments that enclose or are found within coastal archaeological sites fit into one of the categories described above. Harbors and shell middens—depositional environments unique to anthropogenic contexts—are discussed here.

Harbors

Artificial harbors are effectively man-made estuaries or lagoons, where breakwaters have been constructed to reduce wave energy. The construction of breakwaters interrupts littoral drift, and this combined with decreased wave energy can result in net accumulation of sediment within the harbor (Komar 1998; Weigel 1964). An anthropogenic harbor will also include evidence for its human construction and the history of its use. An excellent example of the kinds of information that can be gained from facies analysis of harbor sediments is presented in the work of Reinhardt and colleagues (1994, 1998) based on the underwater excavations at the Roman harbor of Caesarea Maritima in Israel. In these works Reinhardt and colleagues use a combination of sedimentology, biostratigraphy, and geochemistry to define biofacies and harbor facies that are used to interpret the prehistory of the Caesarea Harbor between 21 B.C. and A.D. 1265.

The Caesarea Harbor Facies are defined as follows (Reinhardt and Raban 1999). The Pre-Harbor Facies is composed of high-energy sands (well-sorted medium to fine sand with occasional coarse interbeds) with abundant shell fragments and lacking pottery. This facies was deposited directly on a submerged terrestrial soil or bedrock surface. The Harbor Construction Facies is a cobble rubble (local bedrock and concrete) in a granule-to-sand matrix with abundant biologic erosion or encrustations and pottery sherds. The Harbor Facies is composed of moderately- to well-sorted silt/clay and sands beds with occasional coarse interbeds, organic concentrations, or angular pottery sherds. The Post-Harbor Facies is similar to the Pre-Harbor Facies except that it includes well-rounded pottery sherds. Further excavations in 1997 and 1998 (Reinhardt, pers. comm.) indicate that the Harbor Construction Facies and Harbor Facies also include cobble-sized clasts that are foreign to the region and are interpreted to represent imported ship ballast. The Post-Harbor Facies also included evidence for purposeful filling of the harbor with human garbage. Integrating these data with geochemical and biofacies analyses (proxy data for water depth and changes in salinity) allows the authors to reconstruct the construction of harbor moles, their subsequent destruction by an earthquake in the first or second century A.D., the growth of sand bars on the submerged mole, the purposeful infilling of the harbor in the seventh century A.D., and a return to high energy conditions through its demise in the thirteenth century A.D. (Reinhardt and Raban 1999; Reinhardt et al. 1994, 1998).

Shell Middens

Shell middens are conspicuous anthropogenic deposits of shells, gravel, sand, silt, charcoal, artifacts, and other cultural and geological remains. They may occur as solitary deposits or in association with architectural sites. Shell middens span a broad range of archaeological periods, and some were built during historic times (e.g., Georgia, USA, Crook 1992). They are located adjacent to an aquatic environment that presumably provided the source of the shell materials; shell midden deposits are often intercalated with nearshore sediments (Aten 1983; Stein 1992a). When shellfish are harvested as a resource, there is a very large quantity of refractory refuse (the shell) compared to other aquatic resources (Mason et al. 1998; Stein 1992a). Extensive deposits of shell may therefore accumulate, either purposefully or inadvertently, and the physical nature of shells (porosity, permeability, alkalinity, rate of weathering, and decomposition) will impact the depositional and post-depositional history of the deposit (Stein 1992a, 1992c).

Stein et al. (1992) define a method of facies taxonomy for the stratigraphic study of shell middens using field and lab techniques developed in the study of the British Camp Midden in Washington State. The following characteristics of each excavation unit are described in the field: clast size, clast composition, clast condition, clast type abundance, and color. The excavation units are grouped into facies based on similarities of these characteristics, allowing for the correlation of lithostratigraphic units between adjacent excavation blocks. Larger groupings of lithofacies into layers allowed for broader correlations across the site. Each individual facies was interpreted to represent an "'individual dumping event' when prehistoric people brought material together from some combination of activities and deposited them in one location" (Stein et al. 1992:97). The shell midden is thus treated as an anthropogenic sedimentary deposit for analysis (Stein 1992b). Post-excavation stratigraphic analysis allowed for the definition of ethnozones (stratigraphic units with similar artifactual material), geochronometric units (unit age estimates based on ^{14}C analysis), and ethnochronozones (ethnostratigraphic units deposited during discrete periods of time). Sedimentologic analysis of the deposits (grain size, pH, carbonate, organic, and phosphorus content) was used to interpret the impacts of weathering on the stratigraphy. The stratigraphic and sedimentologic methodology developed by Stein (1992a) was fundamental in interpreting the relative importance of cultural, depositional, and post-depositional processes in the formation of the shell midden.

Geochronological Control: Problems with Marine Radiocarbon Age Estimates

Stratigraphic study and environmental reconstructions are heavily reliant on geochronological control. The most widely used geochronometer for estimating the ages of late Pleistocene and Holocene events is ^{14}C analysis. The method relies upon the incorporation of radioactive ^{14}C into the structure of

living organisms and its subsequent decay to ^{14}N (half life of 5,730 years) upon
the death of the organism. ^{14}C is produced in the upper atmosphere by the interaction of cosmic rays with ^{14}N, and the rate of production is not constant
through time, such that calibration is required to compare ^{14}C age estimates
with calendar dates (Stuiver and Reimer 1993). Additional corrections must be
made if the reservoir from which an organism is deriving its C is either depleted or enriched in ^{14}C (Stuiver and Braziunas 1993). Because of high
turnover rates in the atmosphere, ^{14}C is reasonably well mixed within each
hemisphere; however, the southern hemisphere is depleted in ^{14}C by an
amount equivalent to 40 ^{14}C years (Vogel et al. 1993). As the ocean has a much
slower turnover and mixing rate, it is consistently depleted in ^{14}C. On average,
the depletion of the surface ocean is estimated at an amount equivalent to 400
^{14}C years, but this amount is not constant through time or space (Stuiver and
Braziunas 1993). Stuiver and Braziunas (1993) modeled the average variation in
the depletion of the oceanic ^{14}C throughout the Holocene. The modeled depletion is referred to as reservoir age, R(t).

Spatial and temporal variations in R(t) are expected based on climate-
induced changes in the global carbon reservoirs that are not accounted for in
the model of Stuiver and Braziunas (1993). These local variances from the
global model are referred to as ΔR and need to be accounted for, if marine and
terrestrial ^{14}C age estimates are to be compared. Unfortunately, very few studies have been done that attempt to account for spatial and temporal variances
in ΔR through time. The exception to this situation is the work of Ingram and
colleagues (Ingram 1998; Ingram and Southon 1996; Kennett et al. 1997) along
the eastern Pacific coastline. Modern ΔR values are observed to vary from 220
to 410 ^{14}C years (regional averages reported in Ingram and Southon 1996)
while ancient ΔR values calculated using paired charcoal and shell samples
from archaeological middens showed that ΔR has varied from 870 to -170 ^{14}C
years over the last 5,000 years (Ingram 1998; Kennett et al. 1997). Previously
unpublished ^{14}C age estimates from two charcoal/shell pairs collected from
middens in coastal Peru suggest a minimal range of ΔR values from -400 to
-60 over the past 5,000 years (Table 6.2). DeVries and Wells (1990) interpreted
the Huaynuna pair to indicate that shallow nearshore environments along the
coast of Peru were in equilibrium with the atmosphere. However, Ingram
(1998) and Kennett et al. (1997) interpret similar changes in coastal California
to reflect changing nearshore oceanography, and this explanation is equally
plausible for the Peruvian data.

Ingram and Southon (1996) have also observed that contemporary shells of
different species may have widely varying ΔR values. In modern environments

Table 6.2. Comparison of ^{14}C Ages on Shell and Charcoal from Archaeological Middens in Northern Coastal Peru

	QUEBRADA RIO SECO						HUAYNUNA	
Material	Shell	Charcoal	Charcoal	Wood	Charcoal	Charcoal	Shell	Charcoal
Lab Number (SMU):	1712	1709	1710	1699	1707	1708	2022	2023
$\delta^{13}C$ per mil	+1.42	-24.10	-24.52	-23.58	-23.61	-23.78	+1.1	-17.3
Age ^{14}C yr BP	1010 ± 30	650 ± 25	520 ±40	790 ± 40	780 ± 20	710 ± 25	4474 ± 34	4456 ± 136
Marine ^{14}C age yr BP*	1010-1100		950	1150	1150	1120		4900
ΔR ^{14}C years		45 ± 45	60	-140	-140	-110	-400	
AGE RANGE CAL YR BP								
Terrestrial model†	940-920 680-640	650-560	545-615	725-670	705-670	670-650	4701-4565 5075-5250	5306-4856

* Determined from Stuiver and Braziunas (1993, Fig. 15).
† Using Calib 3.0 (Stuiver and Reimer 1993) and the Stuiver and Pearson (1993) data set.
§ Using Calib 3.0 (Stuiver and Reimer 1993) and the Stuiver and Braziunas (1993) data set. The Huaynuna sample was calibrated with ΔR = -400; the Quebrada Rio Seco sample was calibrated with each of the ΔR values and the sum of the probabilities calculated.

along the Pacific coast, interspecies variances in ΔR of contemporary shells from a single location were as great as 570 ^{14}C years (Ingram and Southon 1996). Interspecies variances in ^{14}C age of shells collected from single depth in San Francisco Bay sediment cores were as great as 1,360 ^{14}C years. To further confound the issue, the interspecies difference in ΔR were not constant either spatially or temporally. Unfortunately, the current state of this research yields more questions than answers. Extreme care must be taken in interpreting any geochronological data based on ^{14}C age estimates from marine carbonate. Ideally, paired charcoal/shell samples would be analyzed (using a single species of marine organism) to determine the variations in ΔR through time at a place, and these estimates used for calibration of other ^{14}C age estimates on the same marine species. At the very least, age estimates from marine carbon should be calibrated using the marine model of Stuiver and Braziunas (1993) with local estimates of the modern range of ΔR values and always maintaining the 2-sigma error estimates.

The Geomorphologic Context of Coastal Settlements

Humans rely upon resources from a regional mix of environments, not simply those proximal to the settlement. The physical bounds of the resource base are dependent upon many cultural and environmental factors. In coastal zones, geomorphologic and geographic controls result in predictable mosaics of environments and ecosystems. As the shoreline evolves through time, the environmental mosaic will evolve, and therefore, the resource base of a settlement will evolve. This section will discuss the sedimentary and environmental evolution of region-scale landforms: deltas, littoral complexes, estuaries, and rocky shorelines.

Deltas

Deltas form where rivers deposit sediment directly into a standing body of water, either the ocean, a lake, or a reservoir. Deltas are progradational complexes of river sediments reworked by littoral and/or estuarine processes. Most delta sediment is fine grained (sand, silt, clay), the coarse load having been deposited upstream. However, where tectonic conditions create short, steep drainage basins that directly enter a standing body of water, the deltas will be built of coarse sediment (sand and gravel).

Deltas are classed into types corresponding to the dominant landforms. Low-gradient deltas built by large rivers are classified as river-dominated (e.g.,

Mississippi River Delta, USA), wave-dominated (e.g., Sao Francisco Delta, Brazil), or tide-dominated (e.g., Ganges-Brahmaputra Delta, India; Elliot 1986; Galloway 1975; Wright 1985). Steep, coarse-grained deltas are classified as fan deltas or braid deltas (Nemec 1990; Nemec and Steel 1988). These types should be considered end-members along a spectrum, and most deltas fall somewhere between the end-member classifications.

Fan deltas are relatively steep features that form where high-relief mountains are located adjacent to the shoreline. Fluvial processes will dominate the proximal fan as it gradually buries the littoral deposits of the distal fan (Nemec 1990). Fan deltas are typical of the steep coastal zone of Peru (Wells 1988, 1992). Wells (1992) showed that a correlation could be made between progradation of the Rio Santa fan delta (Peru) and the chronology of settlement expansion onto the delta through the Holocene. Niemi (1990) documents a tectonically induced transgressive/regressive cycle on the distal margins of a fan delta on that Euboean Gulf Plain (Greece) that resulted in the submergence and partial burial of Roman to Byzantine sites.

Modern delta deposition began between 8 and 5 ka as sea levels stabilized (Stanley and Warne 1997). The rich soils of the deltas (for example, the Yangtze or Nile) supported an abundance of subsistence resources and created a substrate ideal for agriculture (Stanley and Warne 1997; Wells and Noller 1999). Stanley and Warne (1997) document 34 archaeological sites representing every continent (e.g., Mississippi Delta, Orinoco Delta, Danube Delta, Nile Delta, Indus Delta, and the Murray Delta) where the shift from hunter-gatherer and migratory adaptations to agricultural and sedentary adaptations is coincident with early Holocene delta formation. They propose that antecedent and coincident technological developments allowed humans to quickly exploit this productive and newly formed ecological niche (Stanley and Warne 1997).

Littoral Complexes

Where the sediment supply along the shoreline is greater than that which can be removed by littoral drift, broad complexes of beach and nearshore deposits may accrete to the shoreline. Much of the coast of the Carolinas (USA) is made up of such drift, accumulated over multiple phases of sea level rise and fall (Gayes et al. 1992; Moslow and Heron 1994; Riggs et al. 1992; Sexton et al. 1992). They may form down-drift of deltas or along the shore of sediment-rich coasts. As sediment is transported along the coast it forms beach berms and dunes that are aligned with either the swash (wave crest) direction or the drift direction.

Barriers are low sedimentary landforms that extend into a body of water where there is a dramatic change in the orientation of the coastline, for example at the mouth of an estuary or fjord. If the rate of sediment supply is not constant through time, for example when the coastline erodes away a discrete sedimentary deposit, the barrier may form, retreat landward, and then disappear (Carter et al. 1989). With sea level rise, or an increase in storm frequency, coarse-grained barriers may "roll over" landward (i.e., the sediment in the barrier is gradually reworked landward by washover events). Numerous studies have tracked the Holocene evolution of large Atlantic coast barriers in response to changes in sediment supply, sea level rise, and climate variability (Colquhoun et al. 1991). Barrier islands on the Georgia coast (USA) have the remains of precontact occupations from 2500 B.C. to A.D. 1540 (Crook 1992). Crook (1984, 1992) documents increasing social complexity coincident with the establishment of sedentism during this time from shell middens on Sapelo Island, Georgia. While there are changes in the nature of the exploited environments, Crook (1992) believes that shell resources were always of secondary importance on Sapelo Island.

Beach ridges are shore-parallel mounds of littoral or eolian sediment with intervening swales filled with sandy nearshore sediment. Changes in ridge plan-form reflect changes in wave conditions, storminess, sediment supply, sea level, or river mouth/inlet morphology (Anthony 1991; Mason and Jordan 1993; Tanner 1988; Wells 1996). Beach ridge plains in Peru and Alaska have small archaeological sites scattered across them (Machare and Ortlieb 1990; Mason and Jordan 1993; Ortlieb et al. 1993). Ortlieb et al. (1993) analyzed radiocarbon dates from shell middens in northern Peru and showed that the spatial-temporal stratigraphy of the middens was parallel to that of the ridges. At the Santa Beach ridge complex in coastal Peru, very young middens and wind shelters appear to be scattered across ridges of various ages (Wells 1988).

Cheniers are shore-parallel ridges of coarse clastic sediment (sand, gravel, or shells) separated by fine-grained intertidal mudflats or marshes. The mudflats are deposited when the local sedimentation rate is high relative to the rate of reworking; cheniers are deposited when littoral reworking is high relative to the local sedimentation rate. Similar to beach ridges, chenier ridges are common loci for human settlement, roads, and agriculture as they allow inhabitants to "keep their feet dry" above the surrounding wetlands (Sullivan and O'Conner 1993). In northern Australia, prehistoric middens were built on the cheniers, and Sullivan and O'Conner (1993) document clear differences between midden fauna (anthropogenically sorted) and chenier fauna (geologically sorted).

Estuaries and Lagoons

An estuary is a tidal inlet of the sea that is protected from the action of open ocean swell. While "estuary" is the inclusive term, it is sometimes reserved for those inlets where mixing occurs between fresh water and marine water; the term "lagoon" is reserved for tidal inlets with no fresh water source. Estuaries and lagoons are located behind a barrier that absorbs and refracts wave energy. Late Pleistocene and early Holocene sea-level rise resulted in the drowning of coastal valleys such that estuaries were more common and extensive then.

Estuaries are effective sediment traps filled with a mix of fine-grained sediments deposited in a variety of microenvironments (Dalrymple et al. 1992). Mixing of salt and fresh water enhances sedimentation within estuaries by causing suspended clay and organic particles, as well as dissolved solids, to flocculate (stick together) into larger particles.

Lagoons are filled with coarser sediment predominantly supplied by longshore drift. Sediment accumulates in sandbars whose morphology reflects the strength and flow paths of tidal currents (Dalrymple and Rhodes 1995; DeVries and Wells 1990). Where evaporation rates are high, lagoon salinity and temperature may exceed that of the open ocean. If the lagoon becomes stranded from tidal circulation, evaporative pumping will form a salt pan (a.k.a. *sabkha* or *salinas*) where salts accumulate. Mining of the salt from these regions has probably been an important economic resource throughout the Holocene Epoch.

Harbors are either located in natural estuaries or breakwaters are constructed to form an artificial estuary. All processes that occur in natural estuaries will also occur in artificial harbors. The eventual infilling of harbors means that, in the absence of dredging, abandonment is inevitable. Harbors that are located in ancient embayments suffer the same geomorphologic evolution as does the shoreline: they may be stranded many kilometers inland as a result of shoreline progradation or become submerged on transgressive coasts. Stranded harbors are common in the Mediterranean, either resulting from progradation (Ephesus, Foss 1979; Dimini, Zangger 1991), uplift (Lechaion, Wiseman 1978), or subsidence (Kenchreai, Noller et al. 1997).

Dalrymple et al. (1992) described the progression of sediments and ecosystems that occur as an estuary or lagoon fills during and subsequent to a period of sea-level rise. This sedimentary sequence observed on modern progradational coasts indicates that the timing of the shift from erosion to sedimentation is dependent upon the local sedimentation rate. Estuarine ecosystems evolve in phase with the evolution of the sedimentary system. This biologic

Figure 6.5. High-tide shore platform in northern coastal Peru. This platform is flooded only during extreme high tide and storm events.

resource change is then reflected in the changing subsistence remains of coastal occupations (DeVries and Wells 1990; Rollins et al. 1990; Shackleton and van Andel 1986).

Rocky Shorelines

Recessional shorelines are typified by sea cliffs and shore platforms (Fig. 6.5). These erosional shorelines are found worldwide and are particularly common on the sediment-poor coasts of the western Americas (cf., Trenhaile 1987) The morphology of the coast will be strongly controlled by the geology of the coastline. A tidal platform generally occurs somewhere between the elevation of mean low water and extreme high water (Bird 1984:64). Exposed platforms are covered with discontinuous deposits of littoral sediment. The tide pools on these surfaces host a variety of fauna that may be a locally important subsistence resource.

Shell middens adjacent to sea cliffs are vulnerable to loss during periods of rapid coastal erosion (e.g., Huaynuna, Peru, Pozorski and Pozorski 1987). Reworked archaeological debris may accumulate in the colluvium at the base of the sea cliff and then be reworked along the shoreline as littoral deposits. Because active erosion is required to maintain sea cliffs, there is a high potential that early occupation sites in these areas have been lost.

Recognition of Paleoshorelines

A variety of geomorphologic and sedimentary features can mark the location of ancient shorelines. Ancient coastlines will reflect the dominant processes attendant upon the coast during their formation, and therefore they will fit into one of the many coastal classifications discussed earlier. On progradational coasts, the shorelines will be marked by depositional features, such as beach ridges or cheniers (Tanner 1988; Wells 1996). On erosional coasts, paleoshorelines will be marked by notches or platforms and sea cliffs. An example of the recognition of paleoshorelines and their cultural context in Korinth follows.

Complicated tectonics across the Isthmian Plain of Korinth, Greece, result in uplifted shorelines and a stranded harbor along the Gulf of Korinth, and subsided shorelines and a submerged harbor along the Saronic Gulf (Fig. 6.6; Noller et al. 1997; Stiros 1988). Lechaion and Kenchreai were both active ports during the Roman occupation of the region, beginning sometime before 100 B.C. (Wiseman 1978). To walk from Lechaion to Kenchreai one crosses a stair-stepping set of ancient marine platforms and seacliffs, the undulating Isthmian Plain where old shore platforms are deformed and locally back tilted, and finally one drops down abruptly into Kechries Bay (Fig. 6.7a, 6.7b). If you continue to swim offshore from Kenchreai you will observe not only the submerged port and harbor moles, but a number of small notches eroded into limestone bedrock that mark submerged late Holocene shorelines (Fig. 6.7c).

On the northern side of the Isthmian Plain, terrace treads are the remnants of Pleistocene marine platforms, and terrace risers are the remnants of Pleistocene sea cliffs (Fig. 6.7b). The marine platforms are buried by multiple sequences of carbonate conglomerates suggesting that each of the lower platforms was submerged during multiple sea-level high stands. The shoreline angle is defined as the inflection point between the inland edge of the terrace tread and the lower edge of the riser. The shoreline angle position is considered a proxy for the position of sea level when it reached its highest stand associated with the cutting of the terrace tread. Planform maps of the location of the shoreline angle represent maps of paleoshoreline positions (Lajoie et al. 1991). In planform, paleoshorelines are generally concave seaward, with erosional forms similar to a modern shoreline. In contrast, the high riser on the east side of the Isthmus (at 11 km on Fig. 6.7a) is a linear feature transverse to both modern coastline and the Pleistocene shorelines. Investigations of this feature are still in progress to determine if this terrace riser was generated by faulting, shoreline erosion, or fluvial incision.

At the site of Lechaeon, two stranded harbors (one on either side of the mound marked L on Fig. 6.7b) are present (Wiseman 1978). The moles of the

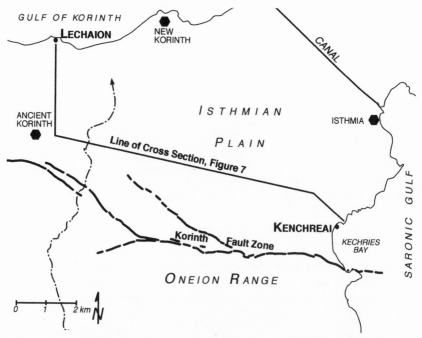

Figure 6.6. The Isthmian Plain research area. The cross sections in Figure 6.7a and 6.7b follow the marked line. The subtidal cross section (Fig. 6.7c) measured on rocky convolute shoreline just northeast of the south end of Figure 6.7a.

exterior harbor are expressed as small inflections of the coastline north of Lechaeon on Figure 6.7a; the remains of these moles now extend only a few meters into the waters of the gulf. The harbor extended inland between the moles to the face of a gravel mound. Most of this exterior harbor is now a gravel-filled plain less than 1 m above sea level. Behind the mound, a protected harbor is stranded above mean sea level. This old waterway is now a flat muddy plain. The remnants of harbor walls surround the mudflat. The blocks in the walls bear *lithofaga* (molluscan) borings indicating that these structures were once submerged in the intertidal zone. The elevation of the *lithofaga* borings (about 1 m) represents the minimal amount of emergence of the harbor (Stiros 1988).

On the eastern side of the Isthmian Plain, the port of Kenchreai is partially submerged below the bay (Noller et al. 1997; Scranton et al. 1978; Wiseman 1978). Submerged floors and architectural features indicate the port has subsided about 2.3 m in the last 1,900 years (Scranton et al. 1978). Scranton et al. (1978) interpret the stratigraphy at Kenchreai to indicate at least three cata-

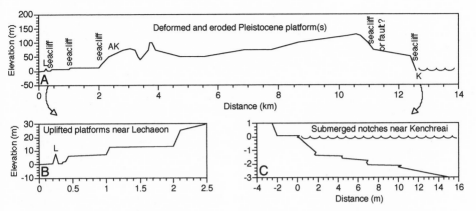

Figure 6.7. Simplified topographic cross sections across the Isthmian Plain. Emergent Pleistocene marine terraces indicate tectonic uplift (relative sea level fall) in the north (left),
while submerged sites and notches indicate tectonic subsidence (relative sea level rise) in the
east (east). L indicates the location of the Roman port of Lechaion; K indicates the location
of the Roman port of Kenchreai, AK indicates the location of the Roman city of Korinth.
Note the differences in scale between the three cross sections.

strophic subsidence events, each accounting for 70 to 80 cm of submergence.
The last event resulted in the submergence of packing crates that still contained the remnants of glass mosaics when they were excavated in the
mid-1960s. Submerged rocky shorelines north and south of Kenchreai have up
to five eroded notches within 2.5 m of the surface of the sea (Fig. 6.7c; Noller
et al. 1997). Below 2.5 m in depth the slope of the seafloor decreases and is
eventually covered with fine-grained sediment. Each notch is a paleoshoreline
cut during the intervening stillstand of relative sea level by a combination of
wave erosion, dissolution, and bioerosion. Combining the geological and archaeological data, we document three significant subsidence events in the last
2,000 years and two late Holocene subsidence events prior to 2 ka. The area
with the highest amounts of displacement during a single event appears to be
centered at Kenchreai (Noller et al. 1997).

Summary

Coastlines are dynamic environments that evolve on time scales ranging from
seconds to millennia. Waves, tides, and currents sort the available sediment
into a predictable set of landforms. Changes in sediment type, sedimentary
structures, and the included fauna can be used to reconstruct coastal environments. Paleoshoreline positions can be reconstructed using the distribution of

landform indicators and facies transitions. Integrating this information through time allows for the reproduction of the prehistoric landscapes settled by coastal people (Wells 2001).

The Holocene transition to a sedentary lifestyle was at least locally coincident with the stabilization of sea level that resulted in a relatively stationary resource base (Stanley and Warne 1997; Wells and Noller 1999). Sedimentary facies changes and ecosystem evolution have resulted in changes in the spatial patterning of sites through time (Stanley and Chen 1996; Wells 1992, 2000) and changes in the subsistence resource base (DeVries and Wells 1990; Shackleton and van Andel 1986).

Acknowledgments

Fieldwork in Peru was supported by the National Science Foundation. Fieldwork in Greece has been supported by the Ohio State University Excavations at Isthmia (Tim Gregory, Director). The research in Korinthia is a collaborative effort with Jay Noller, Richard Rothaus, and Ed Reinhardt. Jay Noller collaborated in the studies of geomorphology and stratigraphy in Peru. Herbert Haas analyzed the radiocarbon samples from coastal Peru. While I am indebted to the contributions of my colleagues, this work, and all errors therein, are fully my responsibility.

References Cited

Albert, R. M., O. Lavi, L. Estroff, S. Weiner, A. Tsatskin, A. Ronen, and S. Lev-Yadun
1999   Mode of Occupation of Tabun Cave, Mt. Carmel, Israel, during the Mousterian Period: A Study of the Sediments and Phytoliths. *Journal of Archaeological Science* 26:1249–1260.

Anthony, E. J.
1991   Beach-Ridge Plain Development: Sherbro Island, Sierra Leone. *Zeitschrift für Geomorphologie* Suppl. Band 81:85–98.

Aten, L. E.
1983   *Indians of the Upper Texas Coast.* Academic Press, New York.

Barton, R. N. E., A. P. Currant, Y. Fernandez-Jalvo, J. C. Finlayson, P. Goldberg, R. Macphail, P. B. Pettitt, and C. B. Stringer
1999   Gibraltar Neanderthals and Results of Recent Excavations in Gorham's, Vanguard and Ibex Caves. *Antiquity* 73:13–22.

Bird, E. C. F.
1984   *Coasts: An Introduction to Coastal Geomorphology.* Basil Blackwell, Oxford.

Bloom, A. L.
1983   Sea Level and Coastal Morphology of the United States through the Late Wisconsin Glacial Maximum. In *Late Quaternary Environments of the U.S.,* edited by H. E. Wright, pp. 215–229. University of Minnesota Press, Minneapolis.

Boggs, S., Jr.
1992   *Petrology of Sedimentary Rocks.* Macmillan, New York.
Carter, R. W. G., D. L. Forbes, S. C. Jennings, J. D. Orford, J. Shaw, and R. B. Taylor
1989   Barrier and Lagoon Coast Evolution under Differing Relative Sea Level Regimes: Examples from Ireland and Nova Scotia. *Marine Geology* 88:221–242.
Clark, J. A., W. E. Farrell, and W. R. Peltier
1978   Global Changes in Post-Glacial Sea Level: A Numerical Calculation. *Quaternary Research* 9:265–287.
Clark, J. A., and C. S. Lingle
1979   Predicted Relative Sea-Level Changes (18000 Years B.P. to Present) Caused by Late-Glacial Retreat of the Antarctic Ice Sheet. *Quaternary Research* 11:279–298.
Clifton, H. E., R. E. Hunter, and R. L. Phillips
1971   Depositional Structures and Processes in the Non-Barred High-Energy Nearshore. *Journal of Sedimentary Petrology* 41:651–670.
Colquhoun, D. J., G. H. Johnson, P. C. Peebles, P. F. Huddlestun, and T. Scott
1991   Quaternary Geology of the Atlantic Coastal Plain. In *Quaternary Nonglacial Geology: Conterminous U.S.,* edited by R. B. Morrison, pp. 629–650. The Geology of North America, vol. K-2. Geological Society of America, Boulder, Colorado.
Crook, M. R., Jr.
1984   Evolving Community Organization on the Georgia Coast. *Journal of Field Archaeology* 11:247–263.
1992   Oyster Sources and Their Prehistoric Use on the Georgia Coast. *Journal of Archaeological Science* 19:483–496.
Curray, J. R.
1964   Transgression and Regressions. In *Papers in Marine Geology, Shepard Commemorative Volume,* edited by R. L. Miller, pp. 175–203. Macmillan, New York.
Curray, J. R., F. J. Emmel, and P. J. S. Crampton
1967   Holocene History of a Strand Plain. In *Lagoonal Coast, Nayarit, Mexico, Lagunas Costeras: Un Simposio,* edited by A. A. Costonares and G. B. Phleger, pp. 63–100. Universidad National Autónoma de Mexico.
Dalrymple, R. W., and R. N. Rhodes
1995   Estuarine Dunes and Bars. In *Geomorphology and Sedimentology of Estuaries,* edited by G. M. E. Perillo, pp. 359–422. Developments in Sedimentology, vol. 53. Elsevier, Amsterdam.
Dalrymple, R. W., B. A. Zaitlin, and R. Boyd
1992   Estuarine Facies Models: Conceptual Basis and Stratigraphic Implications. *Journal of Sedimentary Petrology* 62:1130–1146.
DeVries, T. J., and L. E. Wells
1990   Thermally-Anomalous Holocene Molluscan Assemblages from Coastal Peru: Evidence for Paleogeographic, Not Climatic Change. *Palaeogeography, Palaeoclimatology, Palaeoecology* 81:11–32.
Elliot, T.
1986   Deltas. In *Sedimentary Environments and Facies,* edited by H. G. Reading, pp. 113–154. Blackwell, Boston.
Fairbanks, R. G.
1989   A 17,000-Year Glacio-Eustatic Sea-Level Record: Influence of Glacial Melting Rates on the Younger Dryas Event and Deep-Ocean Circulation. *Nature* 342:637–642.

Farrand, W. R.

2001   Archaeological Sediments in Rockshelters and Caves. In *Sediments in Archaeological Context,* edited by J. K. Stein and W. R. Farrand. The University of Utah Press, Salt Lake City.

Folk, R. L.

1974   *Petrology of Sedimentary Rocks.* Hemphill, Austin, Texas.

Foss, C.

1979   *Ephesus after Antiquity: A Late Antique, Byzantine and Turkish City.* Cambridge University Press, Cambridge.

Gale, S. J., and P. G. Hoare

1991   *Quaternary Sediments: Petrographic Methods for the Study of Unlithified Rocks.* Halstead Press, New York.

Galloway, W. E.

1975   Process Framework for Describing the Morphologic and Stratigraphic Evolution of Deltaic Depositional Systems. In *Deltas—Models for Exploration,* edited by M. L. Broussard, pp. 87–98. Houston Geological Society, Houston.

Gayes, P. T., D. B. Scott, E. S. Collins, and D. D. Nelson

1992   A Late Holocene Sea-Level Fluctuation in South Carolina. In *Quaternary Coasts of the United States: Marine and Lacustrine Systems,* edited by C. H. Fletcher III and J. F. Wehmiller, pp. 155–160. Special Publication No. 48. Society for Sedimentary Geology, Tulsa, Oklahoma.

Gilbertson, D. D., J.-L. Schwenninger, R. A. Kemp, and E. J. Rhodes

1999   Sand-Drift and Soil Formation along an Exposed North Atlantic Coastline: 14,000 Years of Diverse Geomorphological, Climatic and Human Impacts. *Journal of Archaeological Science* 26:439–469.

Higgins, M. D., and R. Higgins

1996   *A Geological Companion to Greece and the Aegean.* Cornell University Press, Ithaca, New York.

Hunter, R. E.

1977   Basic Types of Stratification in Small Eolian Dunes. *Sedimentology* 24:361–387.

Ingram, B. L.

1998   Differences in Radiocarbon Ages between Shell and Charcoal from a Holocene Shellmound in Northern California. *Quaternary Research* 49:102–110.

Ingram, B. L., and J. R. Southon

1996   Reservoir Ages in Eastern Pacific Coastal and Estuarine Waters. *Radiocarbon* 38:573–582.

Jelinek, A. J., W. R. Farrand, G. Haas, A. Horowitz, and P. Goldberg

1974   New Excavations at the Tabun Cave, Mount Carmel, Israel, 1967–1972: A Preliminary Report. *Paleorient* 1:151–183.

Kajiura, K., and N. Shuto

1990   Tsunamis. In *The Sea,* edited by B. Le Mehaute and D. M. Hanes, pp. 395–420. John Wiley and Sons, New York.

Kennett, D. J., B. L. Ingram, J. M. Erlandson, and P. Walker

1997   Evidence for Temporal Fluctuations in Marine Radiocarbon Reservoir Ages in the Santa Barbara Channel, Southern California. *Journal of Archaeological Science* 24:1051–1059.

Kirch, P. V.

1984   *The Evolution of Polynesian Chiefdoms.* Cambridge University Press, Cambridge.

1986   Rethinking Polynesian History. *Journal of the Polynesian Society* 95:9–40.

Komar, P. D.

1998   *Beach Processes and Sedimentation.* Prentice Hall, Englewood Cliffs, New Jersey.

Lajoie, K. R., and S. A. Mathieson

1998   *1982–83 El Niño Coastal Erosion, San Mateo County, California.* Open-File Report 98-041. U.S. Geological Survey, Washington, D.C.

Lajoie, K. R., D. J. Ponti, C. L. Powell III, S. A. Mathieson, and A. M. Sarna-Wojcicki

1991   Emergence Marine Strandlines and Associated Sediments, Coastal California; a Record of Quaternary Sea-Level Fluctuations, Vertical Tectonic Movements, Climatic Changes, and Coastal Processes. In *Quaternary Nonglacial Geology: Conterminous U.S.,* edited by R. B. Morrison, pp. 190–214. The Geology of North America, vol. K-2. Geological Society of America, Boulder, Colorado.

Lightfoot, K.

1997   Cultural Construction of Coastal Landscapes: A Middle Holocene Perspective from San Francisco Bay. In *Archaeology of the California Coast during the Middle Holocene,* edited by J. Erlandson and M. Glassow, pp. 129–141. Perspectives in California Archaeology, vol. 4. Institute of Archaeology, University of California, Berkeley.

Machare, J., and L. Ortlieb

1990   Global Change Studies in Northwestern Peru: A High Potential for Records of Former El Niño Events. *Instituto Panamericano de Geografía e Historia, Revista Geofísica* 32:153–171.

Mason, O. K., and J. W. Jordan

1993   Heightened North Pacific Storminess during Synchronous Late Holocene Erosion of Northwest Alaska Beach Ridges. *Quaternary Research* 40:50–69.

Mason, R. D., M. L. Peterson, and J. A. Tiffany

1998   Weighing vs. Counting: Measurement Reliability and the California School of Midden Analysis. *American Antiquity* 63:303–324.

Moslow, T. F., and S. D. Heron

1994   The Outer Banks of North Carolina. In *Geology of Holocene Barrier Island Systems,* edited by R. A. Davis, pp. 47–74. Springer-Verlag, Berlin.

Nemec, W.

1990   Deltas—Remarks on Terminology and Classification. In *Coarse-Grained Deltas,* edited by A. Colella and D. B. Prior, pp. 3–12. Blackwell Scientific Publications, Oxford.

Nemec, W., and R. J. Steel

1988   What is a Fan Delta and How Do We Recognize It? In *Fan Deltas: Sedimentology and Tectonic Setting,* edited by W. Nemec and R. J. Steel, pp. 3–13. Blackie, Glasgow.

Niemi, T. M.

1990   Paleoenvironmental History of Submerged Ruins on the Northern Euboean Gulf Coastal Plain, Central Greece. *Geoarchaeology: An International Journal* 5:323–347.

Noller, J. S., L. E. Wells, E. Reinhardt, and R. M. Rothaus

1997   Subsidence of the Harbor at Kenchreai, Saronic Gulf, Greece, during the Earthquakes of A.D. 400 and A.D. 1928. *EOS* 78:636.

Ortlieb, L., M. Fournier, and J. Machare

1993   Beach Ridges and Major el Niño Events in Northern Peru. *Journal of Coastal Research,* Special Issue 17, Holocene Cycles: Climate Sea Level and Sedimentation, pp. 109–117.

Pirazzoli, P. A.
1996   *Sea Level Changes, the Last 20,000 Years.* John Wiley and Sons, Chichester.
Posamentier, H. W., M. T. Jervey, and P. R. Vail
1988   Eustatic Controls on Clastic Deposition I—Conceptual Framework. In *Sea-Level Changes: An Integrated Approach,* edited by C. K. Wilgus, B. S. Hastings, C. G. St. C. Kendall, H. W. Posamentier, C. A. Ross, and J. Van Wagoner, pp.109–124. Special Publication 42. Society of Economic Paleontologists and Mineralogists, Tulsa, Oklahoma.
Pozorski, S., and T. Pozorski
1987   *Early Settlement and Subsistence in the Casma Valley, Peru.* University of Iowa Press, Iowa City.
Reinhardt, E. G., R. T. Patterson, J. Blenkinsop, and A. Raban
1998   Paleoenvironmental Evolution of the Inner Basin of the Ancient Harbor at Caesarea Maritima, Israel: Foraminiferal and Sr Isotopic Evidence. *Revue de Paléobiologie* 17:1–21.
Reinhardt, E. G., R. T. Patterson, and C. J. Schroder-Adams
1994   Geoarchaeology of the Ancient Harbor Site of Caesarea Maritima, Israel: Evidence from Sedimentology and Paleoecology of Benthic Foraminifera. *Journal of Foraminiferal Research* 24:37–48.
Reinhardt, E. G., and A. Raban
1999   Destruction of Herod the Great's Harbor at Caesarea Maritima, Israel—Geoarchaeological Evidence. *Geology* 27(9):811–814.
Richardson, J. B., III
1983   The Chira Beach Ridges, Sea Level Change, and the Origin of Maritime Economies on the Peruvian Coast. *Annals of the Carnegie Museum* 52:265–276.
Riggs, S. R., L. L. York, J. F. Wehmiller, and S. W. Snyder
1992   Depositional Patterns Resulting from High Frequency Quaternary Sea-Level Fluctuations in Northeastern North Carolina. In *Quaternary Coasts of the United States: Marine and Lacustrine Systems,* edited by C. H. Fletcher III and J. F. Wehmiller, pp. 141–153. Special Publication No. 48. Society for Sedimentary Geology, Tulsa, Oklahoma.
Rollins, H. B., D. H. Sandweiss, and J. C. Rollins
1990   Mollusks and Coastal Archaeology: A Review. In *Archaeological Geology of North America,* edited by N. P. Lasca and J. Donahue, pp. 467–478. Geological Society of America, Boulder, Colorado.
Scranton, R., J. W. Shaw, and L. Ibrahim
1978   *Kenchreai Eastern Port of Corinth, I. Topography and Architecture.* E. J. Brill, Leiden.
Sexton, W. J., M. O. Hayes, and D. J. Colquhoun
1992   Evolution of Quaternary Shoal Complexes off the Central South Carolina Coast. In *Quaternary Coasts of the United States: Marine and Lacustrine Systems,* edited by C. H. Fletcher III and J. F. Wehmiller, pp. 161–172. Special Publication No. 48. Society for Sedimentary Geology, Tulsa, Oklahoma.
Shackleton, J. C., and Tj. H. van Andel
1986   Prehistoric Shore Environments, Shellfish Availability, and Shellfish Gathering at Franchthi, Greece. *Geoarchaeology: An International Journal* 1:127–143.
Simmons, A. H.
1999   *Faunal Extinction in an Island Society: Pygmy Hippopotamus Hunters of Cyprus.* Kluwer Academic/Plenum Publishers, New York.

Singer, M. J., and P. Janitsky
1986   *Field and Laboratory Procedures Used in a Soil Chronosequence Study.* U.S. Geological Survey Bulletin 1648. Reston, Virginia.

Stanley, D. J.
1995   A Global Sea-Level Curve for the Late Quaternary: The Impossible Dream? *Marine Geology* 125:1–6.

Stanley, D. J., and Z. Chen
1996   Neolithic Settlement Distributions as a Function of Sea Level Controlled Topography in the Yangtze Delta, China. *Geology* 24:1083–1086.

Stanley, D. J., and A. G. Warne
1997   Holocene Sea-Level Change and Early Human Utilization of Deltas. *GSA Today* 7:1–7.

Stein, J. K.
1992a   The Analysis of Shell Middens. In *Deciphering a Shell Midden,* edited by J. K. Stein, pp. 1–24. Academic Press, San Diego.

1992b   Stratification of a Shell Midden. In *Deciphering a Shell Midden,* edited by J. K. Stein, pp. 71–93. Academic Press, San Diego.

1992c   Sediment Analysis of the British Camp Shell Midden. In *Deciphering a Shell Midden,* edited by J. K. Stein, pp. 135–162. Academic Press, San Diego.

2001   Archaeological Sediments in Cultural Environments. *Sediments in Archaeological Context,* edited by J. K. Stein and W. R. Farrand. The University of Utah Press, Salt Lake City.

Stein, J. K., K. D. Kornbacher, and J. L. Tyler
1992   British Camp Shell Midden Stratigraphy. In *Deciphering a Shell Midden,* edited by J. K. Stein, pp. 95–134. Academic Press, San Diego.

Stiros, S. C.
1988   Archaeology—A Tool to Study Active Tectonics. *EOS* 69:1633–1639.

Stoddart, D. R., D. J. Reed, and J. R. French
1989   Understanding Salt-Marsh Accretion, Scolt Head Island, Norfolk, England. *Estuaries* 12:228–236.

Stuiver, M., and T. F. Braziunas
1993   Modeling Atmospheric ^{14}C Influences and ^{14}C Ages of Marine Samples to 10,000 B.C. *Radiocarbon* 35:137–189.

Stuiver, M., and G. W. Pearson
1993   High-Precision Bidecadal Calibration of the Radiocarbon Time Scale. *Radiocarbon* 35:1–23.

Stuiver, M., and P. J. Reimer
1993   Extended ^{14}C Data Base and Revised CALIB 3.0 ^{14}C Age Calibration Program. *Radiocarbon* 35:215–230.

Sullivan, M., and S. O'Conner
1993   Middens and Cheniers: Implications of Australian Research. *Antiquity* 67:776–788.

Sunamura, T.
1976   Feedback Relationship in Wave Erosion of Laboratory Rocky Coast. *Journal of Geology* 84:427–437.

1977   A Relationship between Wave-Induced Cliff Erosion and Erosive Rate of Waves. *Journal of Geology* 85:613–618.

1989   Sandy Beach Geomorphology Elucidated by Laboratory Modeling. In *Applications in Coastal Modeling,* edited by V. C. Lakhan and A. S. Trenhaile, pp. 159–213. Elsevier, Amsterdam.

Tanner, W. F.
1988   Beach Ridge Data and Sea Level History from the Americas. *Journal of Coastal Research* 4:81–91.
Trenhaile, A. S.
1987   *The Geomorphology of Rock Coasts.* Clarendon Press, Oxford.
Tushingham, A. M., and W. R. Peltier
1992   Validation of the ICE-3G Model of Würm-Wisconsin Deglaciation Using a Global Data Base of Relative Sea Level Histories. *Journal of Geophysical Research* 97(B3):3285–3304.
1993   *Relative Sea Level Database.* IGBP Pages/World Data Center-A for Paleoclimatology Data Contribution Series No. 93-016. NOAA/NGDC Paleoclimatology Program, Boulder, Colorado.
Vogel, J., A. Fuls, E.Visser, and B. Becker
1993   Pretoria Calibration Curve for Short-Lived Samples, 1930–3350 B.C. *Radiocarbon* 35:73–85.
Weigel, R. L.
1964   *Oceanographical Engineering.* Prentice Hall, Englewood Cliffs, New Jersey.
Wells, L. E.
1988   Holocene Fluvial and Shoreline History as a Function of Human and Geological Factors in Arid Northern Peru. Unpublished Ph.D. dissertation. Stanford University, Palo Alto, California.
1992   Holocene Landscape Change on the Santa Delta, Peru: Impact on Archaeological Site Distribution. *The Holocene* 2(3):193–204.
1996   The Santa Beach Ridge Complex: Sea-Level and Progradational History of an Open Gravel Coast in Central Peru. *Journal of Coastal Research* 12:1–17.
2001   A Geomorphological Approach to Reconstructing Archaeological Settlement Patterns Based on Surficial Artifact Distribution: Replacing Humans on the Landscape. In *Earth Sciences and Archaeology,* edited by P. Goldberg, V. Holliday, and R. Ferring, pp. 107–141. Kluwer Academic/Plenum Press, New York.
Wells, L. E., and J. S. Noller
1999   Holocene Coevolution of the Physical Landscape and Human Settlement in Northern Coastal Peru. *Geoarchaeology* 14:755–789.
Wilson, D. J.
1988   *Prehispanic Settlement Patterns in the Lower Santa Valley, Peru.* Smithsonian Institution Press, Washington, D.C.
Wiseman, J.
1978   *The Land of the Ancient Corinthians.* Studies in Mediterranean Archaeology, vol. 1. Paul Astroms Forlag, Goteborg.
Wright, L. D.
1985   River Deltas. In *Coastal Sedimentary Environments,* edited by R. A. Davis, pp. 1–76. Springer-Verlag, New York.
Zangger, E.
1991   Prehistoric Coastal Environments in Greece: The Vanished Landscapes of Dimini Bay and Lake Lerna. *Journal of Field Archaeology* 18:1–15.
Zenkovich, V. P.
1967   *Processes of Coastal Development.* John Wiley and Sons, New York.

7

Archaeological Sediments
in Springs and Wetlands

Gail M. Ashley

Potable water sources are foci of human activity, and thus temporary, seasonal, and permanent occupation sites are commonly associated with them. River banks, flood plains, and deltas or margins of permanent water bodies ranging from large lakes to small ponds have long been recognized as areas used by humans. Frequent changes in water level of rivers and lakes typically cover occupation sites with a blanket of organic-rich, fine sediment that slows the weathering process and helps preserve the archaeological record, as well as associated material (bones, plant remains) and structures (footprints, burrows, fire pits, etc.).

Potable water also occurs in relatively small springs or seeps (point-sources) and diffuse areas of groundwater discharge that result in freshwater wetlands (marshes, wet meadows, and groundwater forests) that may cover large expanses (Deocampo 1997; Quade et al. 1995). These tend to be more persistent. More permanent water sources, such as groundwater reservoirs, are less vulnerable to fluctuations in precipitation and evaporation than are surface reservoirs. Lush vegetation and mineral licks attract grazing and browsing animals providing hunting and scavenging opportunities for humans (Griffin and Sattler 1988; Haynes 1967, 1985b; Haynes and Agogino 1966). Wet ground and bogs were likely used to trap animals for easy slaughter. Groundwater forests offered sources of fruits and vegetables and safe sleeping localities for hominids and early humans (Ashley 1996; Peters and Blumenshine 1995). In addition, thermal springs may have had medicinal or therapeutic uses (Griffin and Sattler 1988).

Although groundwater discharge areas are well known in modern times as water sources, particularly in arid settings (Behrensmeyer 1993), the geologic records of them are obscure and have been commonly misinterpreted as lacustrine (Hay et al. 1986; Quade and Pratt 1989). Springs themselves are usually

small in area, and sedimentation rates in groundwater discharge zones are typically slow and irregular (Quade 1986). Thus, it is not surprising that, except
for travertine and tufa deposits, the sedimentological record of springs and related groundwater-affected environments has not been well studied.

This chapter is intended to draw attention to the importance of freshwater
wetlands and springs in archaeological contexts. The objectives are to provide
some background information on geomorphology and hydrology of wetlands,
to present four examples of the sedimentary record associated with archaeological sites (early Pleistocene and late Pleistocene), and to conclude with a
generalized descriptive depositional model. This model is tentative and does
not describe all types of wetland settings. The model will need to be tested in
different geologic settings, but hopefully it might serve as a predictor of yet
undiscovered archaeological sites associated with paleosprings or wetlands.

Environment of Deposition

Hydrology

The hydrology of any region is driven by the hydrologic cycle. The absolute
amount of precipitation is a function of atmospheric circulation and orogenic
effects, and the net amount of water in the system depends on evaporation and
type of vegetation present (both strongly influenced by temperature). Temperature in turn is a function of latitude and altitude, as well as atmospheric circulation. The position of the groundwater table fluctuates with short-term and
long-term changes in the regional water budget (i.e., outflow from a drainage
basin equals inflow, plus or minus storage). Thus, the regional water table can
be found essentially at the Earth's surface in humid areas to tens or hundreds of
meters below the surface in arid lands.

During the time of the emergence of hominids and humans (ca. 5 million
years ago) climate driven by astronomic forcing (Milankovitch cycles) has fluctuated dramatically over thousands to tens of thousands of years (Imbrie et al.
1993). Changes in global climate have triggered increases and decreases in
runoff, fluctuations in the water table, and expansion and contraction of lakes
and wetlands. On time scales of hundreds to thousands of years, feedbacks
between the atmosphere, the ocean, and continental-scale glaciers have produced long, wet periods, times of drought, as well as cooler or warmer intervals. Thus, the appearance and disappearance of springs and groundwater-fed
wetlands on the landscape vary with climate over a range of temporal scales.

A variety of natural geologic settings result in groundwater flowing onto the

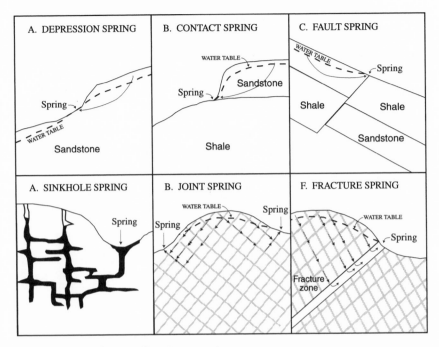

Figure 7.1. Types of springs (from Fetter 1994).

surface (Bryan 1919; Meinzer 1923). Common examples of groundwater dis-charge are springs originating from unconfined near-surface aquifers because of topographic effects (Fig. 7.1a), impermeable strata (Fig. 7.1b), or sinkholes (Fig. 7.1d [Fetter 1994]). Confined groundwater may emanate from faults, joints, and fractures that provide a conduit and exit for flow under hydrostatic pressure (Fig. 7.1c, e, f, respectively) (Fetter 1994). In geologically complex ar-eas, such as rift basins, however, the groundwater is likely multisourced, and the location of groundwater discharge varies temporally owing to shifts in cli-mate (affecting the hydrologic budget) or tectonic activity (Rosen 1994)(Fig. 7.2).

Not all wetlands are fed by groundwater. Some wetlands that were pri-marily rain-fed (ombrotrophic bogs) (Table 7.1) became extensive particularly in the Northern Hemisphere during mid- to late Holocene and contain rich paleoclimatic (Barber 1981, 1993) and archaeological records (Coles 1984; Purdy 1988). They were restricted to areas where precipitation exceeds 1,200 mm/yr (Lowe and Walker 1997). Their origin, starting sometime after 7 ka, is controversial as to whether they were strictly climate related or due at least par-tially to anthropogenic causes (deforestation and agriculture). Some peat bog

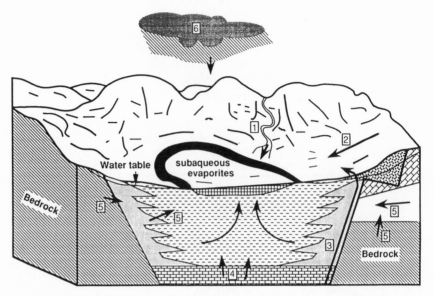

Figure 7.2. Sources of groundwater to a rift basin: (1) channeled flow in permanent or ephemeral streams; (2) overland flow; (3) hydrothermal fluids from a deep source; (4) connate or formation water trapped when the formation was deposited; (5) meteoric groundwater derived from within or outside the immediate basin; (6) direct precipitation onto the surface (from Rosen 1994).

formation may be due to the decline of trees, as trees transpire at greater rates than nonarboreal vegetation and drainage is generally improved by tree rooting. Many Mesolithic and Neolithic age sites are associated with bog sediments (Coles and Coles 1989). Peat deposits are ideal for preservation of fossil evidence (including human remains), wooden structures, clothing, and food stuffs (Godwin 1981). Rain-fed wetlands are not necessarily found associated with rivers and lakes (i.e., in lowlands), and their link to climate is unclear. Consequently, they may produce a geologic record quite different from groundwater wetlands. Because of these differences, they are beyond the intended scope of this chapter.

Springs

Springs are surface outlets for groundwater and commonly the settings for primary production of chemical and biochemical sediment. Composition of spring water varies considerably, reflecting the history of the water (source, flow path, flow rate, etc., Fig. 7.1) (Eugster and Jones 1979; Hardie et al. 1978). In areas of high heat flow, water in hot springs may reach 100 degrees C and is

Table 7.1. Definitions of Wetland-Related Terminology
(From National Research Council 1995)

Bog	A nutrient-poor, acidic-peat-accumulating wetland.
Cienega	Swamp or marsh in the southwestern U.S., especially one formed and fed by streams or groundwater discharge.
Fen (also mire)	Peat-accumulating wetland supporting sedge, moss-dominated communities and coniferous forests; mineral-rich water.
Hydric soils	Soil that is saturated, flooded, or ponded long enough during the growing season to develop anaerobic conditions in the upper part.
Hydrophyte	Any plant growing in water or on a substrate that is at least periodically deficient in oxygen as a result of excessive water.
Marsh	Wetland characterized by frequent or continual inundation, emergent herbaceous vegetation, and mineral soils.
Ombrotrophic bog	Peatland that receives precipitation as a sole source of water.
Peat	Deposit of partially decomposed or undecomposed plant material (mosses, herbaceous plants, trees, and/or shrubs). Accumulates in places that are sufficiently wet to prevent decomposition from keeping pace with production of organic matter.
Phreatophyte	Plant that has a well-developed deep root system that allows it to extract water from the permanent water-table (phreatic zone).
Vernal pool	Shallow, intermittently flooded wet meadow, generally covered by water for extended periods during the cool season but dry for most of the warm season.
Swamp	Emergent wetland in which the uppermost stratum of vegetation is composed primarily of trees.
Wet meadow	Any type of wetland dominated by herbaceous vegetation (frequently sedges) and with waterlogged soil near the surface, but without standing water for most of the year.
Wet prairie	Herbaceous wetland dominated by grasses rather than sedges and waterlogged soil near the surface, but without standing water for most of the year.

typically alkaline (pH = 8–10). Water may be salty if contaminated by surface brines or evaporites at depth. Erupting spring water may reach supersaturation of carbonate by degassing of CO_2 of waters when they flow onto the surface and may form carbonate deposits near the spring orifice (Deocampo and Ashley 1999; Jones et al. 1977). Blue-green algae, bacteria, and cyanobacteria are the most common microbial forms associated with precipitation of carbonate and siliceous sediment (Chafetz and Folk 1984; Jones and Renaut 1998; Scoll and Taft 1964). Spring ponds and marshes may support algae, fungi, diatoms, and a variety of rooted aquatic plants, such as sedge vegetation

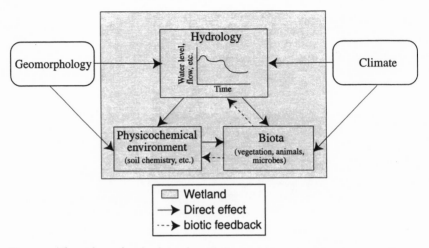

Figure 7.3. The ecology of wetlands in a humid climate: (a) impermeable substrate and/or an organic mat may retain meteoric water in depressions above the water table; (b) the shallow margins of large water bodies commonly support wetlands at the water table (from National Research Council 1995).

Typha, Cyperus, and *Scirpus* in permanent wetlands and *Cynodon* in ephemeral wetlands.

Freshwater Wetlands

Wetlands can occur in any setting where the water table is near or at the surface (Fig. 7.3a). Ephemeral wetlands are linked to seasonal rainy periods or a perched water table, whereas perennial wetlands occur in settings with a more permanent water source. They are often found at the interface of terrestrial ecosystems (such as upland forests and grasslands) and aquatic ecosystems (such as lakes and rivers) (Fig. 7.3b), and thus as part of a natural continuum they are often overlooked (Mitsch and Gosselink 1993). Because wetlands are neither terrestrial nor aquatic, they have not been easily assimilated by the well-established scientific disciplines of terrestrial and aquatic ecology. The exception to this is the recognition of their importance in playa ecology (Bolen 1982; Bolen et al. 1989; Gustavson et al. 1995; Haukos and Smith 1994; Holliday et al. 1996; Urban and Wyatt 1994). Wetlands have been largely neglected by the sedimentary community, and there are no depositional facies models currently in use except those connected with playa stratigraphy (Hill et al. 1995; Holliday et al. 1996; Urban and Wyatt 1994).

Wetlands are typically found in lowlands (on lake margins, distal part of alluvial fans, floodplains, and karstic depressions) and associated with faults,

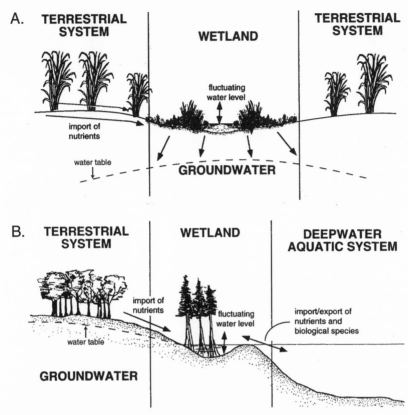

Figure 7.4. The relationships between hydrology, physicochemical environment, and biota in wetlands (from National Research Council 1995). Vegetation provides important feedback to hydrology through evapotranspiration, increase in flow resistance, and to the physicochemical environment by affecting soil properties (organic content, dissolved oxygen) and sedimentation processes (accumulating organic matter, trapping sediment) (modified after Mitsch and Gosselink 1993).

fractures, or perched water tables. The geomorphology of a wetland complex is typically of low relief and comprises a labyrinth of waterways of open water fringed with peats rooted on slightly higher ground (Clymo 1983). On increasingly higher terrain, the vegetation changes from marsh to wet meadow to groundwater forest characterized by a succession of plants with a *decreasing* tolerance for standing water (Table 7.1). A wetland ecosystem is a complex interactive system of water, soil, and organisms (Fig. 7.4) that may ultimately produce a distinctive sedimentary record.

The concept of "wetland" embraces a number of characteristics, including the elevation of the water table with respect to the ground surface, the duration of surface water, soil types (hydric) that form under permanently or temporarily saturated conditions, and various types of plants (hydrophytes) and animals that have become adapted to life in a "wet" environment (National Research Council 1995) (Table 7.1). Variability of wetlands is controlled by hydrogeomorphic characteristics, namely (1) geomorphic setting (lake margin, spring-fed floodplain), (2) source of water (direct precipitation, springs, surface runoff), and (3) hydrodynamics (flow rate, unidirectional or reversing) (Brinson 1993). The physicochemical environment, including pH, Eh, oxygen, and carbon dioxide levels, affects abundance, diversity, and productivity of plants, microbes, invertebrates, and vertebrates. The biotic component, particularly vegetation, on the other hand, can affect hydrology by blocking drainage and retarding runoff.

Water flows and water levels in most wetlands are surprisingly dynamic on time scales of months to years. Flow is initially driven by the hydraulic head of the local groundwater source but later by gravity flow away from the point of discharge (Kusler et al. 1994). The temporal pattern of water level, or hydroperiod, for a specific wetland is part of its ecological signature. Mitsch and Gosselink (1993) found that water levels fluctuate seasonally in most wetlands; those fed by groundwater show the low-amplitude fluctuations, whereas those fed by surface runoff showed high-amplitude and more frequent fluctuations.

In summary, the environment of deposition of springs and wetlands is a direct function of the regional hydrologic budget. The appearances and disappearances of groundwater-fed systems on the landscape in a particular geologic setting vary with climate. They occur under both arid and humid climatic regimes. Because biogenic sediment rather than mineral matter may dominate the depositional environment, the geological records of these systems are not as well known as those of rivers and lakes.

Sedimentation Processes

The sediments in springs and spring-fed wetlands are a mixture of biotic and abiotic chemical precipitates and clastic detritus. The source lithology and the climate are independent variables and strongly influence the resulting geological record (Fig. 7.5). The mineralogy of clastic detritus in areas sourced by igneous, metamorphic, and sedimentary rocks can be quartzo-feldspathic or clastic carbonate in composition. Active volcanism produces pyroclastic debris (ash, lapilli, bombs) that is friable and easily weathered. Weathering breaks down the source rocks into constituent primary particles and secondary minerals (clay minerals and oxides) and contributes dissolved solids and gasses to the groundwater (Hardie et al. 1978). Calcium carbonate deposits (travertine and tufa) are commonly precipitated at the spring orifice triggered by degassing of dissolved carbon dioxide contained within the groundwater. Because of the many processes active in spring systems—biologic (floral and faunal), chemical (evaporation, formation of new minerals), and hydrologic (fluvial and lacustrine)—the lithology of spring deposits varies considerably (Deocampo 1997; Hardie et al. 1978; Reeves and Soper 1959).

The physicochemical environment provides an important linkage between the plant community that depends on nutrients and water chemistry (pH, salinity, and alkalinity) and the animal population that utilizes the wetland for water and food (Fig. 7.5). *Cyperus immensus* (giant reeds), for example, comprises 20 percent of elephant diet in East Africa during the wet season and nearly 30 percent during the dry season. Equally important in wetland ecology is the physical environment that provides the substrate for biological growth, as well as the mechanisms for sediment transport and deposition.

As the vegetation dies and decomposes, a record of the plant community is left in the form of pollen, phytoliths, diatoms, seeds, pods, stems, and roots (Fig. 7.5) (see "Biogenic Components" below). Diatoms may build up thicknesses of diatomaceous earth composed mainly of siliceous skeletal detritus. The fauna also contributes to the record with vertebrate bones and teeth, invertebrate shells, and trace fossils ranging from insect traces to mammal foot prints (Deocampo and Ashley 1997; Laporte and Behrensmeyer 1980).

Detrital sediments ranging from gravels (minor) to clays are transported to the wetlands by colluvial processes under the influence of gravity, eolian processes (gusts of wind, dust devils, storms, or by the prevailing winds), and by fluvial processes. Volcanic airfalls may blanket the landscape with a layer of pyroclastic material that covers and preserves what is on the surface (Pickford 1983). Volumetrically, wind is likely the most important agent for transporting and depositing clastic material to groundwater discharge zones. Mineral sediments are trapped by plants or in shallow water and become part of the wetlands record. In summary, botanical remains, animal remains, and cultural remains that are initially entrapped by the vegetation are permanently entombed by subsequent deposits of sediment and of growing and decaying plant biomass.

Sediments

Grain Size and Composition

Because most of the sediments in spring/wetland systems are either generated within the environment (autochthonous), washed in by colluvial processes, or blown in, the grain size tends to be relatively fine (Deocampo 1997). Sandy sediments may occur in spring-fed channels (Whiting and

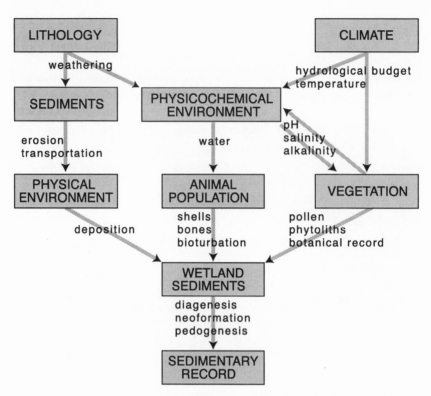

Figure 7.5. Major factors involved in the creation of the sedimentary record of wetlands (boxes) and the minor processes and factors influencing the record (with arrows) (after Deocampo 1997).

Stamm 1995), but the bulk of the record is generally silt and clay-sized material. Analysis of modern wetland sediments from a playa lake in East Africa reveals that they are organic-rich silty clays (50–60 percent clay, 20–30 percent organic matter, and 10–20 percent silt) (Deocampo 1997); however, the proportion of clastic material is expected to vary with the specific geologic setting.

Chemical composition of spring sediments is controlled by the chemistry and temperature of the groundwater. Carbonates are more likely to form in cooler springs; silica sinters and Al-Si gels precipitate in hot springs (Jones and Renaut 1998). Travertine and tufa form low mounds, sheets, coat grains, and fill pores along outflow channels and margins of ponds and marshes (Bathurst 1981). Bacteria, cyanobacteria, and algae aid in chemical sedimentation at springs, forming stromatolites, travertine, and tufas (Renaut et al. 1986). Travertines are laminated with alternating layers of color-banded (white, yellow, tan) limestone and fenestral (openwork) structures (Chafetz and Folk 1984). Tufas are "spongy" and generally less well laminated because they are a

Figure 7.6. Carbonate tufa associated with waxy and earthy claystones, lowermost Bed II, Olduvai Gorge, Tanzania. Plant stems and roots are encrusted and then replaced with calcium carbonate.

mixture of carbonate detritus and carbonate precipitated around plants such as algae or mosses (Fig. 7.6). The carbonate mineral is usually low-magnesium calcite, and the clays are Mg-smectite and sepiolite.

The composition of clastic sediment transported to the wetlands by wind or colluvial processes will reflect local bedrock sources. Hay et al. (1986) determined that in situ silicate formation could be linked to physicochemical properties. He found that clay minerals such as smectites and sepiolite indicated fresher water and lower pH, whereas potassium feldspar and illite formed in more alkaline-saline conditions.

Biogenic Components

Diatoms are unicellular algae with a shell (frustule) made of silica and are found associated with springs and freshwater wetlands. They are ecologically sensitive and useful in studying archaeological sites (Holliday 1995). On the basis of species and community ecology it is possible to reconstruct past pH, oxygen levels, salinity, temperature, and water depths (Battarbee 1988; Gasse 1987).

Chrysophytes are a group of planktonic algae that are covered with siliceous scales. Composition has been found to be strongly related to water chemistry; in particular, assemblage variations provide a sensitive record of pH variations (Cumming et al. 1991).

Phytoliths are irregular-shaped grains of opaline silica deposited within plant cells and provide strength and rigidity to plant leaves and stems. Many phytoliths are characteristic of the plants in which they are formed and may provide important clues to past vegetation (Lowe and Walker 1997; Pearsall and Piperno 1993; Piperno 1988).

Pollen, seeds, and spores are produced as part of plant reproduction. Pollen can be blown in from great distances, thus they tend to represent a regional sampling of vegetation. Some species (e.g., pine) produce pollen in large amounts and thus dominate and skew the pollen record. During death and decay of wetland vegetation, the pollen becomes part of the sedimentary record (Elenga et al. 1994), although pollen varies in its natural resistance to weathering and thus some species may be preferentially preserved or deleted from the record. Pollen, seeds, and spores are best preserved under anaerobic, acidic conditions.

Ostracodes are small (0.4–1.5 mm) aquatic crustaceans that are good paleoenvironmental indicators, particularly for salinity (Lowe and Walker 1997).

Lithofacies: Sedimentary Structures and Bedding

Wetland sediments tend to be massive (i.e., lacking obvious stratification) because of intense bioturbation by plants and animals. Under proper conditions footprinted horizons are common (Deocampo and Ashley 1997; Laporte and Behrensmeyer 1980). Stratification, where present, is vague, diffuse, and subhorizontal. Lithologic units are thin and discontinuous, reflecting the spatial variability of water courses and peat growth in wetlands. Sediments are heavily root marked, and roots can be preserved by replacement of the plant tissue by carbonate, creating root casts and rhizo concretions (Renaut et al. 1986).

Modification Processes

High oxygen demand caused by high bioproductivity (Fig. 7.4) in the marshes and wet meadows creates a reducing environment below the water table. The oxidation-reduction potential (or Eh) of the water controls chemical reactions, particularly with iron and manganese. Manganese is reduced more rapidly than iron; however iron is oxidized more quickly. The preponderance of plant products (organic acids) tends to create a very acidic environment with pHs commonly less than 6 when wetlands are not aerated by animal bioturbation. Preservation of plant material is good in acidic water, and a pH of 5.5 appears to be a threshold. Peats tend to accumulate when pH is less than 5.5 and generally do not accumulate when pH is above 5.5 (Thompson and Hamilton 1983).

Early post-depositional changes produced by groundwater involve continued weathering of minerals, precipitation of new minerals, dissolution-precipitation reactions, and pedogenesis. These low-temperature diagenetic changes are dependent on the mineralogy of the primary sediments, the chemistry of the groundwater, and the ongoing biologic activity. Fluctuations of the water table result in soils being subjected to alternating oxidizing and then reducing conditions producing red and gray mottling (Soil Survey Staff 1994). Bioturbation may disturb the stratigraphy so that artifacts and bones are not in the primary position relative to each other, even though they are not likely to have moved a significant distance. In summary, it is very difficult to generalize the exact nature of the final sedimentary record (Fig. 7.5), but the case studies presented below will provide some specific examples.

Soils

The natural weathering processes on the Earth's surface create soils and thus soil formation is a specific kind of modification process with a suite of processes and resulting characteristics. Most of the original minerals are chemically altered, new minerals form, and organic matter is added by activities of animals and plants. These soil-forming (pedogenic) processes create a variety of soil characteristics (horizons, peds, cutans, glaebules, and slickensides) that commonly overprint any primary stratification. Horizons are subparallel to the surface and recognized by differences in grain size, color, and organic matter. Peds are aggregates of soil material, cutans are "skins" of secondary minerals coating ped surfaces (e.g., clay or organic matter), and glaebules are calcareous or iron-bearing nodules. Slickensides are curved, striated surfaces that develop in wet clayey soils in response to expansion caused by swelling of clay minerals. Wetland soils are distinctive because they form close to (above, below, or at) the water table. Iron is reduced under anoxic (no oxygen) or anaerobic (low oxygen) conditions to produce drab, bluish to greenish gray waterlogged soil (gley). The soils are typically fine grained, with abundant plant remains, and iron-bearing nodules rather than carbonate nodules (Behrensmeyer and Hook 1992; Besley and Fielding 1989; Fastovsky and Mc-Sweeney 1987). The most commonly occurring soil orders are Histosols (organic soils) and Vertisols (characterized by shrinking and swelling of clays).

Case Study 1: Olduvai Gorge (Lowermost Bed II), Tanzania; Oldowan; Early Pleistocene

The Olduvai Gorge is incised into a shallow sedimentary basin that is situated between Precambrian basement rocks of the Serengeti Plain and the Plio-Pleistocene Ngorongoro volcanic complex in the Gregory Rift of East Africa. The 100-m-thick stratigraphic succession of primary air-fall pyroclastic deposits (tuffs) and reworked volcaniclastic sediment contains rich fossil (including at least 65 hominids) and cultural records spanning two million years (Hay 1976; L. S. B. Leakey 1967; M. D. Leakey 1978). New investigations at Olduvai were initiated in order to provide a more complete picture of the environment in which early humans evolved. Paleoenvironmental reconstruction of lowermost Bed II using a landscape archaeological approach revealed a large pyroclastic fan building westward into the basin produced by eruptions from the Ngorongoro volcanic complex that lay to the east (Fig. 7.7a). A lake in the center of the basin expanded and contracted over a wide lake-margin zone at the distal end of the fan. A spring/wetland complex, fed by groundwater, formed on the lake margin during arid periods when the lake level was low. A red soil developed at the distal portion of the fan in a location affected by the water table that fluctuated in sympathy with changes in lake level.

Figure 7.7b depicts three lithologically distinct sedimentary successions representing key depositional environments that developed on the paleolandscape: the alkaline lake environment, the spring/wetland environment, and the pyroclastic debris fan environment (Ashley 1996). The spring/wetlands lithofacies can be traced over a 2-by-1 km area, and these sediments interfinger to the west with lake sediments and to the east with pyroclastic fan sediments. Within these wetlands were small freshwater sources (springs) flowing from the base of the pyroclastic fan. The wetland was a mosaic of rooted vegetation, mud flats, small pools, and streams draining lakeward from the fan. The springs are characterized by tufas of carbonate-encrusted rhizomes (Fig. 7.6).

An excavation (Trench 27) in the spring-wetlands complex in the MCK area of Olduvai Gorge (Hay 1976) exposed 3.3 m of interbedded claystones bracketed between two distinct tuffs, Tuff IF at base and Tuff IIA at top. Quartz flakes and quartz cores, as well as vertebrate fossils, were found in the sediments. Figure 7.8 summarizes the volume of sediment excavated, the composition and grain size of the sediments, lists of fossils, and types of artifacts from each archaeological level. The dominant lithology is earthy claystone characterized by dull, earthy luster. It is white-to-buff, calcareous, and composed of smectitic clay, fresh and weathered volcanic minerals, with fragments of calcified plant remains, phytoliths, diatoms, and pollen. The bedding con-

A.

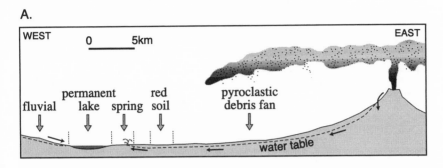

B.

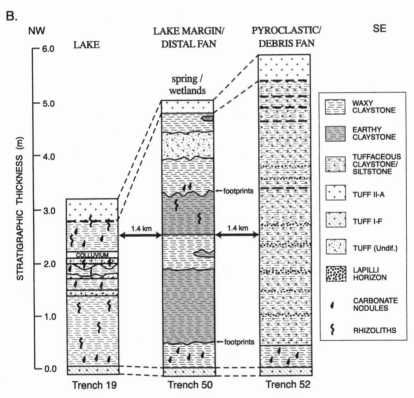

Figure 7.7. (a) Paleoenvironmental reconstruction of Olduvai basin during the early Pleistocene; (b) lithologic successions in the environs of groundwater-fed wetlands, Lower Pleistocene lowermost Bed II, Olduvai Gorge, Tanzania. The sediments are time equivalents as
they occur between isochronous tuffs (Tuff IF and Tuff IIA) and represent the lithologic
changes in a transect across lacustrine, wetland, and terrestrial depositional environments:
saline/alkaline lake, spring and wetlands, and pyroclastic debris fan.

Trench 27 (MCK) lowermost Bed II, Olduvai Gorge Tanzania

lithology	step	level	excavated volume m³	number* of stone artifacts	total weight (g) artifacts	total number of bones	total weight (g) of bones	taxon **
Tuff II A		1	-	-	-	-	-	mammal, bovid
waxy clay		2	0.015	6	11	2	29	mammal, reptile
earthy claystone (calcareous) light gray 5Y 7/1	Step 1	3	1.491	34	3058	57	877	mammal, carnivore, suid, equid, bovid, aves
waxy clay dark olive gray 5Y 3/2		4	0.934	7	92	9	185	reptile, mammal, bovid
earthy clay (calcareous) 7.5Y		5	1.387	50	2500	47	37750	aves, bovid, rhino, equid
← concretion		6	0.514	8	44	20	2693	aves, bovid, equid, mammal
tuffaceous clay light gray 5Y 7/1		7		9	1861	37	1050	aves, bovid, hippo, mammal
siliceous	Step 2	8	0.036	0	0	0	0	
earthy clay (calcareous)		9	0.817	1	262	4	42	aves, bovid, mammal
siliceous		10	0.250	0	0	0	0	
white 10Y 8/1		11	0.554	1	174	2	38	·
waxy clay 2.5Y 3/2		12	0.400	3	0	0		
Tuff IF								

* cores, flakes and flake fragments; artifact data, R. Blumenschine
** bone identification, A. Cushing

Figure 7.8. A detailed sedimentological description of a 4-m step trench excavated in the spring/wetlands lithofacies depicted in Figure 7.7b. The artifacts and fossils recovered in each archaeological level are summarized to the right.

tacts are often footprinted; root traces and root casts are common. Some beds with a larger proportion of volcanic minerals and pyroclastic grains (lapilli and ash) are light gray and more properly called tuffaceous claystone. The other dominant lithology is waxy claystone, an olive to olive-gray to olive-brown claystone with a waxy luster. It is composed of relatively pure Mg-smectitic clay and contains very few fossils and only 1–2 percent clastic detritus, but it frequently contains calcareous nodules of both sparry (crystalline) and micritic (dense, fine-grained) calcite.

Soils are weakly developed throughout the sequence of claystones, but are most obvious in the waxy claystones. Vague soil horizons, prismatic peds, slickensides, and root (or insect?) traces all suggest pedogenic processes following the accumulation of the deposit. Soils are well developed on the adjacent pyroclastic fan (Ashley and Driese 2000).

The depositional environment is interpreted to be a groundwater-fed wetland located on the distal portion of a pyroclastic fan that is periodically flooded by the lake. Episodic volcanic eruptions contributed pyroclastic material to the surface. Waxy claystones, formed in standing water, represent periods of higher lake (higher water table); earthy claystones formed in the vegetated wetlands that trapped pyroclastic air falls, eolian dust, and detritus washed in during seasonal runoff. Dating of the bracketing tuffs (1.75–1.65 Ma) suggests no more than 100,000 years for the accumulation of the 4-m-thick sequence (Manega 1994; Walter et al. 1991). The abundant vertebrate fossil record reveals that a diverse fauna (including carnivores) used the spring-fed wetlands for water and perhaps for food (Fig. 7.8). The abundant artifacts clearly indicate the site was used by hominids. Both Australopithecines and *Homo habilis* are known to have frequented the Gorge during this period (M. D. Leakey 1978). The quartzite cores and flakes were likely obtained at a metamorphic quartzite outcrop located 3 km away (Peters and Blumenschine 1995).

Case Study 2: Pomme de Terre Valley, Missouri; Paleoindian; Late Pleistocene

Paleoindian sites in the central and western United States are found in a variety of sedimentary contexts ranging from fluvial settings to lakes or ponds to caves (Grayson 1993). Many archaeological sites are directly associated with springs, and the following examples from both artesian springs (water under hydrostatic pressure) and gravity-driven drainage seeps summarize their environmental context.

A comprehensive study of the lower Pomme de Terre Valley, Missouri, describes artesian springs in alluvial settings related to the adjustment of drainage basins to postglacial climatic changes and sediment load (Haynes 1985a). The area underwent at least four major cycles of fluvial erosion and aggradation resulting in four terraces (To–T3) (Fig. 7.9). Important archaeological sites containing projectile points at Rodgers Shelter and Phillips Spring occur in the lower, younger (less than 10,500 B.P.) terraces (Wood 1976). River gravels form an aquifer that fed several artesian springs that were active at times of high hydrostatic pressure during lower river levels (glacial periods). Considerable churning by the artesian spring system is typical, so that fossils and artifacts near the spring orifice may not be in primary position. Floodplain aggradation took place under warmer conditions. The springs ceased to flow and were infilled by peat that contains pollen, botanical remains, and animal bones indicating mesic interstadial or interglacial conditions. A typical spring/wetland deposit is roughly circular (1–3 m in diameter) and composed of granular (sand and gravel) tufa surrounded by olive to bluish gray clay and capped with peat.

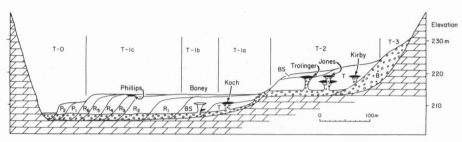

Figure 7.9. Generalized geological cross section of the Pomme de Terre Valley showing the relative stratigraphic positions of spring-laid peat lenses, alluvial terraces, and alluvial deposits: Breshears Valley Formation (B), Trolinger Springs Formation (T), Boney Springs Formation (BS), Rodgers Shelter Formation (R_{1-6}), and Pippins Cemetery Formation (P_{1-2}) (from Haynes 1985a).

Case Study 3: Lehner Mammoth Site, Southeast Arizona; Paleoindian; Late Pleistocene

The Lehner mammoth site is in a fluvial setting that experienced at least three cycles of fluvial erosion and aggradation during the last 13,000 years (Fig. 7.10) (Haury et al. 1959). Thirteen projectiles, mainly Clovis fluted points, and eight butchering tools, as well as many remains of abundant extinct Pleistocene fauna (nine immature mammoths and portions of horse, camel, bison, and tapir) were excavated from the oldest channel gravel (Unit g). Cultural charcoal associated with the artifacts and bones was dated at ca. 10,900 B.P., thus it appears that the site was buried during infilling of the channel in early postglacial time (Haynes 1991). Gravel deposition was interrupted and a wetland represented by an organic-rich "black" algal mat (Unit k) developed in the valley and was later covered with clayey silt deposits (Units l and m).

Haynes (1991) noted that many Clovis sites in the western United States reveal similar fining-upward sedimentary sequences and contain black organic mats (averaging 10,800 B.P. in age). He interpreted the sequences to reflect a rather rapid climate change in the region from "cool and dry" during the brief Younger Dryas episode when the channel was incised and gravels deposited to "warm and moist" when the black mats formed. Marl, mollusc remains, and diatomaceous sediment associated with the vegetative mat at the Lehner site indicate a higher water table and the development of a wetland (Mehringer and Haynes 1965). It appears that the mat fortuitously blanketed the lowland containing the archaeological record and suppressed weathering. Thus, the Lehner mammoth site, like many of the other Clovis sites, may owe its preservation to a groundwater-fed wetland.

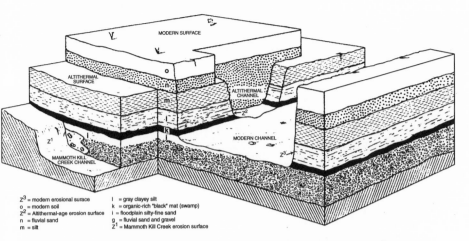

Z³ = modern erosional surace   l = gray clayey silt
o = modern soil   k = organic-rich "black" mat (swamp)
Z² = Altithermal-age erosion surface i = floodplain silty-fine sand
n = fluvial sand   g = fluvial sand and gravel
m = silt   Z¹ = Mammoth Kill Creek erosion surface

Figure 7.10. Schematic reconstruction of the stratigraphy of the Lehner mammoth site in southeast Arizona (modified from Haury et al. 1959). Clovis artifacts and mammoth bones were excavated from beneath the organic-rich mat.

Case Study 4: Yucca Mountain, Nevada; Paleoindian; Late Pleistocene

A detailed description of wetland stratigraphy and sediments comes from an actualistic study of a modern spring system near Yucca Mountain, southern Nevada (Fig. 7.11), although no artifacts were found there. The site is about 30 km from Tule Springs, Nevada, where archaeological materials (quartzite scraper, quartzite flakes, a caliche bead, and a bone tool) were found associated with megafaunal remains (Haynes 1967). The Upper Pleistocene to Holocene stratigraphy at Yucca Mountain comprises five lithologic units and five soils (Quade 1986). The sediments represent a time of changing hydrological and environmental conditions preceding, during, and following the last glacial maximum. Although most of the record was found to be fluvial, a 10-m-thick sequence of pale green calcareous mudstones (30,000–15,000 yr B.P.) with aquatic molluscs was interpreted by Quade (1986; Quade and Pratt 1989; Quade et al. 1995) to represent small water bodies surrounded by a broad, fine-grained alluvial flat. The mudstones correlate with pluvial maximum lacustrine deposits elsewhere in the region and thus represent a moist period preceding the Younger Dryas episode (11,000 B.P.).

The deposits are heavily bioturbated clayey silt with rarely preserved bedding (Fig. 7.11). Secondary carbonate in the form of rhizo concretions replaced aquatic vegetation (*Typha*?) within the capillary fringe (just above the water table). Quade's interpretation of the depositional environment is a scenario of

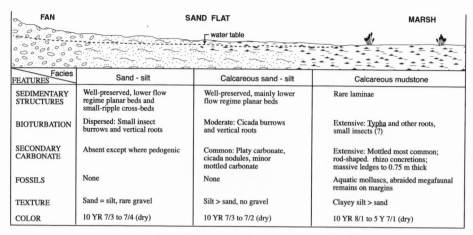

FEATURES \ Facies	Sand - silt	Calcareous sand - silt	Calcareous mudstone
SEDIMENTARY STRUCTURES	Well-preserved, lower flow regime planar beds and small-ripple cross-beds	Well-preserved, mainly lower flow regime planar beds	Rare laminae
BIOTURBATION	Dispersed: Small insect burrows and vertical roots	Moderate: Cicada burrows and vertical roots	Extensive: Typha and other roots, small insects (?)
SECONDARY CARBONATE	Absent except where pedogenic	Common: Platy carbonate, cicada nodules, minor mottled carbonate	Extensive: Mottled most common; rod-shaped. rhizo concretions; massive ledges to 0.75 m thick
FOSSILS	None	None	Aquatic molluscs, abraided megafaunal remains on margins
TEXTURE	Sand = silt, rare gravel	Silt > sand, no gravel	Clayey silt > sand
COLOR	10 YR 7/3 to 7/4 (dry)	10 YR 7/3 to 7/2 (dry)	10 YR 8/1 to 5 Y 7/1 (dry)

Figure 7.11. Detailed lithologic descriptions from a transect across an alluvial fan, sand flat, and groundwater-fed wetlands (marsh) depositional environments (modified from Quade 1986)

a shallow, ephemeral, reed-filled marsh at the distal end of an alluvial fan. Mollusc assemblages from the lower sand flat indicate permanent, well-oxygenated water and seasonal ponds (Fig. 7.11). Table 7.2 lists some representative western North American archaeological sites that are known to be associated with the late Pleistocene wetland deposits.

Discussion

Groundwater discharge zones are fed from reservoirs that are less vulnerable to the vagaries of climate fluctuations than is surface runoff. Thus, springs and associated wetlands tend to be perennial, not just seasonal sources of water for animals (including humans). Thus, it is not surprising that archaeological remains are commonly associated with them.

The waterlogged sediments have chemically reducing conditions favorable for preserving plant and animal remains, at least initially. Waterlogging tends to decrease pH and suppress microbial activity, thereby slowing decay of organic material. However, acidic water tends to dissolve shell and bone and enhances decalcification; thus plant remains are more prevalent than bone in poorly drained, waterlogged environments. On the other hand, bones fortuitously ending up near the spring may be encased in carbonate and preserved. Thus, in addition to the fact that springs/wetlands are an important part of the ecology of humans, their presence is conducive to preservation of archaeological and palaeontological records. Haynes (1991) makes a good case for a re-

Table 7.2. Archaeological Sites with Wetland Contexts

AGENT	DEPOSITION	ALTERATION
Cryoclastism	Frost slabs, spalls, grain-by-grain accumulation	Split/fissured stones, smaller spalls, debris
Collapse	Large blocks and shattered fragments	Crushed debris (of all kinds)
Solifluction	Hillslope sludge (from outside), colluvium	Displacement of earlier deposits (inside cave)
Cryoturbation	None	Churning of strata, rounding of stones
Flowing Water	Flood deposits, karstic imports, surface runoff	Erosion, gullying, travertine
Wind	Well-sorted sand and silt; loess	None
Solution (including hydration, weak acids)	Hydration spalls, grain-by-grain disaggregation; dripstone, travertine	Leaching of $CaCO_3$, rounding of stones, cementation
Pedogenesis	None	Chemical/mineralogical changes, leaching, cementation, root disturbance
Humans and Animals	Artifacts, bones, garbage, body wastes, imported rocks (manuports) and dirt, structures, hearths	Physical disturbance, digging, burrowing, house cleaning, chemical alteration; decreased pH

gional fluctuation in hydrologic budget that accompanied climate change from gradually warming, wet, late-glacial conditions to a cool, dry Younger Dryas episode at ca. 11,000–10,000 B.P., and then immediately back to wetter and warmer conditions at the beginning of the Holocene Epoch. The extinction of the Pleistocene megafauna occurred by the beginning of the Holocene and the high water table was ideal for the preservation of vertebrate fossils and archaeological records from that time period (Haynes 1991). Holliday (2000) presents an alternative model that focuses on aridity following the Younger Dryas (10,900–10,200 B.P.) being important.

The hydrologic budget is likely to fluctuate with time and a lowered water table may expose the former waterlogged sediments to oxidation. Higher ground is better drained than low-lying areas, so that sediment is subjected to aeration and perhaps general reddening or red-and-gray mottling. The oxidizing conditions destroy most plant remains (Retallack 1984). However, in the presence of sufficient mobilized carbonate or other minerals, vertebrate remains and plant roots may be premineralized rapidly and preserved (Behrensmeyer and Hook 1992). Thus, the completeness of the fossil record is in large part a function of physical conditions that promote rapid and permanent burial of organic remains.

The four case studies represent settings widely separated in time (about 2 million years) and, although they occur under different climatic regimes and in different environmental contexts, these settings appear to have served the same functions in focusing human and animal activity and preserving the archaeological record. Springs and wetlands occur in both arid and humid climates, but are probably more noticeable and perhaps more important in dry settings. During wet periods, perhaps rivers and lakes themselves were more important. Modern and late Pleistocene sites still contain organic matter (Deocampo 1997; Quade 1986), whereas the early Pleistocene site at Olduvai has essentially no organic matter. Evidence of the former abundance of vegetation in the older record is suggested, however, by carbonate root casts, phytoliths, and pollen.

The wetland sedimentological records of the case studies are similar. They are characterized by gray-to-greenish silty claystones, associated with tufas and travertines, carbonate rhizo concretions, pollen, diatoms, and insect traces. An overprinting by pedogenic processes is characteristic. Finally, stone artifacts record the presence of humans at the wetland sites, and stone tools and cut marks on bones suggest the wetlands were exploited as scavenging opportunities. Wetlands are relatively low-energy environments, and deposited artifacts and bones may be shifted in position by bioturbation, but are not likely to be moved significant distances and should accurately preserve the spatial context of the archaeological record.

Conclusions

Interpretation of the sedimentological context of an archaeological site must be based upon the composite picture of many properties of the sediment as seen in their vertical and horizontal distribution: variations in (1) grain size, (2) grain composition (mineralogy), and (3) biogenic components. Sedimentary structures, vertical successions, and lateral continuity of facies help complete the picture of the paleolandscape.

Springs and wetlands develop under both humid and arid climatic regimes. They have long served as a focus of human activities, and therefore these environments hold great potential for yielding archaeological records. The sediment record produced in them is distinct; springs have carbonate tufa or travertine, whereas wetlands produce organic-rich, gray-green, silty claystones typically containing records of vegetation (rhizomes, phytoliths, and pollen). Although artesian spring water discharge may locally churn sediment and post-depositional bioturbation may mix surface sediments with the subsurface, bones and artifacts are not likely to be widely dispersed from where sediments were originally deposited.

The archaeological and fossil record is in a large part a function of physical conditions that promote rapid and permanent burial of organic remains. Wetlands can cover occupation sites with a blanket of sediment slowing the weathering process, thereby helping to preserve the archaeological record.

Acknowledgments

The research was supported by National Science Foundation grants (Archaeology BNS 9000099, SBR 9601065, SBR 9602478, R. J. Blumenschine and F. T. Masao, and GEO 9903258 to G. M. Ashley) and L. S. B. Leakey Foundation, the Wenner-Gren Foundation, the National Geographical Society, the Sokkia Corporation, and Rutgers University. I want to thank the hard-working crew of the Olduvai Landscape Paleoanthropology Project and the hospitality of the Olduvai Museum staff, O. Kileo, J. Pareso, and Godfrey Olle Moita. I appreciate Amy Cushing for identifying the invertebrate fossils from Olduvai. I have benefited greatly over the years from discussions with Rob Blumenschine, Kay Behrensmeyer, Thure Cerling, Dan Deocampo, Steve Driese, Craig Feibel, Cindy Luitkus, Lindsay McHenry, Fidelis Masao, Godwin Mollel, Rick Potts, Robin Renaut, and Nancy Sikes. I am particularly grateful to Richard Hay who has been generous with his ideas and unpublished data on Olduvai. I am grateful to the book editors for their meticulous editing and to the anonymous reviewer for very helpful comments.

References Cited

Ashley, G. M.
1996   Springs, Pools and Adjacent Wetlands, a Newly Recognized Habitat, Lowermost Bed II, Olduvai Gorge, Tanzania. *Geological Society of America Abstracts with Programs* 28(6):28.
Ashley, G. M., and S. G. Driese
2000   Paleopedology and Paleohydrology of a Volcaniclastic Paleosol Interval: Implications for Early Pleistocene Stratigraphy and Paleoclimate Record, Olduvai Gorge, Tanzania. *Journal of Sedimentary Research* 70:1065–1080.
Barber, K. E.
1981   *Peat Stratigraphy and Climate Change.* Balkema, Rotterdam.
1993   Peatlands as Scientific Archives of Past Biodiversity. *Biodiversity and Conservation* 2:474–489.

Bathurst, R. G. C.
1981   *Carbonate Sediments and Their Diagenesis.* Elsevier, New York.
Battarbee, R. W.
1988   The Application of Diatom Analysis in Archaeology: A Review. *Journal of Archaeo-logical Science* 15:621–644.
Behrensmeyer, A. K.
1993   The Bones of Amboseli. *National Geographic Research and Exploration* 9(4):402–421.
Behrensmeyer, A. K., and R. W. Hook
1992   Paleoenvironmental Contexts and Taphonomic Modes. In *Terrestrial Ecosystems through Time,* edited by A. K. Behrensmeyer, pp. 15–129. University of Chicago Press, Illinois.
Besly, B. M., and C. R. Fielding
1989   Palaeosols in Westphalian Coal-Bearing and Red-Bed Sequences, Central and Northern England. *Palaeogeography, Palaeoclimatology, Palaeoecology* 70:303–330.
Bolen, E. G.
1982   Playa Wetlands of the U.S. Southern High Plains: Their Wildlife Values and Chal-lenges for Management. In *Wetlands: Ecology and Management,* edited by B. Gopal, R. E. Turner, R. G. Wetzel, and D. F. Whigha. National Institute of Ecology, Jaipur, India.
Bolen, E. G., L. M. Smith, and H. L. Schramm Jr.
1989   Playa Lakes, Prairie Wetlands of the Southern High Plains. *BioScience* 39:615–623.
Brinson, M. M.
1993   A *Hydrogeomorphic Classification of Wetlands.* Wetlands Research Program Technical Report WRP-DE-4. U.S. Army Corps of Engineers, Waterway Experiment Station. Bridgham and Richardson, Vicksburg, Mississippi.
Bryan, K.
1919   Classification of Springs. *Journal of Geology* 27:522–561.
Chafetz, H. S., and R. L. Folk
1984   Travertines, Depositional Morphology and the Bacterially Constructed Con-stituents. *Journal of Sedimentary Petrology* 54:289–316.
Clymo, R. S.
1983   Peat. In *Ecosystems of the World,* vol. 4a, *Mires: Swamp, Bog, Fen, and Moor, Regional Studies,* edited by A. J. P. Gore, pp. 159–218, Elsevier, Amsterdam.
Coles, J.
1984   *The Archaeology of Wetlands.* Edinburgh University Press, Edinburgh.
Coles, B., and J. Coles
1989   *People of the Wetlands: Bogs, Bodies and Lake-Dwellers.* Thames and Hudson, New York.
Cumming, B. F., J. P. Smol, and H. J. B. Birks
1991   The Relationship between Sedimentary Chrysophyte Scales (Chrysophyceae and Synurophyceae) and Limnological Characteristics in 25 Norwegian Lakes. *Nordic Journal of Botany* 2:231–242.
Deocampo, D. M.
1997   Modern Sedimentation and Geochemistry of Freshwater Springs: Ngorongoro Crater, Tanzania. Unpublished M.S. thesis, Rutgers University.
Deocampo, D. M., and G. M. Ashley
1997   Hippo Trails: A Large-Scale Freshwater Biogenic Structure in Arid East Africa. *Geo-logical Society of America Abstracts with Programs* 29(1):40–41.
1999   Siliceous Islands in a Carbonate Sea: Modern and Pleistocene Spring-fed Wetlands

in Ngorongoro Crater and Olduvai Gorge, Tanzania. *Journal of Sedimentary Research* 69:974–979.

Elenga, H., D. Schwartz, and A. Vincens

1994   Pollen Evidence of Late Quaternary Vegetation and Inferred Climate Changes in the Congo. *Palaeogeography, Palaeoclimatology, Palaeoecology* 109:345–356.

Eugster, H. P., and B. F. Jones

1979   Behavior of Major Solutes during Closed-Basin Brine Evolution. *American Journal of Science* 279:609–631.

Fastovsky, D. E., and K. McSweeney

1987   Paleosols Spanning the Cretaceous-Paleogene Transition, Eastern Montana and Western North Dakota. *Geological Society of America Bulletin* 99:66–67.

Fetter, C. W.

1994   *Applied Hydrogeology.* Macmillan, New York.

Gasse, F.

1987   Diatoms for Reconstructing Palaeoenvironments and Paleohydrology in Tropical Semi-Arid Zones. *Hydrobiologia* 154:127–163.

Godwin, H.

1981   *The Archives of Peat Bogs.* Cambridge University Press, London.

Grayson, D. K.

1993   *The Desert's Past—A Natural Prehistory of the Great Basin.* Smithsonian Institution Press, Washington, D.C.

Griffin, D. G., and R. A. Sattler

1988   Alaska's Thermal Springs: A Review of Their Biological and Cultural Significance in the Lifeways of Alaskan Natives. *Journal of Northern Sciences* 2:49–73.

Gustavson, T. C., V. T. Holliday, and S. D. Hovorka

1995   *Origin and Development of Playa Basins, Sources of Recharge to the Ogallala Aquifer, Southern High Plains, Texas and New Mexico.* Bureau of Economic Geology, Report of Investigations 229. University of Texas at Austin, Austin.

Hardie, L. A., J. P. Smoot, and H. P. Eugster

1978   Saline Lakes and Their Deposits: A Sedimentological Approach. In *Modern and Ancient Lake Sediments,* edited by A. Matter and M. E. Tucker, pp. 7–42. International Association of Sedimentologists Special Publication 2.

Haukos, D. A., and L. M. Smith

1994   The Importance of Playa Wetlands to Biodiversity of the Southern High Plains. *Landscape and Urban Planning* 28:83–98.

Haury, E. W., E. B. Sayles, and W. W. Wasley

1959   The Lehner Mammoth Site, Southeastern Arizona. *American Antiquity* 25:2–30.

Hay, R. L.

1976   *Geology of the Olduvai Gorge.* University of California Press, Berkeley.

1996   Stratigraphy and Lake-Margin Paleoenvironments of Lowermost Bed II in Olduvai Gorge. *Darmstadter Beitrage zur Naturgeschichte,* Heft 6:223–230.

Hay, R. L., R. E. Pexton, T. T. Teague, and T. K. Kyser

1986   Spring-Related Carbonate Rocks, Mg Clays, and Associated Minerals in Pliocene Deposit of the Amargosa Desert, Nevada and California. *Geological Society of America Bulletin* 97:1488–1503.

Haynes, C. V., Jr.

1967   Quaternary Geology of the Tule Springs Area, Clark County, Nevada. In *Pleistocene Studies in Southern Nevada,* edited by H. M. Wormington and D. Ellis, pp. 15–104. Nevada State Museum Anthropology Paper No. 13.

1975   Pleistocene and Recent Stratigraphy. In *Late Pleistocene Environments of the Southern High Plains,* edited by F. Wendorf and J. J. Hester, pp. 57–96. Fort Burgwin Research Center Publication No. 9.

1985a   *Mastodon-Bearing Springs and Late Quaternary Geochronology of the Lower Pomme de Terre Valley, Missouri.* Geological Society of America, Special Paper 204. Boulder, Colorado.

1985b   On Watering Holes, Mineral Licks, Death, and Predation. In *Environments and Extinctions: Man in Late Glacial North America,* edited by J. I. Mead and D. J. Meltzer, pp. 53–72. Center for the Study of Early Man, Orono, Maine.

1991   Geoarchaeological and Paleohydrological Evidence for a Clovis-Age Drought in North America and Its Bearing on Extinction. *Quaternary Research* 35:438–450.

Haynes, C. V., Jr., and G. A. Agogino

1966   Prehistoric Springs and Geochronology of the Clovis Site, New Mexico. *American Antiquity* 31:812–821.

Haynes, C.V., Jr., and E. T. Hemmings

1968   Mammoth-Bone Shaft Wrench from Murray Springs, Arizona. *Science* 159:186–187.

Hemmings, E. T.

1970   Early Man in the San Pedro Valley, Arizona. Unpublished Ph.D. dissertation, University of Arizona.

Hill, M. G., V. T. Holliday, and D. J. Stanford

1995   A Further Evaluation of the San Jon Site, New Mexico. *Plains Anthropologist* 40:369–390.

Holliday, V. T.

1995   *Stratigraphy and Paleoenvironments of Late Quaternary Valley Fills on the Southern High Plains.* Geological Society of America, Memoir 1986. Boulder, Colorado.

2000   Folsom Drought and Episodic Drying on the Southern High Plains from 10,9000–10,200 ^{14}C yr B.P. *Quaternary Research* 53:1–12.

Holliday, V. T., S. D. Hovorka, and T. C. Gustavson

1996   Lithostratigraphy and Geochronology of Fills in Small Playa Basins on the Southern High Plains. *Geological Society of America Bulletin* 108:953–965.

Imbrie, J., A. Berger, and N. J. Shackleton

1993   Role of Orbital Forcing: A Two Million-Year Perspective. In *Global Changes in the Perspective of the Past,* edited by J. A. Eddy and H. Oescher, pp. 263–277. John Wiley and Sons, Chichester and New York.

Jones, B. F., H. P. Euster, and S. L. Rettig

1977   Hydrochemistry of the Lake Magadi Basin, Kenya. *Geochimica et Cosmochimica Acta* 41:53–72

Jones, B., and R. W. Renaut

1998   Origin of Platy Calcite Crystals in Hot-spring Deposits in the Kenyan Rift Valley. *Journal of Sedimentary Research* 68(5):913–927.

Kusler, J., W. J. Mitsch, and J. S. Larson

1994   Wetlands. *Scientific American* 64B:70.

Laporte, L. F., and A. K. Behrensmeyer

1980   Tracks and Substrate Reworking by Terrestrial Vertebrates in Quaternary Sediments of Kenya. *Journal of Sedimentary Petrology* 50:1337–1346.

Leakey, L. S. B.

1967   *Olduvai Gorge: 1951–1961.* Cambridge University Press, Cambridge.

Leakey, M. D.

1978   Olduvai Gorge 1911–75: A History of the Investigations. In *Geological Background to Fossil Man,* edited by W. W. Bishop, pp. 157–170. Scottish Academic Press, Edinburgh.

Leonhardy, F. C. (editor)
1966   Domebo: A Paleo-Indian Mammoth Kill in the Prairie-Plains. *Contributions of the Museum of the Great Plains* 1:1–53. Lawton, Oklahoma.

Lowe, J. J., and M. J. Walker
1997   *Reconstructing Quaternary Environments.* Addison Wesley Longman Ltd., Essex, England.

Manega, P. C.
1994   Geochronology, Geochemistry and Isotopic Study of the Plio-Pleistocene Hominid Sites and Ngorongoro Volcanic Highland in Northern Tanzania. Unpublished Ph.D. dissertation, University of Colorado, Boulder.

Mawby, J. E.
1967   Fossil Vertebrates of the Tule Springs Site, Nevada. In *Pleistocene Studies in Southern Nevada,* edited by H. M. Wormington and D. Ellis, pp. 105–129. Nevada State Museum Anthropological Paper 13.

Mehringer, P. J., Jr., and C. V. Haynes Jr.
1965   The Pollen Evidence for the Environment of Early Man and Extinct Mammals at the Lehner Mammoth Site, Southeastern Arizona. *American Antiquity* 31:17–23.

Meinzer, O. E.
1923   *The Occurrence of Groundwater in the United States.* United States Geological Survey Water Supply Paper 494. Washington, D.C.

Mitsch, W. J., and J. G. Gosselink
1993   *Wetlands.* Van Nostrand Reinhold, New York.

National Research Council (N.R.C.)
1995   *Wetlands Characteristics and Boundaries.* National Academy Press.

Pearsall, D. M., and D. R. Piperno
1993   *Current Research in Phytolith Analysis: Applications in Archaeology and Paleoecology.* MASCA Research Papers in Science and Archaeology 10.

Peters, C. R., and R. J. Blumenschine
1995   Landscape Perspectives on Possible Land Use Patterns for Early Hominids in the Olduvai Basin. *Journal of Human Evolution* 29:321–362.

Pickford, M. H. L.
1983   Sedimentation and Fossil Preservation in the Nyanza Rift System, Kenya. *Geological Society of London Special Publication* 25:345–362.

Piperno, D. R.
1988   *Phytolith Analysis: An Archaeological and Geological Perspective.* Academic Press, San Diego.

Purdy, B. (editor)
1988   *Wet-Site Archaeology.* Telford Press, Caldwell, New Jersey.

Quade, J.
1986   Late Quaternary Environmental Changes in the Upper Las Vegas Valley, Nevada. *Quaternary Research* 36:340–357.

Quade, J., M. D. Mifflin, W. L. Pratt, and L. Burckle
1995   Fossil Spring Deposits in the Southern Great Basin and Their Implications for Changes in Water Table Levels near Yucca Mountain, Nevada, during Quaternary Time. *Geological Society of America Bulletin* 107:213–230.

Quade, J., and W. L. Pratt
1989   Late Wisconsin Groundwater Discharge Environments of the Southwestern Indian
        Springs Valley, Southern Nevada. *Quaternary Research* 31:351–370.
Reeves, C. C., Jr., and H. Soper
1959   Calcareous Spring Deposits, Dubois Area, Wyoming. *Journal of Sedimentary Petrol-
        ogy* 29:436–446.
Renaut, R. W., J.-J. Tiercelin, and R. B. Owen
1986   Mineral Precipitation and Diagenesis in the Sediments of the Lake Bogoria Basin,
        Kenya Rift Valley. In *Sedimentation in the Africa Rifts,* edited by L. E. Frostick, R. W.
        Renaut, I. Reid, and J.-J. Tiercelin, pp. 159–176. Geological Society of London Spe-
        cial Publication 25.
Retallack, G. J.
1984   Completeness of the Rock and Fossil Record: Some Estimates Using Fossil Soils.
        Paleobiology 10:59–78.
Rosen, M. R.
1994   The Importance of Groundwater in Playas: A Review of Playa Classification and the
        Sedimentology and Hydrology of Playas. In *Paleoclimate and Basin Evolution of
        Playa Systems,* edited by M. R. Rosen, pp. 1–18. Geological Society of America Spe-
        cial Paper 289.
Scoll, D. W., and W. H. Taft
1964   Algae Contributions to the Formation of Calcareous Tufa, Mono Lake, California.
        Journal of Sedimentary Petrology 34:309–319.
Soil Survey Staff
1994   *Keys to Soil Taxonomy.* 6th ed. U.S. Government Printing Office, Washington, D.C.
Thompson, K., and A. C. Hamilton
1983   Peatlands and Swamps of the African Continent. In *Ecosystems of the World,* vol. 4b,
        Mires: Swamp, Bog, Fen, and Moor, Regional Studies, edited by A. J. P. Gore, pp.
        331–373. Elsevier, Amsterdam.
Urban, L. V., and A. W. Wyatt (editors)
1994   *Proceedings of the Playa Basin Symposium.* Texas Tech University, Water Resources
        Center, Lubbock, Texas.
Walter, R. C., P. C. Manega, R. L. Hay, R. E. Drake, and G. H. Curtis
1991   Laser-Fusion $^{40}Ar/^{39}Ar$ Dating of Bed I, Olduvai Gorge, Tanzania. *Nature*
        354:145–149.
Whiting, P. J., and J. Stamm
1995   The Hydrology and Form of Spring-Dominated Channels. *Geomorphology*
        12:233–240.
Wood, W. R.
1976   Archaeological Investigations at the Pomme de Terre Springs. In *Prehistoric Man and
        His Environments: A Case Study in the Ozark Highland,* edited by W. R. Wood and
        R. B. McMillan, pp. 97–107. Academic Press, New York.

Contributors

Gail M. Ashley
Department of Geological Sciences
Rutgers University
New Brunswick, New Jersey 08903

Bruce G. Gladfelter
Department of Anthropology MC/027
University of Illinois at Chicago
Chicago, Illinois 60607

William R. Farrand
Museum of Anthropology
University of Michigan
Ann Arbor, Michigan 48109-1079

Craig S. Feibel
Paleoenvironmental Research Laboratory
Department of Anthropology
Rutgers University
New Brunswick, New Jersey 08901-1414

Gary Huckleberry
Department of Anthropology
Box 644910
Washington State University
Pullman, Washington 99164-4910

Julie K. Stein
Department of Anthropology
Box 35 3100
University of Washington
Seattle, Washington 98195-3100

Lisa E. Wells
Department of Geosciences
Oregon State University
Corvallis, Oregon 97331-5506

Index